THE WORD
OF GOD

THE WORD OF GOD

HOMILIES BY
LOUIS EVELY

TRANSLATED BY
SISTER MARY AGNES, O.P.

HERDER AND HERDER

1967
HERDER AND HERDER NEW YORK
232 Madison Avenue, New York 10016

Nihil obstat: Thomas J. Beary, Censor Librorum
Imprimatur: ✠Robert F. Joyce, Bishop of Burlington
June 5, 1967

CONTENTS

CONTENTS

THE WORD
OF GOD

PROLOGUE:
THE ANNUNCIATION

OUR LIVES must be led in accordance with the light given to us by Sacred Scripture. Scripture is not merely a history but also a prophecy. It reveals to us not only what is happening today but what will happen continually in the course of time, for God is ever speaking His Word to mankind. Consequently, there will always be calls, vocations, "annunciations," —and the annunciation to Mary should be a help to each one of you in the recognition of your own! —since for us, too, the Word is a contemporary and dwells among us.

How many messages from the Lord, during the course of our lives, and how many messengers also, run the risk, without the help of the Gospel, of being unnoticed! How did you become Christians? How did you remain so? Or, how did you return? How does it happen that you are here now? What made you come? Or not come?

As a matter of fact, all your life is made up of calls from the Lord and the responses that you made. All your life is filled with angels, with messengers, with apparitions which the religious experience of the early witnesses should help us to identify.

And in order to do so more surely, there is a second rule which seems to me as important as the first. If we are to look at our life in the light of the Gospel, it would be very useful for us to read the Gospel in the light of our own life. What I mean is that there are two ways of understanding the Gospel. The first is to under-

11

stand that, at a privileged epoch in history, the divine was manifested in a way that will never happen again. The marvellous was of daily occurrence, miracles were many, dreams and apparitions common. God had changed His policy and manifested Himself to men openly. At the Transfiguration, for example, Jesus was transformed, His divinity appeared, the invisible world became apparent.

That seems very easy, and yet, that way of understanding the Gospel has two serious drawbacks. First, if the religious person sees in the "marvellous" a privileged manifestation of God, then we are forever disqualified, even disinherited. We shall never live a true religious life, a religious life like that of the first witnesses of the life of Christ, because, in our lives, there are no marvels. We shall be living a profane life, a life in which God never manifests Himself, never speaks. It will be life filled with longing for the things of the past where we wish we could have lived, a life on the look-out for all that is most suspect in the religious mentality, such as visions, apparitions, miracles, stigmata, prophecies, and those infallible receipts for recovering lost objects, obtaining special graces, or help in desperate cases.

If God had chosen this spectacular manner of revealing Himself, it would mean that He had changed, transformed Himself in order to appear to us, and then dispensed us from further effort on our part. What I mean is that if God placed Himself within the reach of our eyes and ears, He would not require us to act by faith. If God became evident to our senses, there is no appeal to our heart; if God changes, then we do not change. We would remain static, waiting for some satisfying manifestation instead of working to conform our lives to the Word of God. "He who is of God, hears the words of God. If you do not hear them, that is because you are not of God. My sheep hear, they recognize my voice and they follow."

The other way of reading the Gospel is to realize that everything in it can be found in our life also. Whatever happened to

those first witnesses of Christ, happens also to us, that the evange-
lists have simply translated into the language of their time, using
their own modes of expression, and we are wrong to take too
literally those things which we have experienced as well as they.
We would find the best commentary on the Gospel in meditation
on our own past lives, and it would be a very fruitful method of
interpretation to suspect whatever seems strange and to endeavor
to see in it something that has occurred in our own lives.

Let us try to apply these principles to the Annunciation.

First of all, did Mary actually see an angel?

Notice that there is nothing in the account that obliges us to
believe that she actually did. All that is mentioned is the message. The angel speaks but it is not said that he showed himself.
Mary has received, like each of us, a vocation from God. It is we
who have personified the message by bringing in the appearance
of the messenger. And as we naïvely figure out for ourselves the
attributes of an angel, we disqualify ourselves forever for the
privilege of an angelic message. We have never seen, and we
shall never see, an angel, and hence we run the risk of believing
that God will never send us His call.

But that is not the real question. Whether or not Mary saw an
angel is something secondary. The important thing is to ask
ourselves: How did she recognize him? How did she gain the
certitude that this message, or this messenger, came from God?

Here is where we come upon something of our own experience. In the New Testament, angels are not distinguished by
wings or feathers. They do wear white clothing, but that was the
customary dress of that time. Today they might wear a long dress
or a short one, or a long coat. You have seen hundreds of them.
Just tell me how you happen to be here and I will show you
many angels in your life. Just because they do not wear sufficient
plumage to correspond to your imagination, or to your faulty
interpretation of Scripture, you did not recognize them.

How does one recognize an angel? How does one recognize

that a thought, a meeting, an event comes from God? That is one of the problems of life and that is exactly what Mary had to solve.

How did she do it? The same way that you do, I think.

First of all, she did not allow herself to believe it immediately. She reflected, she asked, she called in question such an extraordinary vocation.

Confronted with a word from God, there are two attitudes, both of them stupid. The one is to say: "I do not understand it at all. It is impossible to see clearly. Let's drop the whole subject." And the other is to say: "It is all very plain. I understand it perfectly. It does not surprise me. I was expecting it." And between the two lies the only reasonable manner of acting, which was ever that of Mary. "She understood not what He said, but she kept all these things, pondering them in her heart."

The Evangelist, in this dialogue with the angel, has dramatized the behavior that is natural to one having faith. Receptivity and reflection; meditation and reasoning; joy and fear; the sense of God and human common sense. And all that took time, just as with us, over and over again, in time, with time, and taking time, for the discernment of the Spirit of God is never done instantaneously.

Then she consulted the Scriptures. She tried to explain her own life and to comprehend what had happened to her by the light of Scripture. All the texts given by Luke and by Matthew are quotations from the prophets, and the Magnificat testifies to the manner in which Mary looked upon her vocation as she studied the long line of spiritual fecundities which had preceded her own.

The second question: Did the message announce the conception, or was the conception itself the message?

The first interpretation seems to be more true to the Gospel where her consent is asked for, and more conformed to the respect which God always shows to the liberty of His creatures.

14

But, at bottom, here, too, the conception is not the main thing. What is important in our lives is not our choice but our consent. The exercise of our liberty is not so marked when we choose as when we consent: the daily acceptance, renewed daily, of a destiny which infinitely surpasses anything that we could have foreseen. Even if Mary had found herself pregnant without any forewarning, she would have still been free, just as we are, to accept in faith, or to submit in fear and complaint to a destiny which she would never know until it was over just how far it would lead her.

So we may think of Mary as finding herself one day in a situation which, to her, was inexplicable and which she could not confide to any one. The graces of God come to us, at times, like bricks. Her deep union with God, her understanding of the Scriptures, her responsiveness to grace, all suggested to her the possibility of a religious explanation of what had happened to her, but she had too much good sense, too much simplicity and naturalness not to be thoroughly confused by such an extraordinary occurrence. She could foresee all the probabilities and feel all the agitation that we ourselves would feel.

To speak to Joseph was impossible. How could a man understand all this?

She prayed. She read, and reread, the Scriptures. She pondered and repeated over and over again all these things in her heart. Little by little, in the light of the Bible, her life became clearer to her, just as the Bible became more clear to her in the light of her own life. She understood and relived all the anxieties of the poor, the persecuted, the sterile, of those beings seemingly so harshly abandoned by God in whom they have placed all their trust, the innocent under suspicion, accused, rejected. She admired their patience, their fidelity to that God who could justify them and yet left them to suffer. She hoped for their vindication, their final justification through the fidelity of God which surpasses that of ourselves.

15

Just at that time she learned that her cousin Elizabeth had also had her life thrown into confusion by an enlargement which obliged her to keep hidden for some five months. Here was a sign, a confirmation, a possible understanding. The Gospel says that Mary hastened to her, being no longer able to keep her secret, to bear her burden all alone.

These two women met and they understood each other. They confided to one another their trials, their reflexions, their prayers, and their hopes. Elizabeth consoled Mary. "Yes, you are right in believing. What has happened to you is truly from God. He is asking more of you than of any one else, but He gives in proportion to what He asks. With Him, all suffering is changed into joy, and every trial becomes a grace. My child is a joy which announces and which foretells what great joy will be yours."

Then Mary sang her hymn of thanksgiving. Mary did not sing her Magnificat after the Annunciation. She was too upset and too anxious. But it welled up from her heart after the Visitation. The real angel that she met was this woman who had suffered like herself and who encouraged her to believe and trust.

And you, too, will sing your Magnificat with Mary when you shall have at last recognized your Annunciation in hers, and seen the promises of God there where you saw only torment.

THE FIRST SUNDAY IN ADVENT

"Raise your heads because your redemption is drawing near." (Luke 21:25–33)

The new year, the true year, the new liturgical year begins today. It opens with a scene of triumph, —the glorious return of Christ, the end of the world, the final judgment.

These grandiose prophecies filled the first Christians with enthusiasm. It was this faith, this expectation, which was something of a shock to their contemporaries, who, like people of today, "lived as those who have no hope." It made them responsive to the warning of Christ: "Watch for you do not know when the Master of the house will return, whether he will come in the evening, or at midnight, or at cock-crow, or in the morning, lest he come suddenly and find you asleep. What I say to you, I say to all: Watch!"

I am certain, my brethren, that the greater number of you do not feel very familiar with these grandiose thoughts. We neither feel uplifted by these promises nor alerted by these distant menaces, and rare are those among us whose religious life is nourished or animated by them. And yet, these events will surely take place. It is of faith that our Lord will return, that He will one day be again upon this earth. It is of faith that this world will come to an end. It is of faith that we shall all be judged, and woe to him, Jesus says in the Gospel, who will be taken by surprise as if he had never been warned, as if he had refused to believe it. We smile with self-complacency at the first Christians who were so simple that they were constantly waiting for the return of Christ, but how shall we appear when that return does take place and we are convicted of negligence in our belief?

17

The Christians of our times can be placed in two general categories, precisely according to their attitude in regard to these great events taught by faith.

In the first, we have the vast number of Christians who do not watch, who expect nothing, who no longer hope. They have renounced all ambition of participating in the universal redemption of mankind. They have resigned themselves to an ever diminishing place amidst the rising currents of the great political and social movements of our times. They have installed themselves in the world and there they live very much confused. They read the newspapers like everyone else, they take part in the distractions of the world like everyone else. They have the same professional standards as everyone else, which is to obtain as much money as possible and spend it exclusively on themselves. They have the same family morals as everyone else, which means not to have too many children nor too many cares, to join the advantages of marriage with the liberty of the celibate. Besides this, they are Christians by education and practice, and entertain no doubt whatever that their manner of life gives them every right to expect all the blessings of the life to come. The glorious return of Christ, the end of the world, the final judgment, these things they regard as exaggerations and too bizarre to merit attention. They certainly do not hope for these things. Their hopes are quite the contrary. They hope for the longest possible continuation of their lives upon this earth and happiness here below. They strive for the best here below and firmly maintain their right to the best hereafter. They resemble a man who has taken out insurance against fire. He does not expect any misfortune, he seldom thinks about it, he takes all reasonable precautions that it does not happen, but if, some day, it should happen, he will not be taken unprepared. So with them. Sunday Masses, more or less complete, confessions without progress, but they are not worried. All is in good order, so they think.

It is not that they refuse to believe in these events which the

Church announces. They accept them with docility but without much interest, seeing nothing in them which concerns themselves. However, when things go badly, when the horizon grows dark, when family, social, or international relations resemble a complicated piece of machinery that has gotten out of order, then they are ready to declare that the end of the world is near. They find in that a ready-made solution for the difficulties which now overwhelm them. Thus they consider themselves dispensed from doing anything, from praying, from working out a solution, or making any effort whatever. They have concluded that they will soon find themselves in heaven, a Christian soul of the primitive Church.

The faith of a Christian in the Parousia has nothing in common with this lax and ill-humored consolation. A true Christian awaits with great pride and hope the return of the Saviour.

First of all, he knows that it is always near, always imminent. He knows that the world depends upon the sovereign will of God. This world has a master, and because of that, it will have an end. At present, all is wrapped in mystery, truths are clothed in figure and in appearances, but some day the revelation will come. We shall see that the hand of God was in each happening of our lives, and when He shall have shattered all the appearances and put true values in their places, we shall be surprised and ashamed and shall strike our breasts because of our lack of faith and shall say: "Lord, pardon me because I did not know what you were doing."

All creation, St. Paul tells us, groans while awaiting the manifestation of the children of God. And we ourselves have our true life hidden in God. It is only when the Lord shall appear that we will know who we are and how closely we resemble Him. Then we shall be relieved of all our infirmities, we shall at last be unable to sin, or fail. We shall finally be able to love Him as we have always desired to do but have never succeeded. We will know how much reason there was for us to believe, to hope, and

19

to love. It will be revealed to us then how God was with us in all our sufferings and had for us the same infinite compassion, affection, and admiration that He had for His Son, dying on the Cross.

But, while fervently awaiting the reappearance of the Lord, the Christian is not inactive. It is this certitude of the Parousia that gives him the courage to work at the preparation of the Kingdom. St. Paul believed that the Lord would return when the entire world should be evangelized. Not knowing the true size of the world, he hoped to achieve this in the space of a human lifetime. It was this hope that set him travelling all the roads of the Empire. He wanted to complete the evangelization of the world before he died so that he might have the joy of seeing his Lord again more quickly.

The first Christians, too, awaited Christ from one moment to another, and that is why they held all their goods in common, rejoicing not only in the loss of their wealth, but in blows, in persecution, and in martyrdom. Christ might appear at any moment, and what a joy it would be if He found them suffering and dying for Him! It was this which gave to the Christianity of the first centuries that extraordinary dynamism which today is found in the political movements when they are looking forward to a "big night." With the Christians it was a "big day," an aurora of love and of peace. About the year 1000 there were great expectations of the return of Christ. That expectation did not, as we are so often led to believe, engender a wave of terror or discouragement. Quite the contrary. The history of that time shows that it was just then that they built the most beautiful churches, founded the most monasteries, and established the "Truce of God" and the "Peace of God," institutions which were far more efficacious than the U.N. in securing peace among men and making the world a worthy place to which God might come.

Thus, for us also, the final triumph of our Lord and His proximate appearance should rouse our enthusiasm for the preparation of His reign. We do not have to look around, like lost sheep, for a Master to follow, a truth in which to believe, nor for the means to save the world. We have a Saviour, a faith, and we know that the world is already saved. God has placed in our hands the means of saving the world, —prayer, the sacraments, and work, —inexhaustible sources of grace. For, after all, the important thing is not that the world should end, but rather that it should fulfill its destiny. The world will not come to an end in some great catastrophe, or some atomic explosion. What we are called upon to accomplish, and in doing so, bring this world to its end, is the fulfillment of the purpose for which it was created. This is what all those fervent Christians, members of the Catholic apostolate in all its many forms, are striving for, working to transform their profession and their surroundings. There are those young married couples who want to make their marriage a vocation to sanctity, all those political and social reformers who want to make this world more humane and fraternal, those priest-workers and those missionaries who announce Christ and carry Him to places where He has never been or where He is no longer. What sustains them is certainly not the contemplation of the results their efforts have already obtained, for the dough of our humanity is hard to knead, slow to rise, and quick to fall. If they had only human ends in view and human encouragement, they should certainly become discouraged. But what stimulates them and renders them invincible is their faith in the words of their Master: "Have confidence, for I have overcome the world." They know how their Master became a conqueror and what price He paid for His victory. Hence they never lose heart, neither in failure, nor in persecutions, nor in suffering, for they know, through the example of Christ, what triumphant resurrections can take place even on the most desolate of Calvaries.

Let us, too, on this first Sunday of Advent, make an act of faith in the eternal victory of Christ, so that this faith may make of us tireless workers for the coming of the Kingdom of God.

THE SECOND SUNDAY IN ADVENT

"Are you he who is to come, or shall we look for another?"
(Matthew 11:2–10)

This is the way in which St. John the Baptist both expresses and prophesies the astonishment and the scandal which the presence and the intervention of God among us always causes. Jesus was an object of scandal for His contemporaries. The religion which He founded and which continues His presence and His work still scandalizes, not only those who come in contact with it from without, but even those who are His followers.

When Christ came into the world He encountered an established religion, natural to the human mind, made for it, and fitted to its measure, —and He overturned it completely. This established religion exalted the majesty and power of God and caused men to fear His justice. The essential thing was to recognize the rights of God and to win His favor by certain well-defined acts of homage: by offerings and by prayers. God punished the bad and rewarded the good. The surest sign of His benevolence was the enjoyment of peace and prosperity. On the other hand, if a man sinned, he could expect the worst chastisements.

This religion is simple, quite natural, very logical, and therefore spontaneous. It is ours at the present time and we must ever be making efforts to rise above it.

This is exactly what St. John the Baptist was preaching. He was proclaiming an event of triumph, the coming of a glorious king who would bring down the anger of God upon the unjust. He announced a clean sweep, with blows of axe and of flail, of all the sins that mankind had heaped up. He foretold one who would redress all wrongs, fill the valleys, and lower the mountains. He believed, as do many of us, that the best way to uproot evil is to destroy the culpable. God would manifest Himself by being harsh to sinners and kind to the just.

And that is why our Saviour was so disconcerting. When St. John the Baptist saw that Jesus was so gentle, so mild, when he learned that Jesus refused to take part in the national struggles, or in political affairs, that He counselled both rich and poor to detachment from material goods, and that He invited both alike to enter His spiritual Kingdom, when he heard Jesus exalt the meek and the peacemakers, and announce the mercy of God upon sinners, poor John the Baptist was perplexed. He did not see in Jesus the fiery avenger whom he had been foretelling, so he ended by sending to Him an embassy to inquire if He were really the expected one or were they to await another.

And Jesus, while praising John the Baptist for his uprightness, his love of justice, and his courage, also said of him that he was the greatest of all the prophets who had gone before him, but such was the difference between the new order which Jesus was to institute and the new religion that He was to reveal, that the least in the Kingdom of heaven would be far greater than John. And Jesus added: "Blessed is he who shall not be scandalized by me!"

For Jesus' teaching was entirely new. He wrought a complete revolution in our religious conceptions. He revealed a religion which no one before Him had ever known and of which we ourselves have yet much to learn. Naïvely as usual, those who were awaiting this revelation, and even he who was appointed to announce it, all believed that Jesus was going to teach what they already knew, the religion they had always known, —a God in accordance with their own ideas, and acting according to their plans, the God of majesty, favorable to the just and without pity for sinners.

But Jesus revealed that God was meek and humble of heart,

23

that God was love, and that His solution to the problem of evil was to overcome the evil, not by violence, but by goodness and gentleness. He revealed that God had resolved to come among men in order to love, to deliver Himself, to give Himself to mankind as a frail little infant, as the physician who goes unarmed upon the battle-field, as a sacrificial lamb. Jesus revealed a religion which required only love, not a faded and sentimental love, but a love inspired by God, exacting, pitiless, crucifying to him who would evade it, but infinitely indulgent, fraternal, gratifying to him who received it.

From then on everything was overturned. Jesus no longer divided humanity into the just and the unjust, —the one to be rewarded, the other to be punished. He divided them into two quite different categories: those who knew how to love, those who believed in love, or those who, at least, tried to love, and, on the other hand, those who refused to love. To His followers Jesus offered only one recompense, something hateful and scandalous—the taking up of one's cross and following Him. And to sinners, He made but one announcement—they would be pardoned and accepted.

Ah, my brethren, it cannot be said too often that such a religion is shocking, terrible, most upsetting. Who among us expects to see a proof of the divine tenderness in failure, sickness, poverty, mourning? Who among us, when suffering comes, recognizes it as his vocation, his call, and that, for him, this is the beginning of his imitation of the Master? Who would not be scandalized by all this? "Blessed is he who is not scandalized."

It is impossible to be a man and not be scandalized by evil. St. Paul suffered from a thorn in his flesh, an angel of Satan who buffeted him, —that is, some physical or moral infirmity which humiliated him and hampered his apostolate. "Three times," he says, "I prayed God to deliver me, and He replied: 'My grace is sufficient for you. For my strength shall be manifested in your weakness.'"

24

Even Jesus Himself suffered in His humanity and learned in His agony this same terrible lesson. "He who, in the days of His flesh, with strong cries and tears, having offered supplications to Him who had the power to save Him from death, having been heard, although He was the Son, learned what it is to obey."

Thus will each of our prayers be answered. We shall not obtain escape from trial, my brethren, but the grace to bear it with love. God will not grant us happiness but, instead, the power to do without it, and to learn, sons and daughters as we are, what it is to obey the Divine Will in our regard.

Such a religion, my brethren, disconcerts us. Just as it astonished St. John the Baptist, so does it astonish us. We accepted it at baptism and again at certain particularly fervent moments in our lives, but daily confrontation with the realities of life hurts us and makes us waiver. It is so far from natural for us to accept the cross! Oh yes, we agree with the principle of it. We know that we should follow our Master. But have you ever noticed that, in actual fact, we judge that the cross that comes to us is never a good one. The cross that we are carrying is either intolerable, or else it is a shabby little thing, humiliating, inefficacious. Always it is precisely the one which we feel that we cannot accept. All the others seem to us to be preferable, such as that of our neighbor, or the one we had before, or that one which we have in our imagination. We would so much rather have another. We would like a cross according to our taste, made to our measure, a beautiful cross, replete with dignity and nobility. But, alas! we must often tell ourselves that, if the cross just suited us, it would no longer be a cross; that, if we refuse every cross that we do not like, we would never accept any at all, and that the cross that God sends us must always be painful and humiliating, paralyzing and difficult, and cause us pain just where we are least armed against it.

All this was experienced by St. John the Baptist. Shut up in prison for long years and at the point of being murdered through the capriciousness of a vicious woman and the weakness of an insignificant little tyrant noted only for his debauchery, the saint must often have asked himself if this were truly the beginning of the Kingdom and if the One whom he had announced would not do something to deliver him.

This was also the experience of the Apostles. How surprised, stunned, and confused they were when Jesus, intending to found the most lasting of kingdoms—a universal Church—being entirely alone, without a friend upon whom He could depend, and knowing that, if He left, all would be lost, chose to inaugurate His work by having Himself put to death. To them, this was not the right moment for that. We, too, find that it is never the right moment for us to be put to death. For our relatives and for ourselves, we find that it is never the right time to die. We shall always be much more useful later on and we are still necessary for all the many tasks which are still unfinished.

But God does not judge thus. God is never of the same opinion as ourselves. God overreaches us and disconcerts us always and it is necessary to conquer oneself in order to put faith in Him.

So St. John remained in prison. He had received some mysterious response that assured him that everything was at its best this way, and that it was just in this way that the Kingdom would be inaugurated and continue to advance. He suffered and he accepted that suffering. He understood and he proved by his death that he expected nothing else, thus showing his fidelity to the One whom he had pointed out.

And let us, too, in spite of our weaknesses and our doubts, and even though we may be tempted all the time to go back on our promises and to haggle over our sacrifices, even then let us also ask our Saviour if it be really He who requires all this. May we not hope for anything else? And in that very moment, as with St. John, He will make us His prophets, His witnesses, His martyrs. Oh, our death will not appear to us as anything beautiful, as anything of great value! There is no such thing as a beautiful cross. As we have failed so many times, so we shall be failures in death. We must follow Jesus even when He stumbles and falls, even in His groans and complaints, and we shall be constantly tempted to plead that the chalice be taken away from us. But if our death be but like this, it will have beauty in the sight of God! Amen.

THE THIRD SUNDAY IN ADVENT

We sometimes wish that we had been born in the time of Christ and we use this as an excuse for our lukewarmness when our conscience reproaches us. If only, we think, we had had the advantage of living with Christ, we would be stronger in our resistance to sin, more confident in the tenderness of God towards us. However, it is practically certain that our sinful habits would not be overcome by the presence of Christ, but they would, in reality, prevent us from recognizing Him. We would not know that He was present, and if He had told us who He was, we would not have believed Him. Not even His miracles would have convinced us. For only those believed in His miracles who already believed in Him. Others were irritated and hardened. A miracle, if it comes from a man who is under suspicion and hated, arouses only resistance. And, above all, we are so light-minded and forgetful that not even a miracle would have made any lasting impression. Thus it is quite possible that Jesus could be quite close to us for years and we might never know it.

This is what is happening now in our own day. Have you ever remarked the striking expression used by St. John the Baptist to announce to the Jews the presence of God in their midst? "There is one in the midst of you whom you do not know."

Our senses enable us to recognize objects. Odors, sounds, contacts all enable us to know what is around us. When we are exposed to bad weather, or if we overtax our strength, we know it. We receive interior warnings and we know that they must not be neglected.

But we have spiritual senses, too, which warn us with great fidelity of the true character of persons, places, and things that we encounter. A place of prayer inspires prayer. We feel it in the very atmosphere, and we react accordingly.

A beautiful ceremony, a Mass celebrated with recollection and devotion, a well-made confession or communion, all lift us out of ourselves and renew our spirits. And it is also certain that a man of prayer, or a saint, possesses a secret power of attracting to himself all who have similar spiritual inclinations. This can be a touchstone to aid us in the recognition of our own status, by asking ourselves what influence the saintly persons we have met have had upon us. Alas, we shall often find that we have lived in their company and have not really known them.

Fundamentally, we all sense and appreciate in another those qualities which we ourselves possess. Each one finds what he seeks and it is to him who knocks that the promise has been made that the door will be opened. And it will be our condemnation if it should be said of us that we lack all spiritual sense because we have no interior life, no religious appetite, that we appreciate only the outward appearance of things because all our interest stops there.

Thus, Jesus was, in appearance, just like everybody else. People who stopped at appearance only saw nothing in Him to make Him different from themselves. He was dressed like other men. He came and went, spoke, walked, and slept like anybody else. The one exception was that He did not sin and this big difference escaped the attention of the crowd.

Only those who had faith, who lived a spiritual life, remarked it, felt moved by it, felt drawn to Him without being able to explain why. At His approach, something stirred deep within them. Feelings of joy, of love, of confusion, immense yet consoling, arose within them. Their hearts burned when He spoke. Strange emotions stirred the creature at the call of the Creator. Those who were of God, heard the word of God with the deepest joy. They were lifted out of themselves. His sheep heard His voice and followed Him. They no longer cared to ask who He was because they knew that it was the Lord. Who else could move them so deeply?

Today, too, Jesus is present in our midst. Jesus, body and soul, God and man, is always with us. He has not left us orphans. "Behold, I am with you all days, even to the end of the world." "Where two or three are gathered together in my name"—as we are today—"I shall be in the midst of them." In very truth, today the words of St. John the Baptist again sound in our ears: "There stands one in the midst of you whom you do not know."

Jesus looks the same today as He did of old. In appearance, He looks like anyone else—a poor person is just like the next one, a priest is not unlike others, a saint looks to us like an ordinary person, a host is, in appearance, just a piece of unleavened bread—and yet, under these appearances, Christ lives, acts, speaks, and prays for us.

Today, still, the light shines in the midst of darkness and the darkness does not comprehend it. Today, still, God lives among His own and His own do not receive Him. Perhaps we are so occupied in not recognizing Him, in offending Him, that we ill-treat Him, insult Him even, as did the Jews, not knowing what they did. This is the reason, St. Paul tells us, that there are among us so many feeble, so many ill, and a great number dead, because they have not discerned in their midst the Body of the Lord.

And yet, there are times when someone among our associates sets out along the path which leads him to the faith. Or from time to time we learn that a man has made a change in his life, that he has cleansed his conscience and reformed his conduct. He is the same and yet he is different. People no longer recognize him, nor does he recognize himself. People are astonished at the change, they talk about it a little, and then pass on. From time to time, a young man or woman renounces marriage, interrupts his career, leaves the world and enters a monastery or a convent. Friends feel a shock of surprise and they stumble out a few words of felicitations full of compassion. These souls have recognized the Master. He has called them and they could not refrain from following that call. But, as for us, we remain where we are and we ask ourselves what happened to them. What did they see that we could not see?

And yet, is it really true that we have never seen the Lord? Has He never made any impression upon our own hearts? Have we never experienced the touch of His healing hand? Have we never penetrated into that zone of hidden force which comes from Him and surrounds Him and in which it is so good to be? Yes, undoubtedly there have been times in our lives when we have tasted how sweet is the Lord. We can recall times when a set of circumstances seemed about to crush us, to pulverize us, and we were protected in some wonderful way. Or someone showed us some unexpected mercy. Or a prayer of ours, said with faith, a retreat, or a confession, and we were transformed. We have not always been insensible. We used to love some person who spoke to us of God, we used to go so gladly to some special church and no other place in the world seemed to us so good. There were occasions when we showed courage or virtue in spite of temptation, when we were generous regardless of those around us, and we know that we were aided and strengthened by Another who approved of our conduct. But—these impressions which came to us from God were passing and we made no effort to continue them.

The error of our spiritual life lies in this, that we do not believe in God. What we believe in is those who tell us to believe in God. We do not seek to meet Him ourselves. We do not believe in His presence; we do not hope to touch Him; we are not attentive to recognize and to retain the impressions which come to us from Him.

We serve God with our will and because it is an obligation. We do not serve Him from our heart. It is the heart which keeps us alive. We are satisfied with emotions and impressions, and then give way to forgetfulness and negligence, and this is why God does not stir our hearts nor make Himself known to us.

It happens to Jesus just as it happens to our friends of long ago. At one time we loved them deeply, but we gradually lost sight of them. For no special reason we have allowed long separations to come between us. We no longer write to them nor reread their letters, nor look through our album of souvenirs. Occasions for meeting them have slipped away. We have allowed ourselves to be absorbed by other things, less agreeable and less according to our taste. Can we love another as much as we loved our old friend? Yet we never think of him, and if we do, we are astonished to find that we have even lost the desire to see him again. It would mean too much change, too much effort, too many arrangements for which we have lost interest, so we lose contact and never renew our old friendship.

This same thing can happen in regard to God. This same thing can render our spiritual life sterile. We can become inattentive to Him, no longer wish to encounter Him, no longer desire to see Him. No one sees God, no one meets Jesus, without having a strong and continual desire to do so.

It is a joy for God to manifest Himself, but, in spite of His omnipotence, He can draw near only to those who hunger and thirst for Him. That is what we lack—a deep longing to see God. It was just this longing, this holy curiosity, this attention that St. John intended to arouse by his words: "There is one in the midst of you whom you do not know." And in us, as well, they should have the same effect. Let us pay attention to them, and allow them to alert us, too, so that we lift up our heads and look around us, seeking Him whom they indicate, Him who is hidden

in the midst of us. Let us pray to St. John that he point out the
Saviour to us so that we may not hear that sad reproach: "Have I
been with you for so long a time and yet you do not know
Me?"

THE FOURTH SUNDAY IN ADVENT

*"John went into all the region about the Jordan, preaching a
baptism of repentance for the forgiveness of sins. So, with many
other exhortations, he preached the Good News to the
people."* (Luke 3:1–6)

Are you aware of the authentic mark of all sincere religion?
Do you know the starting point of all religious renewal? Do you
realize what is the best preparation for the joys of the Christmas
season? It is penance.

Every time that the world has been renewed, each time that a
strong current of grace and joy has brought refreshment to the
world, the means has always been the same—penance. When St.
John the Baptist came to prepare his people to recognize, to love,
and to rejoice in Christ, he found that the best advice that he
could give them was: "Repent! Do penance!" This was also the
initial sermon of Jesus. "The time has come! The Kingdom of
God is at hand. Repent! If you do not do penance, you shall all
likewise perish!" And when the Apostles, after their baptism of
fire on Pentecost, began their preaching of the Good News, they
gave no other counsel but that of their Master: "Repent and ask
pardon for your sins."

There can be no sincere religion without penance, without a
turning to the interior of religion, something just as real and just
as difficult as a conversion to the exterior. There is no true
spiritual life if one does not reach the conclusion that there is still

32

much to learn. There is no vitality in that spiritual life where there is not a periodic recognition of the fact that there is still a long way to go. He who believes himself established, nicely settled, at the apex, and beyond any further improvement is like the Pharisees with whom Jesus could do nothing.

This call to penance annoys and rebukes us. We are completely unsympathetic to the very idea of it, and the word has disappeared from our vocabulary just as the thing itself has disappeared from our preoccupation. We take as much trouble in organizing our distractions as the ancient Christians took in perfecting their penance. What we avoid, they sought.

The big reason for this difference is that we are not conscious of being the sinners that we really are. That is the reason why our spiritual life is so superficial, our confessions so sterile, and our prayers so lacking in fervor. We are not penitents.

We have the idea that all the blame for our defects is due to God. We desire nothing so much as to see Him and to pray to Him, —to know Him and to serve Him. It is He who hides from us, enclosing Himself within impenetrable silence.

This idea is what will prevent us from recognizing and accepting our God—even at Christmas time. We entertain a deep feeling of discontent in regard to God. It is all His fault, we say. He has deceived us. He has not acted as He should. A chasm has opened between ourselves and God. Just as in families where there are quarrels, jealousies, and disputes over the inheritance. They meet one another and speak to one another because it is the proper thing to do, but they do not love one another. Certain subjects are never brought up in conversation because they know that it will mean only further disagreement.

So we act with God. He has not treated us as we thought He should. We have never pardoned Him for permitting such and such a failure, for sending us that cross, that sorrow, that loss, not answering that prayer which we said with such fervor that we have never understood how He could resist us. We have allowed

33

all these grudges to accumulate, and, little by little, a thick wall has come to separate us from God. Oh yes, we still speak to Him, say a prayer now and then, never miss Mass, but our confidence is gone, love is gone, and so is joy. The outer forms remain, but the heart is dead.

However, you can see, my brethren, that the obstacle which must be removed if we are to receive our God is our stubborn clinging to our sins, our holding to our own point of view, our foolish resistance to God, our cherished conviction that it is God who is in the wrong. You must understand that the real preparation for Christmas, the true way to enjoy Christmas, is to fall on one's knees, to strike one's breast, and to confess that God is the One who loves, it is God who knows how to love, and that it is God who is always right. If something goes wrong, it is not God who is to blame but ourselves. He has gone to the utmost limits to win us, to draw us to Himself, to allow us to see Him. Christmas, the coming of God in the flesh, the Incarnation, means just that. It is God's most audacious attempt to give us His Body. The Passion and the Cross mean just this. They are the most moving cry that was ever uttered so that an unresponsive creature could no longer deny that he was loved by God and that the price of his salvation had been paid.

Therefore, all those things about which we complain—sterility and dryness, silence and solitude, the poverty of our spiritual life, the apparent withdrawal of God—all these things are our own fault. It is we who are in the wrong. We are the ones who must be reformed. Our sins, our deficiencies, our repeated refusals to accept the will of God and to trust ourselves to it—these are the things that have erected that wall of separation. It is of little importance that we are unable to say when all this began, nor what is the silly obstacle that we have placed between God and ourselves. What we must do is to repent and to confess our abnormal state. Are we unhappy? Are we lacking in enthusiasm? Are we without grace and love? It is not God who has denied us these things, it is we who have refused them. Let us begin by beating our own breasts, by recognizing our own guilt. Often, it is only after being pardoned that we see where the real fault lies. It is only after absolution that a person understands all the love with which he is surrounded. And only then do we discover how much we were lacking in faith, love, confidence, in prudence and respect, in sincerity and courage.

Advent begins with a history rich in symbolism—that of Zachary, the father of St. John the Baptist. You know that he had always begged God to grant him a child and God had always refused his request. He, too, had been disappointed by God and yet Zachary continued to pray. He was old now, but a religious man, a priest, and even at one time the high priest. Every day he fulfilled the duties of his priesthood, but he had lost confidence in God. His heart was dead even though his lips still murmured the prayer. And when an angel appeared to him to tell him, on the part of God, that he was to have a son, he told the angel that it was not possible. God had heard Zachary when he uttered his first prayer. He was to have a son and that son's birth was to be a miracle. His son was to be a prophet, the greatest prophet of the Old Testament, the Precursor of the Messiah. But, because Zachary's prayer was not heard in the way that he expected, he had ceased to believe that God would hear him, although he continued his prayer. So it became necessary that an angel should punish him and that he should endure a long and severe penance. Repenting of his long incredulity towards God, his heart opened to receive the Gift which God was sending him. And as for us who are praying during this time of preparation for Christmas, but, at bottom, expecting nothing, only a true conversion, only sincere penance, can dispose us to receive the Gift which God has promised us.

God has ever surprised and disconcerted men because He has answered their prayers in a manner quite the opposite of what they expected. But when God came to save the world, it was then

35

that He caused the greatest surprise of all. His relatives, His fellow-villagers, His countrymen, His most enthusiastic partisans—He astonished and disconcerted them all.

And God disconcerts us, too. He has been doing it all our lives, working for our salvation by upsetting all our efforts to escape from Him, by torpedoing all our ridiculous attempts to do without Him. The perpetual antagonism between what God wills and what we will has opened a chasm between us which we must go back and fill in. We shall have to travel back all the road that we have travelled in refusing His will and in doing our own. While we pout and grumble over our fancied hurts, God has promised to send, even to us, an Infant, a frail little Messenger of a great love. But beware! We still have in our hearts all the indifference, all the self-interest, all the stubbornness and ill-will which may one day refuse, reject, and crucify that Infant. If we desire to prepare ourselves to receive Him, if we wish to be among those who will not find Him impossible and insupportable, we must not forget what we are and get down on our knees, strike our breasts, and say: "Father, forgive me, for I have sinned! Father, I have been so stubborn! Pardon me, Father, for I knew not what I was doing, nor what you were doing. I am unworthy of your gifts. Withdraw from me, for I am a sinner!"

And it is on this condition, this condition alone, that, on Christmas, in security, in hope, in love, and in great joy, our Infant Saviour will come to us.

CHRISTMAS—FIRST HOMILY

The joy that I wish you on this feast of Christmas, the joy that I pray will be yours during this Mass that we are celebrating together, is something deep and new. It is not a joy of souvenirs of childhood memories, of Christian customs piously observed, but a fresh, untried joy, the joy of today.

My brethren, this birth at which we rejoice is not principally that of the Infant Jesus, but our own. This night should see something born in each one of us. Every man and woman in the world is called upon to be reborn this night. We are called upon to believe in that unheard of but most necessary thing—that we are capable of a second birth; that a joy, hitherto unknown, can take possession of us, and that we can be filled with a love so strong, so gay, so overflowing, that we know at once that it does not come from ourselves. In St. Paul's words, we have become a new creature. We are all of us renewed, reborn, this night.

There are so very few who really believe in this Nativity! We all seem to have such good reasons for withholding our confidence. This pledge of our hope always comes to us in the darkness of night and in the depth of winter. Salvation flowers in the desert waste.

This Nativity took place the first time in a world that was desperate. Zachary and Elizabeth were certain that they would never have a son. Simeon and Anna feared that they would die before they should see the Saviour. Nicodemus said that rebirth was impossible at his age. Israel had waited so long that all hope was gone. The people of Jerusalem knew very well where the Saviour was to be born. They directed the Magi with skill. They knew their religion and celebrated all the prescribed feasts. But not a single one of them disturbed themselves to go and see. They knew everything so well that it was all the same thing as knowing nothing. We know everything so well that we never learn more. And so the old world, encrusted with sin, slept peacefully as a turtle in its shell.

And yet, it took a little girl of fifteen, with the absolute faith and hope of her youth, to break through all this and to renew the world.

There are few who celebrate the Nativity! (There are many

more who stifle the new-born lest there be a cry of joy and hope.) Those who celebrate the Nativity come from afar. They appear suddenly in the midst of an indifferent people. They set out, leaving everything behind, bearing nothing with them but their most precious gift, and advancing without even knowing to whom they should offer it.

May there still remain among us a few who believe in this Nativity! Let us pray that at least some of us may shake off that habit of believing which is worse than believing nothing. Let us pray that they may begin to heed the new, joyous, and wondrous message of this night.

It will mean nothing to us that the Saviour was born 2,000 years ago if He is not born at the present day as well. It will mean nothing to us that, 2,000 years ago, someone spoke words from God if there be no one, today, who can speak to us on the part of God. It will mean nothing to us that God made advances towards us, that the tenderness of God was shown to us 2,000 years ago, if there is no one among us today whom we can love and compassionate—if we do not love each other at least a little at the present time. The marvel of this present night, my brethren, is that God can return and live among us.

There is ever a need in our midst for a body, for hands to heal, arms to sustain, mouths to speak, and hearts to love. In whom here will this be born tonight?

Oh, undoubtedly this will be a very humble birth, a frail infant whose life is menaced. Wrapped in poor swaddling bands, lying upon straw in a crib. A very poor feast in comparison with the feasts of the world.

But from afar, from everywhere, there are men who will rise up at this light, having a presentiment of this birth, hungry and thirsty for this tenderness, they will go forth blindly to this new-born Child, bringing Him their most precious possessions, although not yet aware of whom it will be given to them to offer themselves.

CHRISTMAS—SECOND HOMILY

When God revealed Himself, He did an unheard of thing. He filled the world with joy.

Look how we have fulfilled the duties of our spiritual life with great effort and weariness. We love God with a discouraged love. We have gradually allowed a veil of misunderstandings and negligences to come between Him and ourselves. Depressed by His absence, rebuffed by His silence, we have come to believe that we are more generous and active than He is. And so we have accommodated ourselves to a God who is mute, because, after all, He gets along very well, and that allows us more liberty to follow our own interests, and attach ourselves to whatever promises to be of use to us, since we no longer expect anything from God.

But when God revealed Himself, He tore away all these veils, He broke through all limitations, He dazzled and amazed everyone. When God showed Himself as God, it was a revelation of great joy.

God was infinitely better than anyone thought. God was young, full of tenderness, charming, infinitely favorable, indulgent, audacious, understanding, gay, happy. God was God!

The Gospel opens with announcements of great happiness. There are announcements, promises, miracles, summonses—a remarkable array. Everyone is astonished, and all receive infinitely more than they had believed possible. Sterile Elizabeth bears a child, incredulous Zachary prophesies, the Virgin becomes a mother, shepherds speak with angels, the Magi give their all, and Simeon no longer fears to die.

What we must learn first of all, the most urgent message, the most pressing revelation is that God is not what we think He is, that He is infinitely better, infinitely more tender, more dazzling,

39

more ravishing, than we have ever imagined. Our greatest and most urgent duty is to exult, to give thanks, to be confused and then exalted, to weep, to laugh, and to kiss His hands and feet. That sorry idol, poor and mean, that we have made of God is broken. All our religion is vain if we are going to pass our days in sadness and in the mistaken notion that we are alone, and sometimes come to the conclusion that we ourselves are better than the God before whom we kneel.

Those who think that they believe in God would hardly recognize the reality in the image that they have created. Face to face with the true God, they come to see that, through laziness, negligence, and lassitude, they have been adoring but an idol. God has vanished from their hearts during this process.

And many of those who have abandoned God have learned, upon seeing what He really is, that they were right in their rejection. They know now that God is far removed from any image, from any idea of their own making, and that it was really their fidelity to Him that made them act as they did. Deep within their souls they have had the conviction that God was better, more powerful, more worthy of enthusiasm than the image that was presented to them.

All have spontaneously recognized this: that He was good, so good that they wished for Him without daring to believe in Him. Wherever He went, there was an outburst of joy. He came, He bent down, He spoke, He called, and everywhere there was joy, hope, and enthusiasm. He astonished them, He satisfied them. He fed the crowd with bread, He gave fish to the fishermen and wine to those who would drink and healing to the sick. Then swaying humanity stood still, held by this happiness. For humanity had suddenly learned that God was good and that it had never had faith in His goodness. Humanity learned that it had never believed in God although it thought so, and those who were sure that they had no faith discovered that they had always been seeking it.

40

The crowd suddenly discovered that they were no longer hungry. A moment before, they would have fought for a mouthful of bread. People were watching each other, watching those privileged ones who had something to eat, they were suffering and sullen. And now, each one has in his hands this miraculous bread, and in holding it thus the heart of each is wonderfully satisfied. Slowly they raised this miraculous bread to their lips, this nourishing bread which came from a few words from the mouth of God. They communicated, eyes were closed, and they were still. It was too much, they were too rich, they were overcome by such wealth and no longer had any desire to eat.

And those who drank were no longer thirsty. From the moment that they had held in their hands that cup—(was it water, or was it blood, or was it wine?)—they knew that their thirst was gone. Up to that moment, of course, they had wanted to drink. Just before that they had believed the feast spoiled, the spouses were humiliated, and the guests displeased. Then there had been that order, a little action, and now each one knew that he was no longer thirsty, that he had never been thirsty. That his thirst, his discontent, had simply been a manifestation of his need for God. God was there, God has been given to us, we drink God.

And the sick—do you know what they learn when they are cured? They suddenly discover that it would have been better for them to remain sick, that they did not need to be cured, that they could be happy in their sickness.

When they now experience that sense of well-being, when their suffering body is no longer a matter of concern, what they come to see is that there lies before them an immense country to conquer, and their cure is but the initial step. They see the love of God covering that country as with sunshine and even softening the sad one which they have just left.

Up to now, they thought they were suffering but from sickness, from their helplessness and the anxiety of their relatives, as well as from fear of the future. But they know now that they have been devoured and tormented by one thing, their lack of confidence in God. Even the unbelievers who deny Him, ignore Him, and curse Him know now that what they lacked the most was the power to believe in the goodness of God. When this is brought home to them, sometimes by a miracle, the tenderness of God overwhelms them and they desire nothing more. They have come to recognize that their greatest need was not a bodily cure. Now they no longer fear a return of their sickness because they know that they are loved.

The hunger from which man suffers is something too great for our imagination. In one of his novels Albert Camus describes a village attacked by the plague. Each one reacts according to his own character to the scourge which spreads rapidly. Some try to ignore it, some to flee from it, some to combat it, and others to profit by it. The village is put under quarantine, and gradually the epidemic dies out. The quarantine was lifted and the survivors made their first trip out of the village. It was then that they realized, as they crossed the meadows and climbed the hills, that what had caused them the most suffering was a certain absence, their exile, an insatiable thirst, and that, in order to be happy, to be truly themselves, to be secure, they needed nothing less than the whole wide world, open and free. They understood that, if they were to live in peace and contentment in their own little homes, they had need to feel surrounded by the whole of humanity.

Our soul is also vast and its requirements immense. Nothing less than God can satisfy us. Our greatest mistake is to think that some one little thing is all that we lack,—is all that we need to make us happy. It may be a little money, a promotion, an opportunity, relief from an illness. Given that, we shall want no more. But we are sadly mistaken. Another sickness will come, some other desire, we shall always be unhappy because the one thing that we need is God. And we always have Him but He does

42

not always have us. When He does, our happiness begins, immediately and without delay. Eternal life is to know the Father and to know the Son, and eternal life begins now, and so does the joy which springs from it. Simeon and Anna tell us on this feast that they no longer fear to die because they have now seen the Lord.

CHRISTMAS—THIRD HOMILY

The Revelation of the Son

A joyous Christmas, my brother, in Him who has brought us all things in empty hands, who instructs us in silence and who renews us completely without any change in the circumstances of our lives, for He has become incarnate therein.

I do not know what kind of Christmas you would like, I do not know if you are delighted or disenchanted, for God's ways are not our ways and He gives us more than we are willing to receive. We sometimes hope that He will work a miracle and transform the unhappy circumstances in our lives and He does something better—He comes to share them.

Jesus comes poorer than the poorest among us. He does not bring riches with Him. The life of Jesus was more monotonous, more confined, more obscure than anything about which we complain. He brings neither adventure nor evasion. Jesus came ignored, unknown, and persecuted, and it is not His way to bring us renown, love, understanding, and admiration.

But He has come to give us all that He is, His Sonship. He is the Son and He has come to reveal to us the Father. He has come to ask us to become His brothers, to partake with Him of His filial relationship, and to learn from Him how a son should love his father, trust in him, and leave everything in his hands.

43

He has in this way revealed to us what we lack most, what we should ask for most of all. We were orphans, we were all suffering more or less from a certain absence, from a hopeless exile, from a nameless sorrow, from a burden too heavy for us. We had broken the vital bond which bound the child to its parent, the creature to its Creator. We were living in a fatal solitude, strangers to ourselves, to others, to the world, to everything that the paternity of God would bring to us, a joyous fraternity.

This is the reason that the Son has come to live among us: in order that each one may recognize himself in that Son, and learn from Him what we truly are, both as poor and as rich as the Son. For joy shines forth from the crib and confidence from the little stable. He has everything as He lies on the straw—He has a Father. What joy, in the midst of destitution, to smile confidently at His Father. What joy to abandon Himself completely, totally, to the will of the Father. A son, with unheard of audacity, wishes to be fully a son in order that the Father may be fully a father. He does not trust to gifts, He will have nothing less than the Giver Himself, so that He may never want for anything. He has come to tell us that to be a son and to have a Father is the whole of our need.

This is the meaning of the feast of Christmas. It is much more than a childish tenderness. The All-powerful has become a little one, the Most High has become the most close. Christmas is the love of God made visible, the revelation of the inmost secret of the Godhead, the love of Father and Son for each other, and the love of the Father for us, His adopted sons.

Coventry Patmore, the English poet, says that the first shock that came to him in the course of a retreat was this: "What a marvellous thing it would be if God were such that my relations with Him could be only those of love and obedience." Then, with a poet's imagination, he went on to picture to himself the sentiments that would follow such a relationship. There was the nobility of being a son, the exact equilibrium of tenderness and respect (loving the one he respected and respecting the one whom he loved), there was pride and modesty (to be a son, and no more than a son), free access to His presence, the delightful sense of dependence upon the Father, trust in His will, repose in His love, and the knowledge that one could rely implicitly in whatsoever He might ordain. These sentiments came to him so easily, so naturally, that he could not help thinking that they must be true. He could never be happy otherwise. And the poet set about seeking the Father because he had discovered that the one thing that mattered was that of being a son.

Let me recall an experience of the last war. In danger, face to face with death, I made this discovery, that my life did not belong to me, that it did not come from me, that I could die, that life was a gift, a loan, gratuitous and fragile. I recall the immense relief that followed this discovery. A heavy weight was lifted from my shoulders. Here, I had been imagining that my life depended upon me, I had been in such anxiety to save it, to procure its preservation, to hide it. All joy had gone out of life because of this responsibility which I had usurped. But now I could breathe freely, realizing that my life was not my responsibility. It was something given to me and would continue, a grace, a prolonged creation. How I regarded my companions with wonder, what joy to meet them again, to be overwhelmed with that beautiful grace of their presence. Never did we love each other so much!

To know that life is something received, and that it was made to be offered, restored, returned, what peaceful repose in hands far more powerful than our own. What relief and what joy! It was a filial joy and it was just this joy that Jesus came to announce to the world. If He was continually happy, enthusiastic, generous, fervent in prayer, tireless in work, courageous in the face of threats and hatred, it was because He knew and loved His Father. "I am not alone. I am never alone. You go and leave

45

me alone," He said to His Apostles in a moment of great sorrow, on the eve of His Passion, "but I am never alone because the Father is always with me." It was from this communion with His Father that He drew His courage. This Presence nourished Him. "I have other food that you know not of," He said to His Apostles. "My food is to do the will of My Father." There are many beautiful passages in St. John which give us a glimpse of this constant contemplation, this respectful love, and this intimate converse with the Father. "Amen, amen, I say to you, the Son can do nothing of Himself, but only what He sees the Father do. All things that the Father does, the Son can do also. For the Father loves the Son and shows Him what to do. I can do nothing of myself. As I hear, I judge. You do that which you have understood of your father. I do that which I have seen of my Father. In truth, he who sees me, sees Him who has sent me." From time to time, this reciprocal affection cannot be concealed: "I bless you, O Father! I give you thanks! Just Father, the world has not known you but I know you. I know that you hear me always!" And the Father Himself cannot resist, and from the height of heaven He exclaims: "This is my beloved Son in whom I am well pleased."

It is this love for His Father that explains His Passion and His death. One might say that from all eternity the Son has sought for some means to express to His Father all His love, all His admiration and all His gratitude. He profited by the days of His flesh to give Him the greatest proof of His love. "There is no greater love than to lay down one's life for those whom one loves. So that the world may know that I love the Father and that I obey the commandments that He has given me, arise, let us go hence," He said to His Apostles as He went to His Passion.

And we, too, shall know that same joy when we feel the Father bend over us with love and say: "Here is my beloved son, or daughter, in whom I am well pleased." We, too, shall know a joy that nothing can dim when we realize that the Father is always looking upon us—poor, lonely, unhappy, even apparently abandoned though we be. He follows us with the same love, the same infinite pity, as well as pride, admiration, and gratitude, that He bestowed upon His Son lying on the straw in Bethlehem or upon the Cross on Calvary.

"Lord," said Philip, "show us the Father. Grant that, upon us in our misery, there may always be the watchful eyes of the Father and it will be sufficient for us."

Lord, grant that, on this feast of Christmas, there may be born in us the love of your Son, and may we ever resemble Him as your sons and daughters. It is in this way that we shall see the Father and that will be sufficient for us.

CHRISTMAS—FOURTH HOMILY

May God bless you, my brothers, you who have come here to gather around Him on this night of Christmas. May God bless you for having come, as did the poor and humble long ago, to be present at His birth and to surround His crib.

And may He bless all those who have taught you to do this—your parents, your friends, your priests. It is their faith which has given birth to yours and which lives again in you. It is for them an honor and a joy.

May God bless you for having heard and responded to His call. For, in spite of appearances, you have not come here of yourselves. Every time that a man draws near to God, seeks God, it is God who has first sought him. The men of good will to whom the angels wished peace in the Gloria of this day's Mass, these are men in whom the good will, the benevolence of God is manifested. Good will arises in man only after he has consented to the grace of God which is offered to him.

May God continue in you and bring to fruition during the

course of this night, the work which He has begun in you by leading you here. Each prayer is a sign that God is working in you. Even the beginning of a prayer is a sign that God is preparing to answer you. Every truth that one discovers is something which one already has, in some way, in his possession or he would not have recognized it. It must be within you before you can recognize it outside of yourself. The two seek each other and become joined. If it is true that one finds only what he seeks, it is also true that one seeks only that which, to some extent, he has already found, which he already has partly in his possession. You seek God only because He has, for quite some time, found, called, attracted you. One prays because one is already being heard.

What shall we receive this night? What grace of God is seeking you out and soliciting your acceptance? With what gift of God are we threatened this night?

We are going to assist at the birth of Christ. Not at the anniversary of His birth. There is no question here of a souvenir, a commemoration, of a pious longing for the favored time when He was born. We believe that Christ is always being born, that He has never ceased being born, that He is not even truly born in many places, in many families, and even in many among yourselves; that He will be born this night, as feeble, as helpless, as much exposed to rejection and ignorance as when He was first born.

If, on your own birthday, you were to say: "I am born today," it certainly would not be true. But divine feasts are not like human feasts. The Church assures you in all truth that it is today—*hodie*—that the Saviour of the world is born. "A Child is born unto us and a Son is given to us." In a few moments, at this Mass, He will be really present among us. Who among us will recognize Him? Who will receive Him?

A new birth upsets the whole household. How long ago was it since there was a birth in your family? How long since you gathered around a little crib? It is an event which transforms a family and changes every one's life. What would happen in your home now if a baby came to it?

But here there is not merely a question of a baby born into a normal family. Here there is question of an infant who holds out His arms to you, begging you to adopt Him. The Father gives Him to you and begs you to accept Him. The Virgin has brought Him into the world only that she might give Him to the world. And she wishes to become your mother in giving you her Child.

It is a serious thing to adopt a child. Who among you would like to adopt a baby? "Impossible!" I can hear you say. "We would no longer have any time to ourselves. We would have to change our whole manner of life."

But this is something still more serious. This Infant is God and it is into your most secret, most intimate self, your conscience, that He wishes to come. That makes us tremble. We fear the approach of God.

This is not entirely because He will exact some modification in our conduct. It is true that, once we admit this Infant, we can no longer live a life of deception, egoism, pride, and hardness of heart.

But the main thing is that He will never leave us to ourselves. That "ego" that we try in every way possible to escape, that hated and yet pampered "ego" at whose feet we throw all the pleasures, all the distractions, all the poisons so that it will leave us in peace, is going to be reawakened by the presence of God. God is going to hold a dialogue with it. The presence of God within us makes us aware of our own personality. We are brought face to face with God, and, because He loves us, He will not permit us to underestimate or be dissatisfied with what we are. It has been said that the greatest charity which we can exercise towards ourselves is to develop a character in which we can be ourselves and accept ourselves. God alone loves us enough to enable us to see ourselves and accept ourselves, by letting us see our value in His eyes. We are so poor in love that it is only with His love, only thanks to His love, that we can love ourselves rightly.

Such a love, discreet and trustful like the love of a child, is the only one which we may admit: "You know how to give good gifts to your children."

This love penetrates into our being. It is the love which unites husband and wife, which causes children to be born, which our fathers and mothers had for us. It is given to us that we may love them more and more, for we need all that God can give us in order that we may love them as much as they have need of being loved.

Only God is capable of keeping this love alive, of bringing it back again after each trial and in all the various stages of our lives. For to love is to hope in another always, to begin anew to believe, to give, and to wait.

This is the birth that we celebrate on this night of Christmas. This is the gift of God which is promised to us—or which we may regard with foreboding—the love of God born in our souls. It is as living as a person, frail as an infant, strong as young life, and it is being offered to each of you.

Let those of us who are preparing to receive communion during this Mass pray that we do not refuse to open our souls to this love.

CHRISTMAS—FIFTH HOMILY

I often say to myself that if, at Christmas, our Saviour were to come to us, it would spoil the whole feast. If Jesus were to invite Himself to our home (even without His family) under the appearance of a displaced person or some old man whom nobody wants because he is old, or under the form of some young prisoner out on parole—that would be the end of our Christmas. The whole thing would be spoiled.

Every time that our Lord comes into one's life, everything is turned upside down. Think for a moment. Look at Zacheus. After he met our Lord, he hadn't a penny to his name! (This also happens at Christmas time to certain fathers of families, but not exactly because of religion!) But Zacheus was filled with joy and a great sense of liberty, and he experienced infinitely more satisfaction in distributing his gold than he had ever felt in acquiring it.

Think of Mary. Never did she feel more poor, more deprived, more despoiled, more abandoned than when our Lord was born. He had chosen the worst moment, the sorriest place. She was a refugee, a "displaced person," and everywhere refused. Yet it was then, in that place, that she experienced such joy that the world does not know of one greater.

It is a bad thing to come to Christmas already satiated with joy. We are too rich in the goods of this earth to rejoice in the goods of heaven. In our comfortable homes, not a thing is lacking, even when the Saviour is not there. We are like children, too occupied with their gifts, their Easter eggs, or their Christmas toys, to look at God and receive Him with both the confusion and the joy, which come from the knowledge of our poverty.

One must be either very poor or very unhappy to find everything in God. We have an abundance of everything save God. Happy are the poor for the Kingdom of God is theirs. Happy those who cannot be made happy save by the divine Other. Happy those who cannot be content with less than God.

CHURCH UNITY

On January 18th begins the Octave of Prayers for Church Unity.

The origin of the Octave is a revelation of the importance

51

of the individual in the plan of God. It reveals the unsuspected efficacy of individual initiative. It is also an example of the means that God uses, and will continue to use, to bring about unity in His Church.

At the close of the 19th century, the established Churches were each absolutely convinced of their own righteousness and also of the crimes of those whom they called their "adversaries." The relations between the Churches were limited to controversies between their theologians, strengthening their own positions and ridiculing that of the opposite party.

While this was going on, an obscure Protestant minister named Louis Watson began to reflect on the scandal of both this attitude and this separation. There is a prayer of Christ's which has not been answered: "Father, that they may be one as we also are one, that the world may believe." It is we Christians who have prevented the realization of that prayer. God has left us free to resist Him. A prayer of Christ is sterile because of us! And this fact makes us responsible for the incredulity of the world.

There is a means, a sure means, to convert the world. Christ Himself has guaranteed its efficacy. There is a means for the 900,000,000 Christians to convert the million and a half persons who have not the faith, and that is to unite—"that they may be one so that the world may believe."

And there is also a means to scandalize the world and confirm it in its incredulity and that is to maintain and to establish divisions.

The men of our day are realists. They base their judgment on what they see. They hear us preach love, and they see that we do not love. They can very well say to us: "Physician, heal yourself!"

This personal conviction of Watson has spread, during the past sixty years, into all Christian Churches. This octave will bring together 900,000,000 Christians, united in one prayer. This octave has completely changed the attitude of these

Churches to one another. Today they salute one another, they visit one another, and they speak to one another. This octave has created the climate of the coming Council.

Why, then, should any one of us feel that it is impossible for him to work for the coming of the Kingdom of God? For each one of us is a direct cause of union or dissension in the Church.

But not by prayer alone. Prayer is important, certainly. Not to pray for union among the Churches would be a proof of unbelievable indifference, egoism, and incredulity.

But prayer, by itself, is not enough. Péguy says: "To pray for victory and to refuse to fight, to me, that is poor reasoning." And St. Thomas More asked of God that, whenever He sent the inspiration to pray for a cause, He would also give the means to work for its realization.

It is not enough to pray for union among the Churches, one must also act.

And what is more, knowingly or unknowingly, we all are working either for the Church or against her.

For, what is true in regard to the world—that the world will be converted if Christians are united—is also true in regard to the Churches, that the Churches will unite if Christians love one another, if Catholics become fervent and charitable.

I will show you what I mean. Look at us Catholics of this city, are we united? Do we love one another? Do we even know one another? Do you know the person beside you, here at Mass? Your neighbor on the street? Your neighbor at work? On the bus? Is there any communication, exchange, sympathy, warmth between us because we are Christians?

Or are we rigorously individualistic? Do we assemble here to be in solitude? Isolated? Protected against one another? Do we look for a quiet corner in which to indulge in our personal devotions without thought for any one else?

Cardinal Feltin has said: "Our Catholics live their common faith each one for himself."

53

Each one for himself and God for us all, is not this the description of our Masses? This Mass today, is it a dinner served at individual tables, or is it a large assembly of warm-hearted and friendly people?

Do you think (and can you honestly hope) that the other Christian Churches are going to make the enormous efforts, the immense sacrifices which their union with the Catholic Church involves, for the single advantage of resembling us? Of being as poorly united as we ourselves are now? Why bother about the union of the Churches if Christians do not love one another? Why union at the top when there is none at the bottom?

What divisions there are among us! What indifference! What ignorance! What jealousies! What quarrels! What barriers! And these exist in families, in neighborhoods, in parishes, in our country, and even between Christians of different races, colors, or nations. And right here, in this church, do we know each other? Do we agree with each other? Do we love each other? Do you know how schisms and heresies come into being? Always during a period of decadence in the Church.

You can easily understand this. There are persons who are not at home in the Church, there are people who feel frozen out in these supposedly fraternal meetings, who have been shocked to see how Christians give the lie to their Faith—so cold, so egoistic, so indifferent to one another. Then, because they do not find in our Church sufficient faith and charity, they begin to look elsewhere and, before long, they have created a Church which seems to them to be more in keeping with what Christ intended.

I once asked a poor old woman why she, who was a Catholic, was now going to the Protestant church. "Now," she told me, "I spend two or three hours every Sunday among friendly people who accept me, treat me with consideration and speak to me."

This was something she had never met with in our Church!

Even at the present day, our tepidity, our torpidity, our preoccupation with ourselves only, engenders divisions, deceptions, and complaints. The source of heresies and schisms is there, within ourselves, and it is always ready to come to life. Then let us heal our own disease before we set out to heal others.

The sole means of achieving Church Unity is a deep search for the sanctity which exists in each church and which is what can unite. We shall come together at the center, not at the outskirts and by marginal concessions. We shall come together when we conform ourselves more strictly to the will of Christ.

Now the will of Christ is very plain. It is that we should love one another, be understanding towards one another, and be interested in one another.

What have we come here to do, at this Mass, for example?

It is not solely to love God and to tell Him so. It is just as much to love our brethren and to let them know it.

"When you come to the church, if you remember that your brother has anything against you, leave there your offering, leave the church, and go first and be reconciled with your brother. Then you may come and bring your gift to the altar."

The joy of a father is to see his children agreeing with one another. I greatly fear that when He looks down from the height of heaven and sees us, each one isolated, unknown, indifferent to everyone else, the Father must say: "I have failed with them. My dearest wish was to have them united among themselves and here they are, thinking to please me by seeking to unite themselves to me as separate individuals."

Christ has foretold us that the world would be converted, not in the least by our saying that we love God. Everybody can say that much, and no one can verify it. What Christ said was that the world would be converted if we bring about that rarest and truest of miracles, if we set about, today, all of us, loving one another. "He who says that he loves God whom he does not see, and does not love his neighbor whom he does see, is a liar," St. John tells us.

He who comes here to unite himself to God whom he does not see, but positively refuses to be united to his brothers whom he does see, is doing the very thing which makes it impossible for anything short of a miracle to bring about the conversion of the world.

Your neighbor is God within the reach of your love, so that you may verify whether your love is sincere and active or merely sentimental revery.

It will be in vain that we have assisted at this Mass if, on leaving, we do not love one another more than we did when we came in.

What good is it for us to assemble here every week, to go through the gestures of union, of communion, if we are determined that there shall be no change either in our heart nor in our conduct when we leave.

The one sign that we have assisted worthily at this Mass is that, upon leaving, we feel closer to one another and we show it by our actions. Does it ever happen that we invite to our table someone with whom we have just been partaking at the table of the Lord?

At least, salute one another, smile at one another, recognize one another.

Our communions! We follow the same ceremonies, the signs of communion; we share the same bread, we come to the same table, we pass the same plate, and after these beautiful demonstrations we go back to our places and occupy ourselves exclusively with our own repast.

Sharing the bread of the Lord rarely moves us to share our own. We recognize the Lord in the breaking of the bread, in that gesture of love in which He gives us His bread, His life. But do we recognize one another by the sharing of our goods? That will cost us dearly! That would be painful! The ceremonies of communion are sufficient. Communion without suffering.

In the college where I was during the war, the community meals became pure ceremonies, something like the Mass. Each one picked over with his fork the slice of the community rutabaga, each one waited patiently, politely, until this was finished. As soon as the *"Ite, Missa est"* came, each one went at top speed to his own room to feast on the good things that he had brought from home—white bread, bacon, chocolate, sardines.

That is, those who could get these things.

Soon the Germans occupied the college, and we had no more private rooms. Some tried to continue their private communion, but it was not practical. One had to eat like this when there was no one else around, and now someone was sure to come in before a person had a chance to swallow the last mouthful. Some ate in their cupboards, like a horse with its nose in its feed-bag!

Finally, someone came up with an idea: suppose we share with one another.

And, from then on, there reigned among us an understanding, a joy, a warmth that we had never known before.

When the college was given back to us and the private rooms were ours once more, everyone was asking: "Father, are we now obliged to remain alone? No more reunions? No more sharing?"

That made us think. These boys had been receiving communion for some eight or ten years. We had instructed them, prepared them for innumerable communions, but we had never taught them to share. For eight, nine, ten years, we had been teaching the rites, the ceremonies, a make-believe communion, and here it had taken the Germans, the occupation, the war, a world-wide catastrophe, to reveal to them the joy of fraternity and of sharing.

We have the greatest respect for the sacred Body which we receive. What respect have we for the sacred Body of Christ of which we are a part?

And yet, which is the more important, the means or the end? The bread, or the person, the sacrament or the reality of which it is the sign?

It means little to Christ to change bread into His Body if this be not the means of changing us into His Body.

That over which Christ longs to pronounce the words of an

57

eternal consecration is not the bread upon the altar, but His members, ourselves—His members who are isolated, paralyzed, crippled, dispersed, broken up into little pieces. These are what His greatest desire is to unite, to revivify, to restore so that He can say at the end of a Mass: "This is my Body."

From our childhood, we have been told stories of sacrileges in regard to the holy Eucharist, about people who profaned the Host, thrust swords into it, and caused blood to flow. But, is it not a greater sacrilege—and it disturbs us so little—to divide the Body of Christ by our disdain, our negligences, our hostilities, and our evil-speaking?

In very truth, it depends upon each one of us whether the Church be united or not, whether it be a testimony of love or a source of scandal in the eyes of men.

The division between the Churches is a scandal, but there is one still greater and that is division in the Church. And it belongs to each one of us to put an end to it.

Would any one, seeing us here at Mass and seeing us leave when Mass is finished, would any one really want to join us and to resemble us? Do we exercise that attraction which in the early days converted the world, —"See how they love one another"?

If this were so, the world would soon be converted and the Churches would very soon be united.

FEAST OF THE HOLY NAME

"He was called Jesus." (Luke 2:21)

When a person tells you his name, when he invites you to call him by his given name, he invites you to his intimacy, he takes you into his confidence. As long as you use the forms "Mr." or "Mrs." or "Miss" you are strangers. You act and speak with circumspection, you are free to conceal yourself behind formality.

But as soon as you begin to address one another by your given names, you are engaged in the bonds of intimacy.

God has told us His Name. God has asked us to address Him by His Name.

What name do you give to God? How do you address Him? What idea have you of God? Or, to put it simply, before what image of God do you pray? Have you found, or have you chosen, a beautiful and tender image of God? Alas! In almost every home, the "Christ" is the one object which is not subject to renewal.

All the rest of your furniture is modernized. Your house is heated by a furnace, you no longer cook with wood or charcoal but by gas or electricity, and you are considering getting a new car. But your crucifix, that is something you have inherited from your parents along with a lot of other old things which you do not want.

Come now, is the image of God before which you pray something beautiful and attractive? Or is it something old, ugly, sad, terrifying? And does not this reveal, of itself, the image that you have of religion?

And His Name?

Many of us call Him "the good God." That is not bad. I do not condemn it. But, after all, that is the family name. All religions believe in God and all the gods are called God.

The true name of God has been revealed to us. God calls Himself Father, and His Son is named Jesus, which means "Saviour." Do we address our God by the name that He has revealed to us? That name is a revelation, a teaching, and it forms in us a certain mentality.

When the Messiah was announced people were expecting a Judge, an Administrator of the Law, an Avenger—almost an executioner—and He is born to us a Saviour.

People got ready to render an account of themselves, they longed to set themselves right with God, and God was there, a little baby, holding out His arms to us, asking of us love, protection, tenderness, and calling us to rejoice.

People believed that God came to reward the good and punish the bad. "The mountains shall be levelled and the valleys filled up," announced St. John. But Jesus has surprised and disconcerted everyone. He came to find the lost, to live familiarly—to eat—with sinners. He revealed that God loves sinners, that He loves the sinner in spite of his sin, that He loves the just, not because of their justice, but that He loves without cause, foolishly, gratuitously, as do all who really love. As our fathers and mothers have loved us, not because of the qualities that we had when we came into the world, but because of the goodness of their own hearts, so warm, so strong, so faithful that they ended by awakening in us a love like to theirs.

Humanity has since been divided, not in the good to be praised and rewarded, and in the bad to be condemned, but in two very different categories.

On one side there are those who believe in love, who are willing to be loved even though they are unworthy of it. These feel that they have need of a Saviour. They are simple enough and humble enough to accept salvation as a gift and love as a grace. And in this category there are many sinners and some few just.

On the other hand, there are those who have no use for love. They prefer to acquit themselves of their duties and keep to the formalities. They want to work for their salvation and merit their recompense. There are also those who do not believe that they can be loved because they have sinned too much, people who think that they cannot be cured because they are too sick. They have despaired of the power of God because they have exaggerated their importance and their singularity, not because they consider themselves just, but because they are sinners.

In which category do you belong?

Do you consider yourself just, honest, strong, in good health, needing nothing from anyone, satisfied with yourself and desirous of having as little to do as possible with God and man? Did you come to Mass this Sunday to satisfy your conscience and to be right with God and irreproachable before men? Or was it to confess your indigence and your need for grace and pardon?

Christ has nothing to do with the just—He came only to seek for sinners. If you proclaim yourself just, you exclude yourself from salvation and you withdraw yourself from the number of those for whom Christ died.

Some Christians will say that they belong to the "happy medium," neither saints nor sinners, neither having committed great sins nor practiced great virtues. Alas, Christ did not come for this "happy medium," He came "to seek and to save that which is lost."

And that is why, even today, publicans and sinners go before us into the Kingdom of God.

Or perhaps you believe yourselves to be sinners? You call out to the Saviour, and do you ask for an extended hand to draw you to the light, to peace, to the purity of Love? Do you realize how sterile you are in love, in faith, and in hope, even towards those whom you think you love the most? How quickly our hearts run out of resources, so quickly wounded, closed, hardened! For is it not in the family circle that there are the worst oppositions, the worst quarrels, the deepest hatreds?

We are feeble and unsteady beings who never keep our promises, who forever give the lie to our proposals, and constantly deceive those who have placed their trust in us.

We have need of pardon, we have need of assistance, of absolution, and of renewal. We have need of a Saviour.

That is why we are here today, on this Feast of the Holy Name of Jesus.

Our Sunday Mass is a reunion of sinners, of sinners who believe in the mercy of their Saviour, in the skill and devotedness of their physician.

He came unto us the Lamb who bears the sins of the world, who carries the terrible weight of all the sinners in the world.

Will you go to Him? Will you rejoice at being invited to partake at His table, of His bread, and His love, in order that you may become capable of sharing your table, your bread, and your love? Are you simple enough to allow yourself to be fed, pardoned, cared for, and cured?

Let us not go to communion like good little children to their reward, but like prodigals to their Father, like the sick to their physician.

Or will you remain at your place, wanting in confidence in this Bread's power to nourish you, in this pardon to cleanse you, in this love to make you happy?

Are you one of those who believe themselves without sin, or their sin without pardon? Then do not call upon Jesus, do not call Him Saviour, because then He has no name for you nor have you any name for Him.

We said in the beginning that the use of the given name introduces us into the friendship of persons. God has told us His Name—Jesus, Saviour, and, by that act, He reveals to us our own name—sinner, lost one, orphan, sick, or even dead. Let us be willing to know ourselves for what we really are, and may we allow Him to call us by these names so that we may, with sincerity, call Him by His Name.

THE EPIPHANY

"Arise and give light, O Jerusalem!" (Isaiah 60:1–6)

The Epiphany is the feast of the manifestation of God. The essential of the Christian religion is that God is revealed to man, that God comes to us, that He makes Himself known to us at our own level, the level of men. The essential of Christianity is that God is known by us under a sensible form.

At first sight, this résumé astonishes us. We are too habituated to saying that God exacts of us faith, obscurity, and obedience. Yet, it is perfectly true to say that God is light, revelation, —Epiphany. That by which the Christian religion differs from every other is that it is a religion of incarnation, a sacramental religion in which God reveals Himself, and is always revealing Himself, to our senses.

The creation of man to the image and likeness of God already signifies this, and indicates the communication possible between Him and ourselves. "When God formed the body of Adam," the Fathers of the Church tell us, "He was already thinking of Christ who would one day become man." Man was created so that he might be permeated by God.

Ever since the days of Paradise, God has been Epiphany. He came to speak familiarly with Adam in the cool of the evening. God made Himself known, God communicated with Adam in a human manner. Adam entered into the confidence of God. God gave Himself. God betrayed Himself. The Passion, that revelation of a love so audacious, courageous, and vulnerable, was begun in Paradise.

Adam rejected this revelation and all became darkness. Sin is a state where God is no longer known nor felt. We know that state well. We are always falling into it. Darkness does not take hold of God. What is more, it refuses to take hold of Him.

But God is not discouraged. God has never stopped speaking. He re-veiled Himself. He lifted that veil of obscurity when He spoke to Abraham and Abraham understood Him. Abraham had the joy of hearing Him with his own ears and of seeing Him with his own eyes. He had the joy of receiving Him within his tent and of assisting at the Epiphany of God in the most incredible of births and in that sacrifice most painful to his paternal heart.

God manifested Himself to Moses in the burning bush, and,

63

on smoking Sinai, He spoke to Moses face to face, as a man is wont to speak to his friend. God spoke by the prophets and God spoke to the prophets, and each one of them was lifted out of himself by the invasion of that most familiar and yet most crushing of presences, the actual presence of God.

The column of cloud or of fire, the Tabernacle, the Temple, these were the first incarnations of God, the first signs given to our eyes and to our hands that God walks with us: Emmanuel.

The veil is lifted more and more until we come to the time of Jesus. Then the veil is rent from top to bottom. "Behold I am with you all days, even to the consummation of the world."

The Epiphany and the Incarnation, these are the two constant needs of the Christian life, says Guardini. The sacraments are sensible signs because there has been an Incarnation and there is an Epiphany.

God has decided to come to us where we are. The amazement of St. John: "That which we have heard, which we have seen with our eyes, which we have looked upon and touched with our hands, concerning the word of life—the life was made manifest, and we saw it" —this is the amazement of a permanent Epiphany to which he invites us to partake in the sacraments.

Happy are the pure of heart; they see God. The normal human state is to see God, to perceive His presence in the things about us, the things that are habitual and familiar. God is with us always. The liturgy is an Epiphany of God for each of us who assists at it with an open heart. The Word dwells among us and we see His glory. A beautiful Mass, a solemn celebration of the sacraments, or of prayers, is a manifestation of God by sensible means.

When, during the Mass, the Gospel is solemnly announced, we reply: "Glory to you, O Lord." But, how many times, when hearing the Gospel, have you benefited by this Epiphany? How often have you seen the glory of God?

I would like to say this: When Jesus spoke, two attitudes were

64

possible, and this is so today. The hard of heart were like indifferent spectators, closed, reticent. When Jesus had finished, they retained nothing, unless it was some objection or a criticism. And we, like them, at the reading of the Gospel, or the homily which explains it, we retain nothing. If we are asked, when we leave the church, what was said, we recall nothing, for we have remained in darkness.

And all the while there was an Epiphany of God. "Who hears you, hears me."

Others, the clean of heart, when Jesus spoke, followed His instruction and permitted themselves to be formed, and even transformed, by His words. His teaching acted upon them. It revealed to them what God is and what they were, how God treated them and how they treated God. They discovered the plan of God, their resistance to it, and His appeal to them. A strange emotion took possession of the creature at the approach of the Creator. His sheep heard His voice and they followed Him. Those who were of God heard the word of God with joy. It aroused within them energies before unknown. Their hearts burned as He spoke. There were deep stirrings of faith and of love, of immense confusion and deep confidence. They were attracted to Him, often unable to say why. When they returned to their homes, so changed, so moved and yet so serene, others asked them: "What did He say? What proof has He given? What was so extraordinary about Him?" They, feeling incapable of giving an explanation, they remain silent the better to savor their recent experience, the better to keep themselves in that state to which He had transported them. And they were content with saying: "No man has ever spoken like this Man."

They have seen His glory. But one must have a clean heart for that. The Mass is an Epiphany of God. But not for those who simply stand there. It is so only for those who take part in it.

The inhabitants of Palestine, at the time of His birth, knew all that they were supposed to know. They knew their catechism.

Nevertheless, they did not see Him. The Magi did see Him. They "knew" infinitely less. But, when they saw this strange light, they believed that it was meant for them. They set out courageously. They *came*. They participated actively in this liturgy of the Incarnation. They came to communicate in the joy of it. They corresponded, they made their offering, and they adored. They saw Him.

From time to time, we too have felt, sometimes in some person, or in some ceremony, sometimes in some gathering or other, that God was there in some special way. God, quite suddenly, became present among us. Visible, palpable. The darkness lifted and we saw something of His glory.

Undoubtedly, these intervals of light are interrupted by much darkness. But if only once we saw the light, that should be sufficient to convince us that the light is always there, and to believe in the Epiphany in spite of the impurity of our own hearts.

FEAST OF THE HOLY FAMILY

"He was subject to them." (Luke 2:42–52)

Every Mass is a wedding Mass. At every Mass we celebrate a marriage—a new and indissoluble alliance, the alliance of God and man. In each Mass God gives Himself to man and man gives himself to God. All revelation represents the union between God and man as a marriage feast, and tells us that God loves humanity as a man loves his wife.

From this you can understand why the first public manifestation of Christ was made at a marriage. It was at a marriage that He announced the great change in the signification of human marriage that He would soon give. The change of water into wine symbolized the transformation of marriage into a sacrament, of the union of Christ with the Church, of God with humanity.

And this is also why the first Sunday after the Epiphany honors the Holy Family. God reveals Himself in the bosom of a human family. Since God wishes to live with us in the intimacy of a family, we should live a family life with God.

Since the Incarnation, and by the grace of the sacrament of baptism and that of marriage, each family relives the mystery of the Holy Family. We are charged to relive in the family circle, all the redemptive love of Christ, all the love with which He has loved and saved His mother and His father, and with which He was loved by them.

In Christ, the husband is responsible for the salvation of his wife. He must love her enough to save her. The wife is responsible for the salvation of her husband. The parents are responsible for the salvation of their children. This is their principal mission, and they will be questioned about it one day. And the children, from the time that their conscience awakens, and more and more as they grow older, become responsible for the salvation of their parents, responsible for loving them enough to save them.

In our human lives, the eternal is created and becomes manifest. The feast of the Holy Family celebrates this value contained in our most trivial daily actions.

Doubtless, very few among us are ready to call their family a Holy Family!

We read in St. Paul: "Women, be submissive to your husbands as to the Lord. Husbands, love your wives as Christ has loved the Church, and be not harsh towards them. Children, obey your parents for that is pleasing to the Lord. Fathers, do not be angry with your children, lest they become pusillanimous. All that you do, do it with a good heart as for the Lord and not for men." (This is what the Church gives us to read in this morning's Office.) We find it all very beautiful, but we feel that we are

67

incapable of living it. How can I see the Lord in my husband? In my wife? In my child?

To be sure, we must have faith for this—faith in baptism, faith in the sacrament of marriage, faith in the love and the presence of God in each one of them.

Even in the Holy Family there had to be faith. Joseph had to have faith in Mary. He had to believe in her in an extraordinary degree, and he certainly had to love her very much before he could bring himself thus to believe in her. Mary had to believe in Joseph. She had to have confidence in his love, his respect, and in the esteem that he had for her. She had to trust to him in the carrying out of the extraordinary vocation which God had given her.

Joseph and Mary had to have faith in their child. Although He was, in appearance, an infant like any other, they had always to believe in the mystery that dwelt within Him. They did not always understand what He did, nor even what He said, as the Gospel of today reminds us, but they had confidence in Him, and His mother kept all these things and meditated upon them in her heart.

And Jesus showed His faith in His parents. He was submissive to them. Although He was entirely devoted to the will of His Father, by remaining thirty years in the family of Nazareth, He showed that one may accomplish the loftiest tasks in the world—honoring the Father, saving mankind, redeeming sin—while still living a very simple, affectionate life in the family.

And do we believe in one another? To love one another, there must be faith. We must continue, in spite of all the disillusionments, to believe in the infinite possibilities, the supernatural riches that reside in the souls of those around us.

The family circle is a paradoxical place where one is loved far above one's merits. There one deliberately violates the law of morality in regard to the affections, which is that we love each one in accordance with his worth. In the family, we love one another without hesitation, infinitely above his worth. And loving like this, being accepted like this, engenders in the bosom of the family incomparably more happiness and goodness than can be found anywhere else.

The family is founded upon faith. If you love your husband, it is not because he is the most extraordinary man in the whole world. Nor the most understanding, the most tender, the most patient, the most generous. Oh no! For if your love for him were because of these things, you would certainly be tempted to change. You must love your husband because he is yours, because you are bound to him by the sacrament of marriage as to a source of indefinite merit and sanctity, and you are nearer to the Lord when with him than you could be if you were with any other being in the world.

You love your wife, not necessarily because she is the most beautiful woman, the gentlest, the tenderest, the least irritable in all the world, but because she is your own wife, for whom you are always responsible, in regard to whom you will render an account on the Day of Judgment.

Parents love their children because they are their own children, those whom God has given into their charge. They did not choose them from an exhibition of the most beautiful babies, nor from among the prize-winners in a contest, but they have accepted them as God sent them, and if they are truly parents they feel in their hearts all that is needed to enable them to do a magnificent work in rearing them.

Children love their parents, not because their parents are without defects, nor because they are the best parents on earth. In this case, we must admit, there would be many occasions for changing. They ought to love their parents because they are their own father and mother, and because they cannot respect the paternity of God if they do not, in spite of everything, venerate this first testimony that He gives them of Himself.

69

This doctrine gives us freedom. In commanding us unconditionally to love each member of our family, we find ourselves freed from all those pretexts which we are constantly using for not loving one another, and for making reproaches and complaints. It also gives free rein to that profound need which we all experience to love in spite of all and at all times. This doctrine tells us that we shall never be finished with the duty of loving. It provides for each of us a career without end of sanctity in the accomplishment of the humble duties of family and conjugal life.

It is when one is loved and does love like this that one finds the greatest happiness and the greatest fulfillment. There is no happiness that can compare with that of a true family circle.

There was a time in our lives when we understood and felt all this. It was when we were little children or when, later, we had a little child of our own. How easy it was to love this little being who had no merits of its own, and who had been confided to our care. How easily we pardoned its unsuspected egoism, its tears, its cries that annoyed everyone else, the work that it gave us. In fact, we never even thought of pardon, it was a joy, and we looked upon the little one with confidence and hope.

And have you not found it true that, during the time when you have loved most, you have received most? We cannot know freshness, expansion, growth, except in surroundings where we feel that we are thoroughly understood and loved.

When I say that, I tell you at the same time what is the surest means of destroying a family, —rash judgment. From the moment that you forget the sacred character of the family, from the moment that you pass judgment upon any one of its members, looking only at appearances—and that usually means looking at another's faults, miseries, and egoism—at that moment you destroy the family. We absolutely must have a strong motive for loving others, otherwise we will never make the immense sacrifices demanded of us by fidelity, perseverance, and conjugal or family love.

A holy family is one where the members are ready to accept things which they do not understand, to pass over conflicts and misunderstandings by appealing to faith. Here they always believe the best of each other, and love each other in spite of disappointment and sometimes suffering. No one is ever lost as long as there is someone who believes in him and loves him. The unworthiest husband, the most miserable of fathers, can yet be saved if there remains in the heart of his wife or of his child enough faith to see God in him and to reveal to him that God who has willed to be present among us.

The world has been saved, the work of redemption was carried on during thirty years, because the members of a holy family believed in each other and loved each other.

THE SECOND SUNDAY AFTER THE EPIPHANY

The Wedding of Cana

"You have kept the good wine until now."   (John 2:1–11)

During these Sundays after the Epiphany, the Church instructs us by various manifestations of our Lord, and today she makes us read the account of His first miracle, the one that He worked at the wedding of Cana by changing water into wine. And it was thus, says the Gospel, that He manifested His glory and His disciples believed in Him.

I do not know if it has ever been given to you to live side by side with a remarkable person, a person of exceptionable intelligence. If you have ever had this advantage, you have certainly

71

come to know what price is paid for it. One feels continually humiliated, contradicted, passed over. You speak of some idea of yours and as soon as he speaks, you perceive that your beautiful idea is nonsense. You propose a plan of action and it becomes childish, ridiculous, the minute he offers his plan. You form a judgment on some matter, and, by the time he has finished speaking, not an argument remains. With God, the situation is, of course, much worse. God is always surprising us. He is unpredictable in all His doings. It is impossible to say in advance just what He will do. You have probably noticed that, in your own life, He has always acted differently from what you would have done. He is constantly contradicting us. We do not recognize Him even in the manner in which He answers our prayers, and what we consider a trial is, in the spiritual life, very often our hesitation in recognizing in the thing which He has sent to us, the very thing that we have been asking for. Generally, afterwards, even we ourselves begin to see that what He has done is the best, and that He knew, infinitely better than ourselves, what was good for us.

Who would ever have imagined, for example, that God, coming to earth to make Himself known to man, He, the Lord of glory, the Father of "immense majesty" as the "Te Deum" says, would choose to appear first as a little infant lying on straw in a crib? Who among ourselves would have believed that God, coming to renew, to repair, to reform the world, would find no better means of accomplishing this than to die on the wood of the Cross between two criminals? And who would have counselled our Lord to work His first miracle at a village wedding, in the midst of that scene of drinking where there was so little thought of a prophet?

Oh! we don't forget that Christ was there and that He brought His disciples to a wedding banquet. But, the other guests had already drunk more wine than had been foreseen, and one glance

72

around the table told Christ the amount that would be needed. This jars with our conventional and virtuous notions regarding what is religious and what is not. We are somewhat scandalized at this intrusion of religion, and of the most pure religion, into the domain of practical life, where things are easygoing and sometimes amusing, and from which we think religion should be excluded, and that we should keep the two apart.

Two very different classes of people have been surprised by this behavior of our Lord. First, the Pharisees and the bigots who feel that religion should be unpleasant, repulsive, and that one cannot be religious unless he is tiresome and annoying. These made a great show of their disapproval at Jesus' attendance at a banquet, at His refusal to oblige His disciples to fast, and they said of Him that He was a man who liked good cheer and drank much wine.

But there was another class who were also somewhat disconcerted, and to which we very likely belong. This was the pleasure-loving people, those who sought amusement and distraction, those who were ever dreaming about leisure and its attractions. These all agreed with the Pharisees and the bigots. These all felt that all joys and pleasures are irreconcilable with the spiritual life. The only difference between them was in their choice. These chose the pleasures without religion and the Pharisees chose religion without pleasure.

What Jesus attacked by this miracle of Cana was just this absurb separation, this sacrilege between the God of nature and of grace, between the God who created the world and all that it contains, and the God who is adored in temples and in churches. It is the same God. We render Him homage by prayer and we render Him homage by eating and drinking, with thanksgiving, what He has created. He has created these things for our pleasure, and we deprive ourselves of the greater part of our joy in regarding these things as thefts, as forbidden things which one takes with something of the spirit of revenge, and resentment, instead of receiving them as gifts which afford all the more pleasure in that they are signs of the goodness of the Giver.

The disciples of Jesus had been disciples of St. John the Baptist. They had been instructed out in the desert and they had followed the Prophet in his fearful austerities—his wild honey and locusts. The first lesson that Jesus gave them was something entirely different. He taught them the first and the most simple virtues—openness to life, with its joys and its friendships. He showed them a disposition which was open, cordial, and audacious, and which made Him from the start the friend of the common people, the peasants, the working men, the gay companions when there was a marriage and hard-working when there was a question of gaining one's livelihood.

In this way, God had truly tried to be agreeable to man in sending him both John and Jesus. This is what our Lord expressed in the parable. "To what shall I compare this generation? They are like to children playing in the market-place, sulky, and to whom their good companions address this reproach: We have played the flute for you and you have not danced, we have sung a lamentation and you have not beat your breast. So it was with John, neither eating nor drinking, and you said of him that he was impossible, that he must be possessed by a demon. The Son of man is come, eating and drinking, and you say of Him that He is a lover of good cheer and a drinker of wine, the friend of publicans and sinners. Wisdom is justified by her children."

Are we these children of wisdom who know how to admire and practice mortification with St. John the Baptist during Advent, with Jesus during Lent, but who also know how to give glory to God for His gifts, to rejoice sincerely and to sympathize frankly in the joy of others, as Jesus teaches us?

Instead of making religion a kill-joy in order to dispense ourselves from practicing it, as the pleasure-loving do, or using it

74

to exalt ourselves and to humiliate and condemn others, as the Pharisees did, have we the courage to live a life that is completely human and completely religious before God? Jesus was that, fully man and fully God.

We are always thinking that, in order to resemble Him, we must become something very different from what we are, that we must torture ourselves, starve ourselves, ill-treat ourselves in every way.

But, in acting like this, we neglect the very thing that we have in common with Him, this human nature which He has made use of in order to draw near to us.

We believe that, in order to come closer to Jesus, we must become more heavenly, more angelic. The truth is, that to become more like Jesus, we must become more like men.

The great obstacle to our spiritual life is not what so many of us think, that we are too human. They say: "I love my family life too much, I am much happier out-of-doors, surrounded by nature, than I am in the church. I love the pleasures of this world, hence I cannot be religious. I cannot have a really spiritual life because I am too human." Not at all. The truth is that you are not human enough.

If we were more human, more generous, more kind, more attentive to others, more compassionate and considerate, we would have a great number of sentiments in common with Jesus, and these would make between us a true community of soul, we would form a real fraternity with Him. Jesus would no longer be a distant stranger to us, a mysterious creature fallen from outer space, without any connection with any known thing upon this earth.

If we had these same sentiments that Jesus had, we would know Him and how He thought and felt.

Every time that we catch ourselves in the midst of great joy, or gratitude, or pity, or love or purity, we can stop for a moment and tell ourselves: "I am experiencing something that Jesus experienced, I am sharing in the same feelings that went through His heart."

If you are sensitive to the things of nature, to the sweet freshness of a little child at play, if you admire truth and hate hypocrisy, if you feel compassion for the tears of a mother, or the despair of a father about to lose his little girl, if you feel for the feeble and the fallen, or more simply still, if you enjoy the beauty of the flower, the freshness of the evening breeze, the peace and silence of the night, that is well, for you sympathize with our Lord, you feel the same emotions that He knew, you enter into that fellowship which He has wished should exist between Him and ourselves. Our daily human life, well lived, would thus lead us to Jesus, instead of taking us from Him, for He chose this life in order to come closer to us.

Contempt for the goods of this world generally leads to our devouring them with avidity and ingratitude, and with a feeling of being under God's condemnation. Contempt of human nature, far from raising us to a truly divine life, generally has no other effect than that of leaving us just where we are—indifferent, frustrated, gross, distracted, and even more neglectful of ourselves.

In becoming incarnate, in becoming flesh, the Word has chosen to place before us a certain number of human values, certain acts and sentiments which are, in fact, divine values, such as love, patience, joy, gratitude, fidelity, enthusiasm, thoughtfulness, and love of the poor and the little ones.

These are human values towards which we must learn to turn ourselves, to incline ourselves, to bend the knee, like the shepherds in the grotto or the Magi at the crib. Only when we become penetrated with respect and a profound esteem for these values, for these virtues which are both human and divine, shall we understand the lesson of the Incarnation.

At Cana, Christ manifested His divinity and revealed His true glory by showing His goodness and kindness of heart. He suffered at the thought of these two nice young spouses being humiliated and put to grief because the wine ran out the first day of their marriage. He sympathized with the simple joy of these hearty guests who would have been disappointed if they had had to stop drinking in the midst of a feast. He changed the water into wine with the same kindness of heart with which He will invite us one day to a banquet where the wine will never fail and at which He will nourish us each day with Bread which strengthens and Wine which will cause us to rejoice forever.

We shall become divine and we shall resemble Him by actions which are as much like His as are prayers and mortifications.

We shall manifest the glory of God, and men will believe in Him by the miracle of our goodness, the ingeniousness of our kindness, and the generosity of our sympathy for those who weep and for those who rejoice.

THE THIRD SUNDAY AFTER THE EPIPHANY (I)

"I have never found an Israelite with faith as great as this." (Matthew 8:1–13)

The Gospel of today is truly a Gospel of Epiphany. It reveals Jesus to us as the Supreme Lord, the great Assembler of the People of God, He who can enable us to surmount all our divisions, our excommunications, our ostracisms. Jesus here manifests Himself as Saviour and brings back into the religious community those whom everyone thought excluded—a leper and a pagan.

God created the world in unity and in love. It is the devil who has brought in division and discord.

Sin has not only broken the filial bond between man and God.

77

It has also separated husband and wife. Adam received Eve with an exclamation of joy, like every man before a good woman. "Behold! Flesh of my flesh and bone of my bone!" But you know how he separated himself from her in refusing to take any responsibility for her fault. If he had defended her, if he had claimed for himself part of the culpability, he would not have been chased out of Paradise since there would still have been love, still have been union, still have been charity.

Original sin has separated brother from brother (Cain and Abel), parents from children, Noah from his sons, men from one another, and there is the tower of Babel. Each of our faults, each of our sins, has brought some new division into the world. There are barriers of race, barriers between the classes of society, barriers of color, of language, of nation, and—alas!—even of religion. All are crystallizations, the fossils of our sins, of our lack of love.

How many barriers, how many divisions there are among us! Each one here has an immense need of being loved, of being appreciated, and yet, how badly we respond to the needs of others! Each one complains of the barrier to which he must submit, and ignores, or justifies, that which he imposes upon others.

Christ has come to abolish all these divisions, to break to pieces all these barriers. He has been sent in order to reunite in one single body all the children of God who are dispersed. All the children of God: the black and the white, employers and employees, the Americans and the Russians, the believers and the unbelievers. They ignore Him and they are dispersed. Although they are in good faith, they are behind the iron curtain.

Christ has but one aim, to reunite them. And He shows us this in today's Gospel by bringing back into the religious community two excommunicated, two untouchables, two banished from society, two whom all the pious and healthy of Israel believed it a duty to keep at a distance.

78

And then He eulogizes this pagan and places him far above all the traditional believers, all the faithful who believed themselves saved because they had interwoven into their lives certain practices of piety and who now heard that they would be cast out into darkness, there to weep and grind their teeth.

This is certainly not a pleasant lesson to hear, but we must not deceive ourselves, my brothers, for it is aimed at us, priests and faithful, who think ourselves saved because we follow a religion, because we have been baptized, because we find ourselves here at Mass this Sunday.

Christ had a great affection for the pagans. He longed to get away from his own sorry, sleepy community, so fed up and satisfied with itself, and go to new souls, souls that were fresh and impressionable. Among His own, these faithful, He found that souls were dull, accustomed to religious practices, hardened by routine, practicing their religion without joy, without interest.

When, for once, He came upon an enthusiastic and generous act of faith, He found it in a pagan. It is said that this is the only time in all the Gospel that Christ was in admiration of anyone, and this one was not a believer but a pagan.

Are we sure that Jesus was not thinking of us when He made this sad observation: "In truth, I have not found like faith in Israel, among my faithful!" Oh yes, these words are aimed at us. All religion, even the most true (and the Jewish religion was the true religion at that time), runs the risk of degenerating into pharisaism, routine, and dullness.

If we practice our religion without any effort to renew our lives, to improve our conduct, to become more faithful, to be converted, we run the risk of finding ourselves some day more pagan than if we had never had the faith. For he who has nothing can yet receive, but he who believes that he has everything, how are you going to get him to receive anything?

Do not think that I exaggerate. There are people whose religion prevents them from becoming religious. Be on your guard against professionalism! In religion, there are no professionals, only amateurs. Are you amateurs? Or are you professionals?

Recall that Christ did not find faith among those who proclaimed themselves religious. He never met more opposition than from the devout, the bigots, the professional religious. And faith sprang up in abundance among the amateurs, the pagans, the heretics, the fallen women, the ignorant.

This should make us uneasy. (There is a means of protecting oneself against God even with religious things: certain habitual practices, rites, assurances. Thus one cuts down the cost, one limits his gifts and his inquietudes. No questions are asked.)

If I may refer to my modest experience, every time that anyone has asked me a religious question that was really interesting and fruitful, it has nearly always been asked by an unbeliever. Never has any one of the faithful asked me a question about religion. The faithful do not ask questions. They believe that they know everything, or they are not interested. They do not desire to know or to do anything more.

A pagan can still ask questions, go to the bottom of a problem, find a truth which demands of him a complete gift of himself. But, as for us, we are protected by our traditional faith from such exaggerations.

Yes, one can make use of God to do without Him. Yes, a religion of habit and tradition can prevent us from becoming religious.

Let me ask you a question. If you were suddenly to learn that you were not baptized, that your baptism was not valid, would you ask to be baptized tomorrow?

At that I believe the greater number of you would reply: "Just a moment. I would like time to think. I would like to look into the matter. I want to take this seriously." "Very well, but why don't you do it anyway? It is certainly reasonable, why don't you do it?" "Because I have already been baptized."

Then it is your baptism that prevents you from reflecting, from seeking information, from asking for further instruction in your religion. The fact of your baptism then dispenses you from ever taking the responsibility of your baptism. Because you have a religion you have ceased to be religious.

How long is it since you read a religious book? How long is it since you learned anything in regard to your religion? How long is it since you opened the Gospel? How long is it since you really prayed? A quarter of an hour, or half an hour of personal prayer? A pagan who was seeking God would do these things, or a person who was in some desperate trouble, or a repentant sinner. But never one of the faithful at Sunday Mass!

That is why the publicans and sinners continue to go before us into the Kingdom of God. Take an example. None of the converts that I know ever go to Mass without also receiving holy communion. They have been instructed and they know what the Mass is and that the normal way to participate in the Mass is to communicate. They have read the words of Christ: "If you do not eat the flesh of the Son of man and drink His blood, you will not have life in you." "As the living Father has sent me, and as I live by the Father, so he who eats me shall live by me." They have read that and they have believed the words of Christ. So they communicate every time that they go to Mass.

But those who are Christian by tradition or habit, as you know, communicate less frequently. They have always acted that way in his circle. They have their own religion and that prevents them from believing in Christ. They have their own religion and that does not allow them to become religious. They have their own religious habits and these stand in the way of their being sensitive to or impressed by the words of God.

A severe lesson is given to us on this subject by the Jewish people. They were in possession of the true religion of their time, just as we have the true religion of our time. They believed in their parents, in their priests, in their prophets, and in their religion. And these were good parents, true priests, and inspired books, and notwithstanding all this, God was in the midst of them and they no longer believed in God.

They possessed excellent religious organizations—practices, rites, preachers, sacred books; but all these, which should have stimulated them, alerted them, prepared them to recognize Christ, to love Him, to have personal contact with Him, all these became simply exterior observances, having no effect on their interior lives, but leaving them torpid, indifferent, satisfied that the possession of these things was all that was needed to procure their salvation.

Our Lord gave them a brutal awakening when He told them that many of them would be rejected and would come to themselves in the midst of weeping and gnashing of teeth.

They had believed for so long that they no longer believed. They had prayed for so long that they no longer prayed. They had hoped for so long that they no longer expected anything, and they were very disagreeably surprised by this revelation of what they had been hoping for. *As history repeating itself*

For us also there is an uncomfortable lesson in today's Gospel. We have but one chance to be saved, and that is to live by a faith which leads us personally to God, which enables us to find God in everything that speaks to us of Him.

Some of you are probably tempted to say: "Oh, all that you are telling us is much too complicated for me. Faith is much more simple. I believe what I have always been told, I do what we have always done at home."

That is just the trouble. The Jews did what they had always done, they believed what they had always believed, and they did not believe in Christ. They did not recognize Him for what He was.

This "simple" faith makes us like those Jews who persecuted Christianity in its beginning. The reason for their hostility was their fidelity to family or national habits. And what is meant by this "simple" faith but an unwillingness to look into anything, to study its meaning for fear of having to change some of our habits?

In reality, faith is a quest. All true faith means a difficulty surmounted.

As long as you believe simply because your parents and your surroundings have been Christian, it is impossible to determine whether you believe in God or in those who have spoken to you about Him.

As long as you have no doubts about the faith, it is because your opinions coincide quite naturally with the dogmas of faith and your own ideas accord with the ideas of God, but, at the same time, it is impossible for me to determine whether or not you believe in God or merely in yourself.

It is just when we come upon a difficulty, upon some difference, some opposition, either apparent or real, between what God tells us and what we ourselves think, just at this moment when, as a general rule, you think that you have lost your faith, that you have, for the very first time in your whole life, the opportunity to make a real act of faith—to give yourself over into the hands of God, to abandon yourself to Another, to give up your own ideas and accept His ideas and to enter into His world.

The Centurion of the Gospel did just that.

He set out on the road, he left behind his own national background, for he was not a Jew but a Roman, and he was seeking out a Jew. He left his own religious background, for he was a pagan and he had faith in Christ. He entrusted himself completely to Him, disregarding his early education, his family surroundings, and his own habits.

And no one will ever be saved without going through something of the same experience, a conversion to the interior meaning of religion which is just as real and just as costly as any exterior conversion.

The words of Christ may seem to us painful and terribly exacting, but they do, nevertheless, signify something to arouse

83

joy and enthusiasm. They tell us that God has His servants everywhere in the world, even where one would least expect to find them. They tell us that many who are now behind the iron curtain or the bamboo curtain have perhaps a faith that is far stronger than that of those who are now in the Church.

For salvation is offered to the whole world; to pagans, schismatics, and heretics. And even to Christians who are humble enough and simple enough to take it as the Church invites them to do, who are willing to take the words of the Centurion and say to Christ: "I do not know how to believe in you, but say only a word and my soul will be healed if its incredulity; my soul will be healed of this habit of not believing which has insinuated itself so secretly into my habit of believing; my soul will be healed of this miserable habit of not praying which has crept so silently into my old habit of praying; my soul will be healed of this spirituality which is sleeping in death, strangled by habits which have paralyzed me and kept me from coming to you."

THE THIRD SUNDAY AFTER THE EPIPHANY (II)

"My sheep hear my voice and they follow me."   (John 10:3)

One can recognize Jesus by His demands. Placed before Him, it was impossible to be unmoved by the authority which He exercised over hearts. "My sheep hear my voice," He says, *"and they follow me."* His most extraordinary words seem so natural when they come from His lips. One allows oneself to be conquered, doubts disappear, and one is sure that even the impossible will come to pass. Or else one yields to fear, one shrinks back into oneself and the old familiar habits. Either one yields, or one becomes hardened. Each meeting with Jesus leaves us either better or worse. We are never the same.

Jesus has many ways of making Himself known and of attracting souls to Himself. He is the light which shines even today in the darkness, and the darkness does not understand it. He it is who made the world, and the world knows Him not. He comes even today, every day, among His own, and so few of them receive Him.

There is in Jesus a fount of love which gushes up on all occasions for everyone and everything. Often we think that we are too human to be really religious, that we are too sensitive, too tender-hearted, too moved over nothing, too attached to our surroundings. We are too earthy, so we think, for us to ever have any spiritual life. But if we had known Jesus, we would have recognized in Him one who knew how to love much more and much better than we ever can. Jesus noticed everything, took an interest in the humblest of creatures, like that poor woman who gave three pennies. He marvelled at next to nothing, He exulted, He gave thanks for the things of which we think nothing, He grew tender and melted with pity at every misery, He divined every distress. Above all, the love and confidence that He showed caused others, from whom nothing good was expected, to show forth unsuspected depths of faith and generosity. Then each could see better the emptiness, the egoism, the blindness, the poverty of his own heart, and no one was any longer tempted to say, as we do, that he loved so much that he could not be a Christian. We all delude ourselves so easily. We believe that we love much and are capable of loving much more, if only other people were more lovable. We put the blame on the faults of others, or on the mediocrity of our surroundings, and we dream of a very different life where at last we can give full vent to our power of loving. But, when we come to Jesus, we discover that it is love that we lack rather than the occasions of exercising it. We learn that we have limited our sympathy, not to the merits of those about us, but to the feeble capacity of our own poor hearts.

Jesus loved nature. Take, for example, those country scenes

which we have not looked upon for many a day, those trees, those valleys, the sky above, and for which we have never given thanks. He loved every one and every thing and we pass them by without a thought. He loved them, He sought them out, they did Him good, and He could never do without them. Jesus lived in nature. He was born in a grotto and died on a mountain, and the whole Gospel is full of accounts of long apostolic journeys in the open air. He speaks as one who is very observant, who could foretell the weather by the signs in the sky, who knew the thoughts of the men in the fields, who knew the beauty of the wild flowers and the habits of the birds of the air. It was in the outdoor world that he found rest and to it He went after a fatiguing day in which He had been constantly harassed by the crowd, with its quarrels, its complaints, its demands, its unreasonableness, its lack of comprehension, its hardness of heart. He would go for long boat rides on the lake with His disciples, there to breathe in the freshness of the air, and enjoy the silence of the sea. There were times when He sent away everyone and climbed the hills in order to pray. Night came on and He was there alone. So many passages in the Gospel reveal all this to us. For example: "In the morning, Jesus left the house and went to sit by the side of the lake." How often have we not done the very same thing, when, rising early for once, we have gone down to the beach, washed by the high tide, to breathe air which no one else had yet breathed and to watch the coming of a day which we were the first to see. What were Jesus' thoughts? What did He think as He let His glance wander over that untamed sea, still so much like it was in the beginning, when, new and fresh, it came forth from the hand of God? All things were transparent to Jesus. He saw through them to the divine realities, in the likeness of which they had been created.

He saw the water, the water of the seas and of the springs and of the wells, and He saw that it was good. "Give me some of your water," He said to the Samaritan woman. "But that is not the true water, I am the one who gives the true water, the water which will slake thirst forever, the water which becomes a bubbling and enduring fountain in him who drinks it." He saw the vines with their branches, covered with leaves and ripening fruit, and He exclaimed: "I am the true vine and my Father is the vine-dresser." He saw bread, the golden brown loaves, so nourishing and so plentiful, and He said: "Bread is good. Ask it of your Father every day. But that is not the true bread. I am the Bread which came down from heaven and which gives life to the world. He who eats this Bread will know eternal life." He saw fathers and mothers, and He said: "How good you are to your little ones! It is extraordinary how you, bad as you are, can be so good to your children." But He added: "Even so, you are not fatherly nor motherly enough. No one knows the Father but the Son and he to whom the Son reveals Him." He saw the roads and the winding pathways, and He said: "I am the true pathway, the Way, and the Truth," and thus He revealed how everything created was in imitation of God and for His glory.

See by what simple things you would have recognized Jesus. You would have known that He loved much more than you do the most familiar things, and that only from Him can you learn to love them as you should.

Is it difficult, for example, to grow tender towards a little child? To know the appeal of his youth, his gaiety, his generosity, his confidence? All those who have felt this, all those who love children, can say to themselves that they feel something that Jesus felt, that they share these sentiments with Him. By becoming His disciples, they will learn to love the little ones even more. You all know that famous passage in the Gospel where He reproved His disciples when they would keep the children from approaching Him. But there is another one, even more significant which perhaps you do not know. It was during a moment of sadness when Jesus was trying to confide to His Apostles the anguish that He felt at the thought of His approaching death.

The Apostles did not understand this confidence, nor did they dare to question Him when He seemed so sorrowful. So they fell behind and let Him walk on ahead alone. Before long they were engaged in a violent and animated discussion about which one among them would be the greater in the Kingdom to come. When they stopped to rest Jesus asked them: "What were you talking about?" Not one of them dared to answer Him because they knew that He would never permit any discussion on this subject. Then Jesus went to find a little child in order to bring home to them His lesson and to show them an example. As you may imagine, the child, brought into this circle of grown men, was ill at ease. He began to blush and to shrink back and perhaps to cry. Then Jesus bent over the child and caressed him, consoled him, and reassured him, and did not go on with the lesson until He had embraced the little one.

With Jesus things were very simple and yet very serious. At first, it seems that we are dealing with things that are purely human and then we find that they are really divine. We share, or do not share, His sympathies, we like or we criticize His actions, all seems so human and, in reality, we are dealing with God.

Jesus had His friends, and they were very dear to Him. Above all, He loved St. John whose youth, enthusiasm, and purity charmed Him. Throughout the fourth Gospel the author never designates himself by any other name than that of "the disciple whom Jesus loved." And that affection was so apparent, so evident, that everyone knew who was meant. Jesus loved Lazarus and Martha and Mary Magdalene. Have you ever noticed how, in the Gospel, every time that Mary Magdalene is mentioned Jesus defends her? This is certainly a mark of a loving and faithful heart—never to allow anything to be said against the one who is loved. He defended her against Judas who accused her of wastefulness in regard to the perfume that she poured over His feet. He defended her against Martha who accused her of being lazy when she sat at His feet instead of taking part in the work of the house. He defended her against Simon, the Pharisee, who invited Him to his table and who, seeing Mary at the feet of Jesus, said to himself with disgust: "If this man were a prophet He would know who and what kind of woman this is that He touches, that she is a sinner." Then Jesus, knowing his thoughts, said to him: "Simon, may I tell you something?" He replied: "Master, speak." "A man had two debtors. One owed him $500 and the other fifty. As neither had the money to pay the debt, he forgave them both. Which of the two will love him more?" Simon, being a usurer, replied: "The one, I think, for whom the most was forgiven." "You have judged correctly, Simon. When I came into your house, you did not give me water for my feet. And ever since I came in, she has not ceased to wash my feet with her tears and dry them with her hair. You did not give me a kiss, but she . . ." See the tenderness of Jesus. How He was aware of every mark of affection and hurt by unkindness. Have we not received Him with the coldness of Simon, and is it not to us also that He addresses the reproach made to Simon: "You have not given me a kiss?"

Truly, it is not difficult to come to Jesus. It is sufficient to want to love, to believe in love, to accept being loved, and to consent to love in our turn. Where is there cause for fear and avoidance of Him?

When God decided to become man, He had to choose in what human way He would come. He had to choose the appearance of His face, His body, and all that belonged to it. From the very first, He rejected anything that would be striking, unusual, such as great wealth or power. All that He wanted was love, and all those who have loved love, all those who desire to love, all those who have hunger for and who thirst after a love which will purify our own—all these feel irresistibly drawn to Him, to meet Him and to eat the Bread which He is ready to give to them.

THE FOURTH SUNDAY AFTER THE EPIPHANY

"Why are you afraid, O men of little faith?" (Matthew 8:23–27)

The Gospels for these Sundays after the Epiphany recount for us different manifestations of our Lord, different ways in which, little by little, He made Himself known to His own. In the Gospel which we have just read, Jesus reveals Himself as Master of heaven and earth.

You know the scene. It is night, and twelve men are bent over their oars. With startling suddenness, a tempest has burst upon them. The Lake of Genesareth is something of a long corridor down which the winds rush. The Apostles were experienced mariners, and they recognized at once that this was a serious situation. They had lost all control of their boat, and the huge waves were pouring over the sides, so that the boat was filling rapidly with water. Feeling sure that they were lost, they awakened Jesus. Then they saw something that they never forgot as long as they lived. Jesus stood majestically in that boat tossing on the waves and surrounded by those men clinging to the rowers' benches. He commanded and the next moment the Apostles found themselves in the midst of silence, on a quiet sea, in a boat that was still. They were stunned. They feared. They looked upon Him wide-eyed. It was a manifestation of the Lord.

However, this Gospel has a more profound meaning. Have you noticed that this manifestation of power came about at the request, at the prayer of the Apostles, and that they were chided for it? "Why are you afraid, O men of little faith?"

This reproach of our Lord surprises us. We would have thought just the contrary. We find their behavior very natural in the midst of danger and we would have regarded it as an act of

90

faith, this having recourse to the Lord when threatened by evil.
Jesus blames what we would have praised. He reveals that the
prayer of the Apostles was, in fact, a prayer of distrust, of disquiet,
of doubt, and He teaches them that they ought not to have been
troubled by such a little thing, for, with Him there, they had
nothing to fear. No one can perish when in the company of
Jesus; He can save them even while He sleeps.

This lesson probably passed unnoticed in the midst of the joy
that they felt over the miracle they had just obtained. But it calls
for our reflexion, for we have the occasion more often of seeing
the tempest rage than of seeing it miraculously calmed, and of
seeing Jesus asleep more often than of admiring the Master
imposing His will upon the elements.

How is it that Jesus, who came into the world to reveal the
mission given Him by His Father, did not make use of the means
which seems to us so natural, that of unquestionable miracles?

The Jews expected of our Lord miracles of great power, they
clamored for signs in the heavens, the overthrow of their enemies, universal domination for themselves. Jesus refused these
signs, and the few miracles that He did perform He did with
regret, or through pity and goodness, in secret, recommending
silence, and always knowing that He ran the risk of distracting
them from the truth that He came to reveal which was of far
greater importance.

Now we, like the Jews, want miracles. Either consciously or
unconsciously, we expect miracles. We find this such an easy
solution to our problems, and insofar as we do not see the reasons
why God, who could so easily favor us, absolutely refuses to do
so, there arises between God and ourselves a certain misunder-
standing which ought to be removed.

The first reason for this refusal is that a religion of miracles
would place God at the service of our interests, our caprices, or
our appetites. What is the final purpose of religion but to detach
us from the world with its deceitful pleasures, its human affec-

91

tions which must some day be broken, in order to attach us to another world and another life to which the love of God invites us?

Now all these miracles which we desire—cures, temporal success, comfort in sorrow and relief in suffering—would result in attaching us still more to this life which we must leave some day, and, by making it less painful, less disquieting, less sorrowful, these miracles would keep us from preparing ourselves for the other life for which we were made and where we will be forever happy. Jesus knew these people who followed Him in order to obtain favors from Him. He told them: "You follow me but it is not because you have seen a miracle, and by perceiving God in this wonderful exhibition of goodness, strength, and love, you are devoted to Him. No, it is because you have had bread to eat and your hunger is satisfied."

For Jesus knew that the miracles that He worked turned attention away from His person. In Jesus, the divine showed in every word, look, or action. Sincere and sensitive souls constantly received the impression of it. Those who were more gross and superficial were interested only in the benefits received—they had eaten bread. God respects the liberty of souls. He is not a ruthless conqueror who imposes his will upon others, who enslaves his disciples by brute force, or by some threat, or by artful words. God offers Himself. He speaks to the heart. He has come to reveal the dispositions hidden in the depths of the heart of each one of us. Even today it is there that He reveals Himself, and now as of old He reveals Himself only to those souls who freely choose to have Him. The disciples whom Jesus desires to have are not those who grow enthusiastic over prodigies, but those recollected and attentive souls to whom Christ is revealed not by flesh and blood, but by a whisper, a murmur, an attraction which comes from the Father. "No one can come to me unless the Father who sent me draw him."

This is the manifestation, this is the epiphany that He desires. Even the Magi had to offer their gifts to an Infant in swaddling bands and lying upon straw. He desires that we put our faith in a man whom we see sleeping during a tempest and dying on a cross.

But the important motive, which underlies and dominates all the rest, is the fact that a miracle in the physical order is a revelation of power. Now Jesus desired to reveal only God's love. The miracle that Jesus was continually working, the miracle that He worked the more as the physical miracles became less, and in proportion as He became the more feeble, the more despoiled, the more abandoned into our hands, was the prodigious miracle, the unbelievable revelation of the love of God for us. It was the extraordinary tenderness with which God has so loved the world that He has given His only Son to save the world, and the Son has become obedient even to the death of the Cross.

Those who clamored for miracles in their own interest were incapable of perceiving this miracle of love. "Save us, we perish!" These, ignoring the love which God is showing them, wish to profit by His presence only in order that they might the more easily do without Him. The true miracle, the true revelation of Jesus was not on Tabor, where He was transfigured for a few minutes before three witnesses. The true miracle was the Incarnation, the Passion, Calvary with its unheard of humiliations which God desired to suffer in the sight of the whole world for love of us. We do not comprehend this miracle, that anyone could invent, that anyone could be capable of loving us like that. This miracle means little to us because we know nothing of love. We are displeased with Jesus. He has disappointed everyone—His parents, His village, His people, His most enthusiastic partisans. And us, too. We are tired of His goodness, of His patience, of His tolerance. We find Him sleeping. We are tempted to say to Him what was said by His enemies: "No one does a thing in secret when He wishes it to become known. Show yourself to the world. Come down from your Cross and all will believe in you!"

But Jesus does not come down. "You do not know of what spirit you are," He says. "It is when I shall be lifted up from the earth that I shall draw all things to myself."

It is in remaining a prey to suffering and to outrage that He continues to testify to the invincible power and the unheard of patience of God, the seriousness with which God has loved us and the unbelievable confidence which He has in us. It is in remaining upon the Cross, it is in continuing to turn upon us His glance from eyes filled with tears and blood, that He will succeed in reaching our better selves and placing us voluntarily, willingly, upon our knees before Him.

If the entire Church, with the Pope at its head, if all the bishops, clergy, and laity were to prostrate themselves in prayer and beg of God His triumphal coming as Judge upon the clouds of heaven, I can tell you truly that they would not obtain this favor. (No one knows the day nor the hour which the Father has fixed.) But, in no matter what church or shack, where the humblest—I dare to say even the worst—priest pronounces the words of consecration, there God is, docile in our hands, in our grasp, there He is again, come among us to love and to suffer. There He is, delivered over to our negligences, our distractions, our rudeness, our baseness. There He is as He loves to be, there He is as He loves to appear, to reveal Himself to us. There He is once again, sleeping, so calm, so silent, so patient.

For understand, that all the value, all the purpose of our faith is to place us in real contact with Him sleeping there, and to render us attentive to this revelation of the Father which draws us to Jesus.

Let us pray that we may become capable of believing in what Jesus does in silence. Let us not pray that we may see miracles, but that we may have need of no other miracle but that of being so deeply loved. Let us pray that we may respond by another miracle, that of believing, that of loving in our turn. And of receiving the grace to recognize Jesus in that secret rendezvous where only those who love are to be found.

THE FIFTH SUNDAY AFTER THE EPIPHANY

The Good Grain and the Cockle

Last Sunday we saw our Lord manifest Himself as a wonder-worker. We saw His epiphany as Master of heaven and earth. Today He manifests Himself as Teacher and we cannot but admire the extraordinary wisdom of His teaching. For this He makes use of a parable so simple and so clear that every child can understand it, and so commonplace, it seems to us, that we have never taken the trouble to think about it.

This is the parable of the good grain and the cockle. The Kingdom of God is likened to a field in which the owner has sown good seed, but, while men were asleep, their enemy came into the field and sowed cockle which is a violent poison. When the seeds had sprouted, the cockle was noticed in among the good grain. Scandalized at this, the workmen asked the owner: "Did you not sow good seed in your field?" The owner replied: "An enemy has done this."

The reaction of the workmen to this is immediate. It is the same with us. "Do you want us to go now," they say, "and clear out this cockle?"

The reply of the owner is startling. "No," he says, "lest in uprooting the cockle you cause damage to the wheat. Let them both grow. At the time of the harvest I will tell the reapers, 'Gather first the cockle and bind it into bundles and burn it, then store the wheat in my barns.'"

The deepest truths are contained in this simple parable. Jesus resolves the enigma of sin, the existence of evil in the world, in the Church, and among men.

He prevents and refutes our scandal at the presence of evil, and the patience of God in dealing with it.

Not many epochs have been as scandalized as ours by the consideration of the power of evil in the world. It is a commonplace saying that, in the 19th century, in their enthusiasm over the discoveries of science, men declared that they no longer had any need of God. They hoped that civilization and education would suffice to make men adhere to the moral law. "Every time that you open a school," said Victor Hugo, "you close a prison."

Science would be able to suppress famines, sickness, and, possibly, death itself. We have all had sad experience of the outcome of these illusions.

Before the war, we knew that there was such a thing as evil. We pictured it to ourselves as lurking in the dark corners of the world or in the secret of consciences. What was our stupor to see it erupt one fine day, armed with so many tanks, planes, cannons, and men, and with one mighty outburst injustice submerged the whole of Europe.

Many unstable consciences took pride in and felt admiration for this victory of science against which they had never been warned. The disillusionment was cruel and the world has not yet recovered from that catastrophe for which it was so ill prepared.

There is no worse pessimism than an optimism based upon a lie. Our century, just as sentimental and romantic as the 19th, has settled down into despair as the preceding one was lifted up in its illusions. But that does not mean that it will be converted. In the 19th century, things went too well, God was useless. In the 20th century, things are so bad that it is impossible to believe that there is a God.

Why does He permit all this evil?

It is like children in a quarrel. Each one considers himself in the right. No one has the good sense to recognize his own culpability.

All the literature of our times tries to justify man and throw all the blame on God, to denounce with horror the cockle that has grown so quickly while we were asleep.

The men of our times are saying that we have arrived at the 25th hour, where all counter-action, all salvation is impossible, and there is nothing to be done but stand by and watch the unavoidable process of destruction. To this scandalous notion Jesus offers a strengthening optimism. The owner is good, and it is good seed that our Father has sown in His field.

Sin is the work of the devil. He is ever present among us. He is far stronger than we are, but infinitely less powerful than God. Against those who are not asleep but wide awake in their faith, keeping close to their Saviour by love, against such the devil has no power. He can do nothing.

These are already saved and delivered from evil.

But, in this parable, Jesus is mainly concerned with the scandal that arises when we see the patience, the silence, the passivity of God brought face to face with the activity and the triumph of evil.

You know the classic objection brought against God. If God is all-powerful, then He is not good because He could suppress evil and He does not do it. Or else God is good, He has pity on men, He hates evil, but He is unable to stop it, so that shows that He is not all-powerful. To this dilemma Jesus responds with profound wisdom—the good and the bad are inextricably bound together here below.

Actually, there is no way of separating the one from the other. We are not capable of distinguishing all the good that there is in what seems bad, nor all the bad in what seems good. In suppressing the bad the good will suffer, just as in pulling up the cockle the good grain is damaged.

97

It is necessary that evil should remain upon the earth. It has a mission to fulfill, a work that is necessary until the end of the world, a mysterious service to render to the good. This entwinement of good and evil upon this earth is a mystery, but reflexion can bring much light to bear on the subject.

Physical evil, such as physical suffering, for example, inevitably follows upon the fact that we are beings who are endowed with the power of sensation. Whatever lessens our suffering also lessens our power to enjoy.

Suppose, for example, it were possible to separate these from one another. Suppose some medicine were found that would do away with all pain. The result would be that there would be no more warning signals of danger, which is what the sense of pain really is. We would be the unconscious victims of sickness, accidents, and danger of every kind.

The man who does not feel suffering is blind, for is not suffering, in reality, a light? Moral suffering—sorrow—is a source of much spiritual progress.

What can anyone do with a child who is devoid of feeling? The son who cares nothing for the tears of his mother or the reproach of his father?

What kind of creature would he be who is indifferent to shame, who is satisfied to be more beastly, dirtier, lazier than everyone else? In fact, without the powerful stimulus of moral suffering, humanity would grovel in satisfied indifference.

And sin?

If man is capable of loving God, of devoting himself, of believing, of trusting, of continuing to hope in spite of everything, this is because he is free, because he has the liberty to do evil, to sin and to shut himself up in despair. In removing the cockle of sin, you would, at the same time, destroy the good grain of the virtues.

What kind of world would this be if men were to serve God

like slaves, or perhaps, if each failure were immediately visited with some violent and physical punishment, teaching us to serve God out of terror and never out of love?

But sin is even more intimately bound to good than you think. The cause of sin is the pride of man who believes that he is sufficient unto himself and can do without God, that he can become independent just as God is. And the consequence of sin is, in general, humiliation. Our weakness is uncovered, our powerlessness is manifested, and the outcome of our sinfulness shows us how great is our need for God.

Man is a being, so Jesus has told us, who does not know what he does, but he generally learns this after he has done it. It is in paying the consequences of sin that he acknowledges, like the woman, that "the serpent deceived me."

This is a reflection that I often make when I see so many men and boys grow tired of the spiritual life. They become indifferent, without either conviction or difficulties. They do not know what sin is. It is like that parable of the barren fig tree, which the owner wanted to cut down, but the workman intervened and begged him to let him try once more. "Let me put manure around it, then perhaps it will bear fruit."

So with many of these simple fellows, ignorant of their own innate weakness because they are so good-natured, or because their lives have been so protected, God permits them to fall into some very humiliating sin, or even some grave scandal, and this reveals to them how weak they really are and how much need they have of God.

God is not afraid of evil, He is not scandalized by sin. God employs it in the service of good. If you would like to know the esteem that God has for what we call "the goods of the earth," all you have to do is to look around and see to whom God gives them. To His enemies, most often. And if you want to know the opinion that God has of suffering, see to whom He sends it. To

His friends, in good measure. If you want to know what He thinks of sin, look where He goes to find His friends—among the sinners, by preference.

Jesus died to save men from sin. When sin is no longer in the will of man, it no longer exists, or better, there remains only its happy consequence, a humble recognition of the goodness of God and of our need for Him. God would not have permitted the evil if He were not powerful enough to draw good out of it. Thus sin does not do any injury to the Kingdom of God but contributes mysteriously to its benefit. St. Augustine says: "To those who love God, everything is useful, even sin." Jesus has said the same but, above all, He has lived it. Jesus is the good grain to which the cockle of sin, of suffering, and of evil is no longer inextricably entwined. He is the eternal image of the good grain, the Bread of Life, the Wheat of God, mixed with the cockle of the Cross.

He reminds us always that evil has been conquered, that sin has no power, that we need no longer have fear for He has brought about the redemption of the world and the triumph of the just. He ever recalls to our minds all the good that has come from so much evil.

Bearing in mind His Resurrection, we should be more faithful and await with confidence the wise judgment of the Father of the family.

When the day of the great harvest comes we shall know why it was necessary that so much evil should be left amid the good, and why Infinite Wisdom was so patient. From now on, if we will place our trust in Him, our lives will be happy, and our sufferings much easier to bear, for, in truth, man suffers less from the evils which come upon him than from the worry and anxiety that he endures because of them. It is not the presence of the cockle which bothers us so much as the paralyzing doubt regarding its origin. "Lord, did you not sow good seed in your field? How is it that there is now the cockle?"

100

There are many among the sick who think that they do not believe in God, when in fact they drive Him away, ignore Him, and are sulky towards Him. If, by some miracle, they are cured and thus brought face to face with His love and His goodness, they come to know that what really troubled them was their inability to believe in the goodness of God. They feel that now it would cost them little if their illness were to return. They feel that their greatest suffering was not their sickness, the fever, the care, the anxiety about the future, the despair of relatives, but that the real suffering was their doubts concerning the goodness of God.

And the rest of us would find our woes become far less the day that we realize that the Father of the family has sown only good seed in His field and that it is because of His infinite wisdom and infinite goodness that He bears so patiently with the cockle.

SEPTUAGESIMA SUNDAY

The Workers of the Last Hour

"I choose to give to this last as I give to you."   (Matthew 20:1–16)

This parable, so encouraging for sinners and so discouraging for the "just," is the best trap for catching us in our pharisaism.

For, either we recognize ourselves as sinners, and our Lord fills us with hope and joy. It is never too late to mend. We have no right to despair in regard to ourselves. We are feeble and inconstant, even in sin. God is strong and persevering and He never renounces us. Who knows? After so many calls from the Father of the family, and such deafness on our part, we may yet hear Him one day, and He will give us all that we have wasted, all that we—and others—thought irrevocably lost.

Or, on the other hand, we consider ourselves "just"—and Christ told us that He has not come for the just. We feel that we have served God for so long that we well merit our recompense, and even a greater recompense than those who have not been subjected to the same trials as ourselves. We have made such-and-such sacrifices for God, we have patiently endured so many Masses, have forced ourselves to go to confession, and we have given up pleasures and suffered renunciations so that now we have come to feel envy towards and be jealous of those miserable workers of the last hour. "They have it easy. They are in luck. If we had known, we would have waited, too. We would not have gone to so much trouble."

What a pity! Such an attitude condemns the life that we have lived up to now and called Christian. In speaking like this we prove that we have not really known the God we pretend to serve, for, if we did, our attitude would be something very different.

We would be saying: "What luck has been ours in knowing and serving God for such a long time! By a free gift of His we have had the joy of living in His intimacy ever since the beginning of our lives. He has done us the favor of calling us among the first. His choice of us is something we shall never understand, for we have done nothing to merit being chosen and pardoned in preference to them."

And we would show great compassion towards these last called, these late comers, and we would beg the Father of the family to give them the same salary as to ourselves. We would ask Him to compensate, by the graciousness of their reception, for a long separation, a long privation, a long solitude.

In reality, our taking scandal at the generosity of the Master is our own condemnation. It proves that we have served Him badly. that we have known nothing of His goodness and His generosity.

It reveals that we ourselves are workers who have not even yet been called, that we are really workers—of the twelfth hour!

102

SEXAGESIMA SUNDAY

On Making Good Use of the Word of God

Today, instead of making our usual examination of the conscience of the preacher (has he taken too long, or been more tiresome than usual, did he repeat, or did he contradict, was he double-tongued?), the Gospel invites us to make our examination of the consciences of the auditors.

Jesus tells us that, if the Word of God remains without fruit in our case, it is not the fault of the seed, nor even of the sower ("Who hears you, hears Me."), but it is the fault of the earth on which it falls, that is, the dispositions that we bring to it.

The Word of God possesses infinite strength. It is a fire which is capable of covering the whole earth in an instant. It is a sword so sharp that it separates the thoughts and feelings of the heart. It is a seed which, scattered by twelve poor men, and forever seeming to be lost in the earth, grows and multiplies a hundred-fold.

How is it that its fecundity seems lost in our midst?

It certainly is not because the seed has not been sown! How many sermons have we not heard, how many catechism lessons, exhortations in the confessional, retreats and days of recollection, and how many religious books are published! Never has the Word of God been so widely disseminated, and yet we all have the impression that it is something we never heard before in all our lives.

Then, ought not the blame to be placed upon our own dispositions? Every preacher has had the sad experience of being neither understood nor listened to, and Jesus Himself has had more of it than anyone else, and He invites us to seek within ourselves for the reason why the teaching which has been given to us with such prodigality has borne so little fruit.

Have you ever thought of examining your dispositions when you listen to a sermon? St. Paul told the faithful who intended to receive the Bread of Christ: "Examine yourself before you eat this Bread. For he who eats and drinks, eats and drinks his own condemnation, not discerning the Body of the Lord. That is why there are among us so many sick, infirm, and even many dead."

But the Word of God ought also to find in us some preparation, some discernment, some respect, and without this it will not nourish our souls. May it not be said of us that we are of the number of those who do not know how to discern the Word of the Lord?

The first group of auditors, Jesus tells us, are like the highway, macadamized by habit. The seed falls here without penetrating at all. They have heard so many sermons and none of them has ever made any change in them. They expect nothing and they receive nothing. The Word of God annoys them, and they regard as time lost that given to its proclamation. It is the time when they sit down to catch up a little on their sleep, or else go over their favorite dreams, their usual worries, or their plans for the future. What a revelation it would be if we could see the thoughts with which many entertain themselves while God is speaking to them and trying to touch their hearts!

To Jesus the souls of His auditors were transparent while He spoke to them and He denounced Satan who, like a sinister crow, was always on the watch and flew to pick up the seeds before they could sink into the soil and take root, then replacing them by seeds of his own, poisonous and of no use.

Have you ever remarked the fact—and our Lord gives it as a proof of the existence of the demon—how quickly we forget the Word of God? Ask someone what the Gospel was last Sunday. As a rule, they have not yet left the church after Mass before they have forgotten it entirely.

But let them go to the theater or to a movie and they can recount the whole film, they can go over the most striking scenes, even in their prayers they are pursued by the music which they have heard. Only the Word of God slips away without a trace.

The second group is that of the superficial. These are sensitive and enthusiastic souls but they have no depth. They do not know themselves and are ignorant of the resistance that their bad habits offer to the Word of God. They get excited easily and believe themselves converted because their emotions are stirred. If it should happen that they shed a few tears, they feel that they have given proof of great virtue. Everything that is said to them affects them, but nothing ever changes them. They hasten to repeat to others the thoughts that made some impression on them, and thus in giving them away, they lose the benefit they might have reaped if they had allowed them to penetrate. They praise the preacher to the skies, but because they are so proud and attribute to themselves such great merit for having listened to and approved of him, they believe themselves dispensed from acquiring anything further.

The third group is the deep, rich soil in which the Word can germinate. These possess reflexive minds and a formed character. But they hasten to check its growth for fear of the hold that it might get over them. They stop their ears by so much agitation, so much work, and find their present life so filled that they feel that they have the right to neglect their eternal life. They are interested in too many things to occupy themselves with God as well. They are too intelligent to bend before the simplicity of the Gospel. They always find some objection to make, some reason for contradicting it, some defect to ridicule, some excuse for not thinking any more about it. While they are listening, they are carrying on a debate in their minds with the preacher, and the victory is always theirs.

These are the worst. Their lack of cooperation is entirely voluntary. They deliberately cultivate the thorns of their pride, their agitation, their mockery, in order to check the growth of the seed which they regard as a menace.

Finally, what is that good soil which hungrily absorbs the good seed and allows it to germinate into action? What is that field where the Word of God bears fruit?

I fear to tell you. They are those who have recognized themselves in one of these three categories. But not those who stand around complacently waiting for someone to speak about them and eulogize them before the whole world.

Rather, they are the ones who receive the Word of God as a revelation, as a personal interview, those who allow themselves to be concerned, to be unmasked, to be dislodged from their security and their good conscience. They are the ones who take to themselves what is said and who recognize themselves, saying: "I am the one whom he means, it is my conduct that is being denounced, I am the one who is being condemned, that is what I must change."

They have received the Word, not as coming from man but from God.

In them it penetrates, it germinates, it ripens and bears magnificent fruit.

Happy are those who hear the Word of God and put it into practice!

FEAST OF ST. JOSEPH

Many of the saints have suffered more from the works of their biographers than from the hands of their persecutors. The fathers have stoned the prophets, as Scripture tells us, but their sons have built them basilicas, carved statues, and written lives which justify even more violent treatment.

St. Joseph is one of those saints who have suffered most from the zeal of his admirers. They have been pleased to represent him as old, worn out, dusty, almost patriarchal. They have taken from him every vestige of youth, character, or prominence, so as to

106

render unlikely and even disgusting the project of a marriage between this tired old man and a young girl.

Happily, the picture which our time offers is quite different. Today we picture St. Joseph as a young man, a fiancé, a young husband of a young girl of sixteen years. Our time feels that one can be a Christian even while one is young, that a Christian should remain young, that every Christian should be militant, not looking for retirement, that the greatest sin, as St. Paul puts it, is to be "the old man," with old-fashioned ideas, without hope, rheumatic of heart, and frozen of faith.

Cardinal Suenens says that it is a tradition not in keeping with the faith that has given to St. Joseph this factitious character of an anonymous old man of effacing habits and behavior.

How is it that we think that Mary would have chosen for her fiancé and husband an old man who could never have become, as head of the Holy Family, the model and the ideal of our own families?

We are free, and it is much more natural, to imagine St. Joseph as young, and even handsome, and to believe that Joseph and Mary loved each other as spouses. We may even believe that Mary would not have chosen to place her own life and that of her Son in the hands of someone who could not be the true head of the family, who could not be its protector, and whom she could not really love.

Perhaps you will suggest that, in view of the virginity that she wished to preserve, such a marriage would have been a matter of prudence.

Not at all! Of false prudence, yes.

Do you think that, for two spouses bound to the great sacrifices that conjugal chastity demands, it were better that they did not love one another?

Quite the contrary. One can renounce a certain form of love only because one has found a better. All the difference between restraint and renouncement is there.

107

Restraint is an unnatural refusal, a malicious constraint, an insupportable privation because it is without compensation.

Renouncement is the passing over to a better love, to a new manner of loving which permits one to make the sacrifice of the first. It reveals a greater and more attentive tenderness, which renews and sanctifies love. Certainly, it was not prudence for Mary and Joseph not to love each other. On the contrary, they had to love each other in order to be able to bear together so many trials and sufferings.

It is because he loved her that Joseph retained his faith in Mary and that he did not, in spite of everything, denounce her.

He knew and loved Mary too well to harbor a suspicion of her for an instant. He knew how upright she was, how transparent her soul, how unwavering in the face of duty and how pure. To him who truly loves, a thousand objections cannot make a single doubt. For him who does not love, a thousand proofs cannot make certitude. "The spouse," says the Canticle of Canticles, "recognizes his bride by a single hair of her neck."

When he found himself confronted by the mystery of this extraordinary conception in regard to the one person in all the world of whom he was most sure, the problem which tormented him was not a problem of love. To love is to have confidence, it is to believe and to give credit. It was rather, according to the Gospel, a problem of justice and of discretion. Not daring to interfere in something that God had not revealed to him, certain that his bride was without reproach, he contented himself with a simple withdrawal and formed no judgment in regard to her.

His faith in Mary was to protect, strengthen, and be the teacher of his faith in God. And when it pleased the Lord to take him into the secret, Joseph was still worthy of Mary, for he had never doubted her.

Notice well that this faith on the part of Joseph owed nothing whatever to the angel. As always, the angel arrived on the scene when it was all over. Neither to Joseph nor to us does God send

His angels in order to dispense us from struggling with, and reflecting upon, our own problems. For a long time Joseph was suffering and searching for a solution. When he had found one he had resolved upon a course of action. Joseph's anguish and torment had ceased (since he was asleep) when the angel came to reward him. The angels of God come only to those who are capable of receiving their messages.

The angels of the Annunciation are always flying over this world in search of some soul who is attentive, open, and docile enough to receive the Word of God. They do not present themselves before the eyes of the distracted, but deliver their messages to interior and peaceful souls. It is where the waters are most calm that the slightest breath of air can cause the ripples. The truly angelic work took place in the depths of the souls of Joseph and Mary.

To each of us, too, a work, a call, a vocation is given. Some hear and at once set about putting it into execution. These are the ones who are attentive and ready. But if you are going to wait for the visit of an angel before you budge an inch, you will wait throughout your whole existence.

They knew many other trials and in them their love deepened and matured as does all true conjugal love.

When God enters into our lives He usually begins by turning everything upside down. His graces are somewhat like a shower of stones hurled upon us. One might say that St. Joseph is a patron particularly fitted for our time, for he lived, like ourselves, in the midst of catastrophes. Persecutions, massacres, exile, displaced persons, poverty—he knew all these things that have happened to us or that threaten to happen in the future.

Let us try to understand that St. Joseph is our patron and the Blessed Virgin is our model because they resemble us, because they have lived lives very much like our own, because they have borne the same trials, the only difference being that they bore them better than we do. If not, if they were angels in disguise, or creatures overwhelmed with extraordinary graces, they would be of no use to us.

How many times there must have come to their minds and to their lips that question, that reproach that is written for our joy, in the Gospel—the same that we are so often tempted to make but which we would not have allowed ourselves if they had not authorized it by their example. "Lord, why have you done so to us? Why do you treat us like this? For we have sought you, sorrowing."

They themselves lost Jesus. They could not find Him. They did not know if they would ever find Him. They, too, knew solitude, the absence of their dear one, the silence of that familiar voice. They too knew what we think happens only to ourselves—the disorder, the anguish, the suffering of one who has lost his God.

But they sought Him for three days. They did not give way to discouragement. They did not abandon Him although it seemed that He had abandoned them. And they found Him. Their faith was rewarded. It did not deceive them. Their fidelity had its recompense. They found Him, as always, there where they ought to have guessed that He would be. And they knew that, at bottom, it was they who were far from Him, from His natural home, and not He who had left them.

If, when we have lost our contact with God, when God seems to have abandoned us, if we, too, give three days to prayer, to seeking for Him, I think it will be with us as it was with them, that having partaken of their sorrow, we shall also partake of their joy.

There is that other sentence, placed in the Gospel of our feast, for our consolation, and for our fraternity with them: "They did not understand what He said to them"! Do we understand anything of what God has done during our lives? Of the way He guides us? Of the way He treats us? They were stunned, puzzled, unhappy. But, and it is here that they set us an example, "Mary kept all these words, pondering them in her heart." Confronted by some event, some trial, or with some Word of God, there are two reactions which are dangerous—one, very stupid, is "I understand everything"; the other, hostile, "I understand nothing, there is nothing about it that is understandable." The only modest and sure attitude is that of the Blessed Virgin, to let mature, let ripen in the way that pleases God, in the depths of one's heart, those things which God alone can make clear to us.

Mary and Joseph lived by faith.

In the Holy Family, just as in our own families, there was the daily need of confidence in one another, faith in one another, and giving credit to one another.

There was Joseph's faith in Mary. He loved her and was proud to love her so much that he never had a doubt concerning her.

There was Mary's faith in Joseph. She loved and esteemed him and admired him enough to believe him capable of a love strong enough to be pure, to be worthy of her trust, to be the protector of her Son. She believed that, in spite of sacrifices, or rather because of them, they would become a more united and happier family than any other in all the world.

There was the faith of Joseph and Mary in Jesus. They did not always understand what He did nor what He said, but they had confidence in Him, they remembered what He said, they meditated upon it, and they had the wisdom of those who have sufficient light to bear with their darkness.

There was the faith of Jesus in His parents, for "He obeyed them."

Thus it is that every true family lives by faith. Every true family is a place where one is loved infinitely more than one deserves. To love and to be loved like this is the source of more happiness and goodness in the bosom of the family than any exact weighing of merits and exact rewards can produce. A true family is one where the members are willing to accept the fact that they do not understand everything, and where disagreements and misunderstandings are overcome by the spirit of faith. Here

111

they are always ready to renew their trust in one another, their love for one another, regardless of past deceptions or sufferings.

No man is ever lost as long as there remains someone who believes in him and loves him. A woman remains young as long as her husband loves her. A man keeps his sense of value as long as his wife believes in him. And a child's future is secure as long as his parents prepare him for it and share his hopes.

The world has been saved, the work of redemption has been accomplished during thirty years because, in a little family, the members believed in and loved each other. Unto the end, the Holy Family lived by that faith.

Joseph died before anything was accomplished, when, as yet, nothing notable had taken place. He had to accept God's extraordinary entry into his life, and then pass thirty years seeing nothing extraordinary accomplished.

He had no need of a miracle, an explanation, any proof, he simply believed. He is the image of all those older relatives of ours who died before the victory was won, of those soldiers who believed when we doubted, but who have gone and left us to enjoy what they have won. They sowed and others reaped.

He is the model of those disinterested workers, of all those who know how to occupy themselves with the things of God and the interests of others without thought of their own affairs, without seeking payment for their devotedness, all the while remaining willingly in the shadow, like St. Joseph, who never said a word, never worked a miracle, of whom, so far as I know, there has never been an apparition, but who has quietly kept the place which God entrusted to him.

May St. Joseph, who with such chivalrous disinterestedness reared a child who was not his own, and who respected the woman who was placed in his care, obtain for us many young men who will care for the children of others as though they were their own, who will know how to respect in every woman the one whom they will one day marry, and in that one may they

112

always see a resemblance to the Virgin which will ever give to their love that pure and respectful character which was that of St. Joseph for Mary and which has made of him a great saint.

QUINQUAGESIMA SUNDAY

The Cure of the Blind Man

"Lord, that I may see!"   (Luke 18:31–43)

As His Passion drew near, Jesus tried to forewarn His Apostles against the scandal of His failure. He foretold it to them several times and in such a way as to show them that His weakness itself was a proof of His power. Perhaps He also attempted to confide in them, to seek their understanding, to share His burden with them. "I have a baptism wherewith I am to be baptized and I am in anguish until it be accomplished."

The response of the Apostles is disappointing. Jesus takes them into His confidence. He foretells His sufferings. He shares with them His most intimate secrets. They are not interested. They do not understand and they do not take the trouble to ask any questions.

We are scandalized and we condemn them as egoists and cowards.

And it does not occur to us that that is exactly the way we ourselves feel. Lent will begin this Wednesday. At this announcement who among you feels any great interest, courage, resolution, or faith?

Some of us have probably made plans for Mardigras. Who has made his plans for Lent? Who is impatiently waiting for this time of renovation and closer following of Christ?

The Lenten announcement arouses in us exactly the same

113

sentiments as in the Apostles—we are not expecting anything, we are not interested, and we do not even try to understand.

We are told that Jesus is about to take up His Cross, and each of us is invited to follow Him, or run the risk of betraying Him. The Trappists, the Carmelites, the Carthusians, the Dominicans, all increase their penances. The children decide upon their Lenten mortifications. And we, are we preparing to make a change in our lives? Are we, at last, to become Christians? When should we do so if not on this occasion?

But there is something greater still. These words of Christ which seem to us to be so sad, so discouraging, are, in reality, the announcement of the greatest joy. In this announcement of our Lord, have you noticed the words that should have filled the Apostles with joy? That should have given them confidence in the face of every trial and kept them faithful to the end? "And the third day He shall rise again."

Jesus assures them of His resurrection, His final triumph over His adversaries, His presence among them always, and instead of exulting with joy, they are so stupid that they stand there dejected and without any response.

And we, are we responsive to that radiant assurance of a resurrection? Do we believe a resurrection is even possible? Do we hope for some renewal? Are we expecting something from God?

The Gospel continues with the account of the cure of the blind man. Only one person asked Jesus, as He passed along, for light. Only one blind person knew that he could not see. A single person knew himself to be blind among all this crowd of blind who did not know, and that single one was cured.

We are all blind. We are all like the Apostles, without spiritual understanding, torpid, dull.

Let us be like that blind man, let us become conscious of our real state. Let us say to Christ with sincerity: "I am totally blind.

114

I understand nothing in regard to Lent. I have no desire whatever
to suffer. The Cross and all mortification make me shudder with
horror. I have no desire to follow you. All that repels and
discourages me."

But if we acknowledge our blindness we shall obtain our cure.
Jesus will enlighten us also and give us the perception of God, a
spiritual vision, the revelation of the designs and the desires of
the Father.

Then, for the first time, we shall begin to understand what He
is saying to us: "Behold, we are going up to Jerusalem, and all
that was foretold by the prophets regarding the Son of man shall
be accomplished. For He will be delivered to the Gentiles, and
will be mocked and shamefully treated and spit upon, they will
scourge Him and kill Him, and on the third day He will rise."

We shall be overcome by sorrow and by joy while awaiting
Him. A great hope will carry us along. We shall passionately
desire to be faithful. And, like this blind man who was cured, we
shall follow Jesus, glorifying God.

ASH WEDNESDAY

What a strange resolution for Lent our Lord, in the Gospel,
advises us to make! Not to have a long face, not to publish our
efforts, not to make others the witnesses of our privations by our
bad humor. But, on the contrary, to use perfume, to look pleasant, and to place in God our treasure, our heart, and our joy.

For the first Christians, the proclamation of penance was
"Good News." God is about to pardon our faults, God is coming
to us "full of tenderness and compassion, patient and infinitely
merciful" (as the prophet Joel says in the Epistle of the Mass).
"The Kingdom of God is at hand. Do penance and believe in the

Good News." So preached St. John the Baptist. God is going to reveal to you His tenderness. You are going to be rid of your faults. You are going to rise above your failures.

For us moderns, all this is bad news! Lent is beginning? Bad news! Do penance? More bad news! Go to confession? Worse still!

If, in some assembly of Christian men and women, someone begins to speak of penance, or of sacrifice, immediately all faces darken, and the temperature drops too. Everyone begins to fear for what is most dear to him—his purse, his cigarettes, the movies, the television. Each one is afraid to think of God!

What can be the reason for such a reversal? You are here because you wish to be here. In earlier times, only those took up the cross and did penance who had committed great crimes. They were the "public penitents."

On Holy Thursday, at the Mass during which they were readmitted to the community, these sinners seemed so happy, so innocent, so converted that they fairly trembled with happiness and fervor. Seeing them, the rest of the faithful felt sorrow and regret that they had not been subjected to a like penance, and they wished to know the same renewal. The following year, they, like you today, asked for the cross and for admission to the company of the penitents.

Why, then, are we so gloomy?

The reason is that we are thinking only of ourselves, of our mortifications which cost, of the cross which we fear, of the sacrifices which are repugnant to us, and of the confession which we will have to make.

We do not think of God who is awaiting us, who has called us, and thanks to whom all will turn into joy if we turn our hearts to Him.

There are two kinds of religion between which we must choose, the one is true and the other is false. The false one, the pagan one, is the one in which we offer to God painful, sad, and miserable things which we impose upon ourselves for His sake. And this kind of religion is miserable, sad, and painful. No one has any desire to know more about it because no one wants to do any more.

It all ends up by giving us, in regard to God, the mentality of a dissatisfied benefactor. When one looks over one's past, one says to oneself: "How much I have done for Him! Look at all that I have sacrificed for Him! And what has He done for me?"

The other kind of religion, the true one, regards what God has done for us. It looks at the great and marvellous things that He has done in spite of the poverty and littleness of His servants. Of this kind of religion one never knows enough. The more one learns, the more one wants to learn. It is the religion of the Magnificat, of the Psalms which chant the marvellous works of God. It is the religion of the Creed, in which there is not a word about ourselves but which proclaims the works, the inventions, the marvellous enterprises of God to show us, to persuade us, that He loves us.

Hence penance does not mean a turning towards oneself, a burying of one's nose in one's sins. What do you find attractive in that? How is that beneficial?

Penance is a turning of oneself to the true God, a finding of God, a coming to know Him, to recognize Him, to marvel at His tenderness, to receive and to rejoice in His forgiveness.

There is all the difference between the two conceptions that there is between Judas and St. Peter.

Judas recognized his sin. He even made his confession. He admitted: "I have sinned. I have betrayed innocent blood!" But he stopped there, and the weight of it was so heavy that he went and hanged himself.

Peter looked at Jesus. That look of Peter was turned towards Jesus and met His look—he saw his God humiliated, yet tender and loving, calling to him and awaiting him. He responded, in his turn, by tenderness and love, by sorrow and joy and immense hope—by a true repentance. He was no longer clinging to his sin, he was quite detached from it, for he had found One who is infinitely better than sin and despair.

We are Christians if we have come in contact with that God and met His glance. We are Christians if we believe what we should know after so many years of experience—that God loves us.

We are not Christians because we practice all the mortifications of Lent, go to Mass every Sunday, nor because we are virtuous, honest, and pure. Not even because we love God. Every religion helps one do that.

But we are Christians because we have that strange, unusual, unheard of persuasion that God loves us, that God loves *you,* that He takes delight in the love of your heart, that He is pleased with your attention and hurt by your refusal.

The true God loves men. Man can do without God, but God cannot do without man. A son can forget, can deny his father or mother, but parents will never deny their child. "And even if a mother should forget her infant, I will not forget you, says the Lord. See I have graven you in the palm of my hand. You are always before my eyes." The hunger that man has for God is as nothing in comparison with the hunger that God has for man.

You will be asked only one question in heaven: "Have you believed in the love that God has for you?" And the saints will reply with St. John: "We have known the love of God for us and we have believed in it."

God's love for us is gratuitous. God loves us before we loved Him, and even without our loving Him. God loves us even as sinners. God has no need of our sacrifices in order to make Him love us. God loves us even if we make no sacrifices nor any mortifications during Lent. He does not love us because we are worthy. God loves us, like all those who love us truly, such as our father and mother, not because of the good qualities that are to be found in us, but because of the goodness, generosity, and

118

fidelity of their own hearts. They are so tender, so loving, so persevering that they are sure that one day a like love will spring up in our own hearts.

Our soul is a joy to God not because of what we do for Him, but because of what He can do for us.

Nothing is more dangerous than premature sacrifices. Nothing is more dangerous than to try to outdo God in love without having first learned what His love is. Nothing is more pharisaic than to wish to be worthy of being loved by God before having accepted the fact that God loves you even when you are unworthy.

Christian teaching is not the teaching of sacrifice, but, on the contrary, the teaching of the paternity of God. God is a father. To be a father means to be the one to love first, to take the initiative, to teach love by loving.

God gives. He is not one who takes, nor one who receives. It is His joy to give. He has created this world and all that is good and beautiful in it for us to use with gratitude. He rejoices when we appreciate His gifts and discover in them a proof, a reflection of His goodness.

And when one of you likes something, God is pleased to have found, at last, a man who agrees with Him. For it was God who said that His creation was good. "And God saw that it was good." Then, begin by persuading yourself of that goodness, of this paternity of God. There is not enough chocolate in all the candy stores of this city, there are not enough cigarettes in all the tobacco shops of this city, there are not enough pies and cakes in all the bakery shops of this city to convince you of this truth and make it penetrate. God wishes nothing from you, God is not somber and disagreeable, God is not jealous of your poor little pleasures, He desires only to sanctify them, and to make them even greater. God does not desire renouncement, or privation for its own sake, but only in order that He may reveal to you something better than that which you already know.

For God gives in order to teach us to give. If God gave to us in order to receive from us, He would not be giving us anything. God is not one who receives but one who gives. To those who have confidence in Him He reveals the joy of giving, for it is "better to give than to receive."

Hence, your Lenten sacrifices are not sterile privations, not painful and bitter renunciations, "dead losses," doing without beefsteak or cigarettes. This will be a Lent of sharing with others, and therefore of joy, of fraternity, of generosity. You will share your food with someone who has none, your clothing with those who have too little, and you will be astonished at the joy that it will bring you and you will be far happier than you are now.

No "mortifications" this lent. Most of us are only too "mort" as it is, too gloomy, too inert! Choose some "vivifications" this Lent. Pray a quarter of an hour every day, go to communion more often, meditate on some good religious book, read, or better, listen to the Gospel, go and make a good confession, one that will make of all your faults "happy faults." All our faults ought to become "happy faults," faults which but recall to us the goodness and the tenderness with which we were pardoned.

But how rare this is!

It costs God nothing to pardon sins. That is the least of His tasks. His most difficult one is to get you to desire, from time to time, your own pardon, to have some wish to be pardoned. That pardon, that need to be pardoned has to overflow mightily from His heart before it can reach your heart and arouse you, with tender insistence, with incessant solicitations, with loving invitations, to the thought, the desire, the courage to go and ask for pardon.

And that is not all. That pardon must so invade you, so agitate you, so carry you away, so unsettle you that you set about granting your own pardon to everyone, and you even pardon yourself, and God, too, for having sinned. Thus the sterile and proud regret for our faults is transformed into amazement at the merciful tenderness with which only God could pardon our sins.

It is only in this way that you will discover the true God, the One who will dispense us from sin, the One who will make us so happy that we will prefer Him to sin, and seek to avoid all that could distract us from Him.

For, if you are going to try to do without God, you will need your chocolate, your cigarettes, your dances, your movies, you even have need of your sins to fill up so empty a life. What would there be in your life if you did not have your sins? That insupportable emptiness must be filled, be it with sins or with other things of which you are not so proud, nor satisfied with in the end, but which are better than that terrible emptiness.

But God will make it possible for you to do without all these things. If God is living, if God loves you, if He calls you, if He receives you with affectionate rejoicing, then He can fill your life. He can nourish you, He can cause you to rejoice, to be filled with enthusiasm all day long. Consequently, we have no need to sin. We are much happier without it.

In God we have placed our heart and found our treasure and our joy!

THE FIRST SUNDAY IN LENT

The Temptations of Christ: Matthew 4:1–11

Christ relived, in the space of a single lifetime, all the history of the people of God. That history had no other purpose but to prepare the people to recognize and to understand Christ when He came. It was entirely prophetic.

Like Israel, Jesus fled into Egypt. And also like Israel, He

121

passed through the desert before beginning that Exodus which He would complete, deserted, on the Cross.

The desert is a strange place. One goes there to find God and one encounters the devil. The Holy Spirit pushes you there, and it is so that you may be tempted by Satan. There one fasts and there one dreams of feasting. God reveals Himself, and meanwhile the world becomes embellished with all the prestige of an absent thing.

The significance of the temptations of Christ becomes clear if one studies the Bible, especially Genesis and Exodus.

At His baptism, Christ became the new Adam, the Son of God who is going to preside over a new creation. Hence, He is tempted as was the first Adam.

To the first Adam, the devil proposed supernatural powers that would enable him to rival God, without any need of faith, love, and obedience. With Christ he tries the same tactics, and urges Him to make use of powers which he supposed Christ to possess, in order to enjoy the satisfaction of food, ostentation and ambition.

Miserable temptations, which Christ repulsed with a word, the Word of God.

Real temptation would come to Christ later, in the solitude and agony of Gethsemane.

There too, a single word would have sufficed for the Father to send Him twelve legions of angels to serve and to deliver Him from His enemies, but He renounced His own will entirely, placing His trust in complete obedience.

Adam had sought to become Power without love. Christ was lifted up on the cross to repair that fault and became Love without power.

It was in this way that He reëstablished Paradise. "He lived among the wild beasts," says St. Mark, "and the angels served Him."

THE SECOND SUNDAY IN LENT

The Transfiguration

"Lord, it is good for us to be here." (Matthew 17:1–9)

We have just read the Gospel of the Transfiguration. What do you think of it? What do you remember of it? What have you learned in regard to yourself? Will your day, your week, your life be in any way modified?

There is this strange thing in regard to the Gospel. One can read it a hundred times and yet never come out of his spiritual sleep. And often, the more one reads . . . the more one sleeps.

A stranger—a Hindu or a Buddhist, for instance—who might have heard it read, would have been interested and would be curious enough to ask for an explanation. But never a Christian.

It is always that way. What one thinks one knows best is just the thing about which he knows least. When parents think that they know their children and that there is no need whatever of keeping an eye on them, of listening to them, of encouraging their confidences, you can be sure that some day or other they are going to learn things that will astonish them. And if children think that they know their parents, they are treating them like old pieces of furniture which we use and never remark their value until some stranger comes along and admires them.

If a wife thinks that she knows her husband and, above all, if a husband is sure that he knows his wife, if they do not attend to one another more and more, if they no longer feel any need for consulting one another, of speaking together, one may well conclude that they no longer love one another and that, as a matter of fact, they no longer know one another. And it is then, unfortunately, that they begin to know someone else.

123

Such is the alarming effect of habit. That which breaks up a home, kills love, undermines faith and the Church itself is not the crises, the sins, or the revolts, but simply routine.

What significance has this Gospel of the Transfiguration for ourselves? For the Apostles were just like ourselves, creatures of habit. They were living daily with Christ and, in spite of that, or better, because of that, they did not know Him. They needed a vision, a Transfiguration, exactly as we need a shock, a light, a revelation, so that we may wake up to what we are about to do, here, this Sunday, at the Mass of the Transfiguration.

The Gospel is not a history of things past, it is a prophecy which tells what will happen always, even what is happening today. You yourselves are foretold and foreseen in the Gospel. It explains to you what you are. It reveals to you what you are doing, what you are doing without knowing it. Forgive them, for they know not what they do. But we ought to know.

The Gospel is always true; God is always the same. And men are also always the same. The Gospel is the life which God leads among men. It tells how God treats men and how men treat—or mistreat—God.

The Apostles were accustomed to our Lord. They saw Him every day. They ate and drank with Him, and they were up to their necks in work, and, besides, they heard numberless sermons. And the more they heard, the less they were impressed and the less attention did they pay to them.

The Fathers of the Church tell us that a supernatural light always shone from our Lord's face but that the distracted and darkened eyes of those about Him never noticed it. They say that the Father never ceased giving testimony to Him, that it could be seen by every movement, by every word, that Christ was His Beloved Son, but that the slow and heavy minds of men could not understand this. Moses and Elijah and all those prophets they knew by heart, or thought they knew by heart just as you think you know the Gospel by heart, gave testimony to Him, an-

124

nounced Him, described Him, prefigured Him by their lives more than by their words, but no one paid attention.

Finally, our Lord decided that it was impossible to continue like this. He took them apart and led them far from the crowds among whom they were persons of importance, of bustling activity. They were the ones who organized the miracles, distributed the recommendations, picked out the ones whose turn it should be to receive attention. Our Lord led them away from all this and up a high mountain, into solitude, up a mountain where there was nothing but rocks, a place of deeper silence than this church to which the Lord has led you this morning.

There they became calm, they learned to keep silence, they were relieved of their worries and their ambitions. They were alone with Him and they began to pay attention to Him, to look at Him, to see Him, and they began to notice Him as He really was.

And we also need a vision, a Transfiguration, in order that we may observe that we are so habituated to believe in Christ that we no longer believe in Him, so habituated to prayer that we no longer pray, so habituated to hearing Him spoken of, or what is worse, so habituated to speaking of Him ourselves, that we no longer know Him, and we can well ask ourselves if we ever knew Him, for the day is long past when He was alive to us.

The means of receiving this grace is indeed very simple and it is always the same as it was in the days of the Apostles. Prayer, silence, solitude; give a little time to the Lord, to Him alone. How long is it since you have spent an hour in prayer? How long is it since you have consecrated to the Lord an afternoon or an evening? This time which you grant so willingly to no matter whom, to no matter what meeting, to no matter what show—see how much time, if any, you have refused, or harshly disputed, with the Lord. You would not find it hard to spend three hours in meeting a celebrated person or in listening to a lecture by a person of importance. Not at all! But three hours in learning that your Redeemer is alive, three hours in learning that the Lord is near, three hours in making the acquaintance of Him who is ever in the midst of us and whom we know not—impossible!

But if you have done this most extraordinary thing, you know something of Him, and if you do it often—an unbelievable miracle—you will come to know, little by little, either in the calm of the great outdoors, or in the peace of a little chapel, much more, and your eyes will be opened. You will begin to see very clearly both God and yourself. You will know what you are concealing, the evil that you do knowingly or which you refuse to know. You will hear His voice, that voice which is always speaking to you and which you make such great effort to silence. His will shall become plain to you. His presence will become so real as to be almost oppressive. His face will become so beautiful and tender that no other has ever been so attractive. Then you too will say to Him, as so many others have done before you: "Lord, it is good for us to be here! Ah, if only I could stay here always like this! If only I could always remain the same! Let me set up my tent here and dwell here forever!"

Basically, that is what should take place now, that is what should take place at this Mass if we assist at it with mind, heart, and eyes wide open. Jesus becomes present here by our fraternity, by our assembling here in His name. The prophets, St. John the Baptist, Abel, Abraham, Melchisedech, and the Apostles bear witness to Him. His Father is there, and, instructed because we have listened to Him, in a few minutes we are going to dare to say: "Our Father." We are going to assist at a transubstantiation. We can communicate with Him heart to heart. How can we be otherwise than good here? How not wish to dwell here always? Ah, if that miracle could come to pass, that we should have no desire to go, that we should wish to stay even after the Mass is finished. That would be the decisive sign that we have understood what it is all about, that we have given it our attention, and that,

126

for once, we have gotten out of our routine and that we know what we are doing.

We do not leave safely until the moment comes when we long to remain.

For the Lord will say to us then, as He did to Peter, James, and John: "Do not speak of this vision until the Son of man be risen from the dead."

Which means: Do not rejoice because of this vision; do not be puffed up by this vision; do not let yourself indulge in the belief that all is in safety because you have had this vision. Go now and return to your home, to your housekeeping, to your children, to your work, to your shop, to your neighborhood. Go and live your vision, go and give testimony, accomplish your Passion in union with mine, your resurrection and that of those about you, and then you will know forever that your vision was good and authentic, and that your religion was living and true.

THE THIRD SUNDAY IN LENT (I)

The Demon

The Gospel of today, like that of the first Sunday of Lent, ought to astonish us, ought to shock us, ought to scandalize us, if any reading of Scripture were still capable of awakening in us any reaction at all.

In this Gospel, Jesus speaks of the demon as of a reality. And He really seems to believe in it. That being who is looked upon as something to cause adults to smile, or to scare the children into good behavior, Jesus considers to be a force in this world. He calls him the Prince of this world, the adversary with whom He Himself must contend.

We no longer believe in the demon. In our days he has

127

executed his most skillful maneuver, which is to move about in secret, and to cause doubts regarding his very existence. Even priests no longer preach on this subject. They know well that it is no longer popular. And who am I, then, to try to persuade you of his influence if the very Word of God does not convince you?

Nevertheless, it suffices but to open the Gospel to see that, from the beginning of His mission, Jesus is struggling with a power for evil that is incredibly active and widespread. Everywhere Jesus uncovers it, puts it to flight, dethrones it. And when Satan, after having been foiled by Christ, in order to retain his grip on his Kingdom, hurled against Him all those whom he had in his power, all men who were submissive to him, that unbelievable thing was revealed, that, in reality, everyone, priests and lay people, rich and poor, Jews and Romans, the high priests and the bad thief, were all his subjects. In very truth, Satan was the Prince of this world, and then, as now, no one suspected it.

Do you believe that the people who heard Jesus and did not believe in Him, who rejected, condemned, and crucified Him, were very much worse than ourselves? Not at all. They did it, just as we do it, with all sorts of good reasons, with a good conscience, letting themselves be led by popular opinion, just as we do when we do not believe in the devil. They took sides with the crowd, acted through fear or self-interest, let themselves be maneuvered by someone else. They did it as we do it, by not knowing what they did. They served the devil and they knew it not.

The Church believes in the devil. She baptizes infants (and you became Christians only because you swore to renounce his service). She multiplies her exorcisms. She blesses everything presented to her in order to consecrate it to God. This is not because she thinks that we are all possessed by the devil, but because she knows the network of sin in which we are all enmeshed as soon as we come into the world.

God loves and gives the power to love. God unites and draws

128

together. He has willed, from the very beginning, that husband and wife should form a single and indissoluble body. Jesus came to bring together, in one single body, the children of God who are scattered. But the devil divides and separates. Recall how Adam, after having received Eve with an exclamation of joy— "This is flesh of my flesh and bone of my bone"—after his sin submitted to the influence of the devil and, in cowardice, separated from her. Recall how he threw the blame upon her, as in every quarrel between husband and wife: "The woman you gave me, she is the one who gave me to eat." It is Satan who divides the spouses, who divides the parents from the children (Noah and his sons), brother from brother (Cain and Abel), and man from man (Babel). The world of the present day, tragically divided, incapable of love and agreement, is an evident manifestation of the influence of Satan.

The same applies to those who do not believe in Christ and also to those who do not believe in the Church. It seems to me that there is a very evident proof of the existence of the demon in the fact that the presence and the action of evil in the world far surpass the capacity and the wickedness of the men who accomplish it. There is something so studied, so well organized, so remarkably skillful in the activity of evil in the world that it proclaims its author.

In general, men sin through stupidity. "They know not what they do." Afterwards, they realize that they have no wish whatever for what they have brought about.

But the devil is remarkably intelligent. He is lucid, Lucifer!

Let us consider, for example, the barriers between the different classes of society, between those of a different language, different race, different color. Take a group of normal men, good, humane, reasonable. Let one of them differ from the others by the color of his skin, or the language that he speaks, or by the mere fact that he was born on the other side of some arbitrary border, and he becomes at once an enemy, an irreconcilable adversary.

Or here is something even stranger. In the college where I am stationed, the seniors are passionately interested, at a distance, in the great movements for universal fraternity, decolonization, aid to undeveloped countries. But, within the college, the boarders despise the day scholars, and the day scholars return it with interest, and the classical students disdain those taking the technical courses. They would kiss the feet of an African or a member of some primitive tribe, but if a student took up English in preference to Latin, he was definitely classified in their esteem.

Look at the moral situation in the world of business. In many professions it is literally impossible to be honest, where all is done by commissions and bribes, recommendations and the bartering of influence. Every one of those concerned in it deplore it individually, but the structure is such that no one can do anything about it.

Or take the field of education. How many boys from the working class get into the universities? Why is it that money sustains so many dullards in a way of life which does not suit them, in which they are unhappy and useless, and why does the lack of money deprive so many others of the development of which they are capable and society is deprived of men of ability who are so badly needed?

Let us look at the world situation—famine joined to overproduction. One third of the world is surfeited, and it is ours, the Christian world, while the other two-thirds suffers from hunger and gives signs of exhaustion and utter lack of resources.

And this is not due to malice, hatred, or oppression. It is the result of forces which elude the individual. These are kept from knowing, they feel powerless to act against it, they are caught in a system that eludes their power to control, they are the playthings of a diabolical power that makes use of them to carry out its plans.

How is it possible to spend millions to send rockets into space while so many peoples upon this earth lack the most indispensable things? There is rivalry regarding the colonization of the moon, the conquering and settling of Mars, and we have not yet begun to humanize our own planet.

The expense of armament would suffice, here and now, to double the income of all the undeveloped countries. The cost of a single super-bomber, either American or Russian, would make it possible to cure and to suppress the disease of leprosy throughout the entire world, while the cost of the last world war would have permitted the construction of comfortable homes for every family in our hemisphere.

What is worse, humanity is beginning to look with calmness upon the possibility of atomic war. Men calculate the chances of survival, they prepare various organizations "just in case," they dare to use this as an argument in international discussions. Do you not see in all this the influence of the first one who in all the history of the world preferred his own ruin, his own annihilation, to the act of faith and love that was asked of him? Do you not detect in this cold callousness with which humanity considers its own suicide, something of the foolishness, the blindness, the inhuman pride which recalls the first universal catastrophe, the first revolt, and the first rebel?

Confronted by these proofs of systematic perversion, evil, and superhuman pride, one begins to feel that evil is some One, rather than some Thing, someone who is extremely evil and extremely strong, and that we are but feeble creatures of flesh, compromised and involved in the revolt of one much stronger than ourselves.

Doubtless there are those who believe too much in the devil and they run the risk of letting themselves be fascinated by him and distracted from God and from themselves by an obsession regarding his influence. It is infinitely more important to believe in God than in the demon, and to know that God is near us and tries us for the sake of good far more than the devil does for the sake of evil. But to ignore or to deny the existence of the devil is

131

a dangerous thing. It is the best way to be of service to him and to become his plaything.

Do you believe in the devil? Have you ever observed him at work in you and round about you? Have you ever felt the terrible might of evil urging you on and, at times, getting beyond your control? Have you ever been astonished at what you can become capable of? Your words, your thoughts, your desires, your imagination, your deeds?

Don't think that the devil will ever show himself to you. That would be useless. All that he needs is a fit of anger, a little spite, or some desire for revenge. He needs but a little money or a little flesh to have us at his mercy.

One does not have to know a man very long before one finds the hole in his armor, the worm in the fruit, the vice or the disgrace that he is hiding, the blood—his own or that of someone else—with which he pays for his success or uses to sign his contract.

I recall those families that we used to know when we were children. From a distance, or at first sight, they seemed to us so charming, so united, so irreproachable, so much better, so much happier than our own. And then, every time, and often at the very moment when we were expressing our admiration: "What a happy family you are! What a stylish father! What a good mother!" Then we would learn the truth, the hidden divisions, the secret shame, the crushing misfortune, and we would go home saying to ourselves: "How dreadful! The poor people! We are much better off than they are. We are the ones who are lucky!"

Since I became a priest, I have become accustomed to these confidences. Whenever a person comes to me with a confidential manner, I find myself expecting such revelations. Oh, I do not foresee them, I do not imagine them, I do not even suggest them—that would be odious. They are spontaneously offered and they are always unpredictable. The heart of each man encloses secrets that are impossible for him to bear alone.

132

Indeed, we all go around wearing masks. We all try to appear good, honest, respectable. But, interiorly, we are all full of incertitudes, ruins, covetous desires. The youngest are still doubtful, but the others know, or soon learn, beginning with the oldest.

Jesus, who knew what is in man, never trusted Himself to men. He has told us how He judges us: "You who are evil"—and that is a statement of the truth that is refreshing in the midst of the hypocrisy that surrounds us. We are never closer to pardon and salvation than when we own that we are sinners.

And it is Jesus who has said those dreadful words: "All those who have come before me are thieves and robbers, coming to pillage, to slaughter, and to destroy!" Thieves? Robbers? Us? But when Jesus tore the mask from the least worthy of His auditors, when He said to them before everyone, before the adulterous woman, "Let him who is without sin among you cast the first stone," the crowds saw with astonishment how deceitful are appearances, and what, in reality, man is.

The life of a man, seen from the interior, is not usually beautiful. All the evil that we have done knowingly, all the evil that we have done unknowingly, and all the precautions that we have taken to hide it, even from ourselves. All the base motives for which we have done good, —it is always our vices which furnish the greatest motivation to our virtues, and no one does good so joyously as one who has a bad reason for doing it. And all the good and beautiful causes for which we have done evil, nourishing our monsters with both hands in the dark, with our faces lifted to the stars.

And, above all, there is our own frightful interior misery, our blindness towards God and towards others, our indifference to the ills from which they suffer, or, perhaps, the insane joy which we sometimes experience upon learning of their misfortunes and their failures, not forgetting our irresistible urge to assert ourselves and impose our own will which is the stimulant of all our words and actions. Our coldness and our ingratitude in regard to the beauty of the world and the goodness of life. Our terrible poverty of faith, hope, and love. Our unimaginable hostility to God, the severity with which we criticize everything that He does, our revulsion to all that He sends us, our apprehension of all that He prepares, our discouragement in all that happens to us. There is our resolution to sin, our basic determination to prefer ourselves, to suffice for ourselves, our preference for unhappiness by ourselves rather than for happiness with Him and thanks to Him.

Is not this what you are? Are you not frightened by your capacity to be like this? So much worse than you ever realized, so much worse than you have any wish to be? Do you not see that you are in bondage to a being who is strong, and who accomplishes his work and his will in you, and that only One who is much stronger can deliver you?

We were delivered at the time of our baptism, but, since then, as the Evangelist says, the evil spirit has returned, and brought with him seven others, more evil than himself, and they lodge there at their ease.

In very truth, man does not live out his life alone. He is incapable of absolute independence. Either he gives himself to God or is enslaved to the devil. In good, as well as in evil, it is not we who live but it is either Christ or Satan who lives and reigns in us.

Ah, it is only when one sees oneself caught in these frightful complications of evil that one begins to understand, and to long for redemption, and one calls upon the Redeemer. It is when we become convinced that we could never escape by our own efforts, that we could never make any change, that we could never deliver ourselves, that we must become other than we now are, that we must live a different life, that some One else must give His life for us, it is only then that we begin to comprehend something of the joy of being redeemed.

Without this, we understand nothing of the Passion of Christ, of His sufferings and death. Nor do we understand that the slightest faults that we bring weekly to confession deserve this great chastisement and require this reparation. Nor do we comprehend that our lives as saved, redeemed, baptized are worth the terrible price that they have cost.

We make a pretense of being sorry over our state of sinfulness, caused by whatever it was that Adam did in the darkness of prehistoric days, and then we make a pretense of rejoicing over our redemption by the mysterious intervention of Christ who was substituted for ourselves. Our religion is past, our religion is actually lost, between these two hypocrisies.

From the moment when we have the testimony of the Holy Spirit within our own conscience, or better, and, alas, more frequently, when the pitiless evidence of events reveals to us our own blindness, our own feebleness, our own complete instability before God and before others, from the moment when we despair of ourselves, of our false security, and of our superficial virtues, when we know that, regardless of outward appearances, we are surrounded by dangers and weaknesses that may at any moment cause us to become like one of those for whom we feel horror and pity, —it is then that we can open our hearts to the joy of being loved, of being pardoned, redeemed, protected, and saved.

Then it is that we begin to comprehend and to desire a true paschal communion, to have a longing to throw ourselves into the arms of our Lord and to remain there, united to Him, protected by Him, and one with Him.

After this we shall no longer be shocked or scandalized by the Passion, we shall go over the Way of the Cross, we shall kiss the wounds of the Saviour, we shall take hold of Him, we shall be encouraged by all the proofs of His love for us, and we shall know beyond all doubt that nothing less than all that suffering, all that blood, was needed so that we might at last become free, living and loving God.

THE THIRD SUNDAY IN LENT (II)

The Demon

Do you not recognize yourself in today's Gospel? A person who has received a light, a revelation regarding himself or his manner of life?

Do you not recognize yourself in that man who was liberated from the demon some ten or twenty years ago by baptism, or by a conversion, or a retreat—a group of Christians who were fervent but who have now fallen back into a more cruel slavery than before?

Perhaps he has tasted how sweet the Lord is, perhaps he has instructed, converted, enlightened others, and there was sincere and happy communication between God and himself, and yet, it may happen that—after some years—he will find it as difficult to believe in Christ as if he had never known Him.

"And the second state of that man is worse than the first."

Here is another experience of the existence of the demon which is also described in the Gospel. "There is a kind of demon who is not cast out except by prayer."

That means that there may be in us a demon who is absolutely opposed to our giving ourselves to prayer, and who has succeeded in preventing us from making any true prayer for months and even years. I am not speaking of those short moments of absent-mindedness which are our "Our Fathers" and "Hail Marys." I am speaking of true prayer which means attention, which is a true meeting with God.

Do you pray ten minutes a day? Close your eyes. Answer interiorly. Fine! Now you know the answer given by all your neighbors. It is the same as yours. Yes, we are Christians. We all believe in God. We practice our religion . . . but we never speak to God. Do you still doubt the existence of the devil?

136

There is something else. Try to pray. Yes, decide to pray. Make up your mind to pray, during this Lent, for ten minutes every day. Do you notice how your demon is agitated, frightened, and beginning to protest?

Not only will you not pray, but you do not want to pray. You are quite decided that you will not pray. It is impossible for you to pray.

This is what the Evangelist tells us of a certain man who was bound, thrown to earth, even paralyzed by his demons. We are all busy people. We all have much to do, too much to do.

Notice! This means that we are entirely given up to our own caprice, to our foolishness, to our demon. We always have some choice between the things to be done, and so we will always have reasons, excuses, pretexts for not doing what we do not want to do. We will always have reasons, and good reasons (even good works!) for not taking time to give to prayer.

And God has, in your esteem, the place that He has in your time. If you have no place for Him in your time, it means that He has no place in your esteem.

You find time for whatever you consider important; your clothes, your meals, your newspaper, the radio, television, the cinema, those things are sacred. There is your coiffeur, your friends, even your parents. If God has no time in your day that is because He is, for you, without importance.

Your employment of time is determined by your judgment of value. If you have no time for God that is because He has no value.

Without time for prayer every day you are practically an atheist. Oh, yes, an atheist with deep sighs, with great sadness, with much melancholy. "Ah! if I could only pray! If I only had the time to pray! When can I pray?" But the fact is that you do not pray.

It is the same thing as when a husband is unfaithful to his wife. He thinks of his wife with remorse and great tenderness.

137

He knows that she has reason to complain of him, that she has an infinity of virtues and merits, that he is the last of the last. So he brings her a gift. But she is not deceived.

If you never pray, and yet long for God with regret and sadness, this is because you have been unfaithful to Him.

A good number of Christians are like savages when it comes to prayer. They have had no experience, no training, no apprenticeship. They do not know what prayer is, they have no words, no thoughts, no ideas that will furnish matter for prayer. They remain gaping and empty before God. The mouth speaks out of the abundance of the heart, but they are silent because the heart is empty. Then they soon give way to discouragement. They are empty and mute towards God because they have never spoken to Him.

Another experience. When Christ spoke of the Eucharist for the first time the people said: "This word is hard and who can understand it?" And from that moment many left Him.

You should communicate at every Mass. That participation in the Mass which is normal, useful, and counselled is accomplished by receiving communion. The Church teaches it and Christ tells you to do so: "Unless you eat the flesh of the Son of man and drink His blood, you have no life in you. . . . As the living Father sent me, and I live because of the Father, so he who eats me will live because of me."

You hear these words, you know this teaching, and yet you do not communicate.

The majority of Christians of the present day, in our churches on Sunday, abstain from communion. They have their own religion which they prefer to that of the Church. They have their own habits which prevent them from believing in the Word of Christ. They oppose Christ and the Church with an obstinacy that is prodigious. They exercise in His regard a sort of prophylaxis. "Prudence!" they exclaim, "not too much intimacy, beware of contagion, let us keep our distance." Their religion is decidedly aseptic. It will never kill them.

138

Oh, yes, they believe in the Eucharist, but they never receive it.

The unfortunate thing is that the demons also believe in the Eucharist, they know the Real Presence, too, and neither do they communicate.

Faith without works is dead, St. James tells us. And so with you. It will be of no use to you to believe in the Eucharist if you do not put that faith into practice. There are many instances of this kind in the Gospel—the mute demon who kills love and friendship by keeping silence, by placing between you and the others a deep pit of silence, of lies, of misunderstandings. When a person still tries to explain himself, or as long as the argument continues, there is hope. There is still an exchange. But when a person wraps himself in silence, it means that there is no longer any hope of an understanding between them.

There are the seven demons of impurity that Christ chased out of Mary Magdalene, the desperate demon, the legion of demons who possess this young man, or that young girl, frantic for pleasure, excitement, liberty. "Often they had bound him with fetters and chains"—(they put him, or her, in boarding school)—"but the chains he wrenched apart, and the fetters he broke in pieces, and no one had the strength to subdue him. Night and day among the tombs—(the coffee houses)—or on the mountains—(it does not matter where as long as it is original)—he was always crying out—(this is the best way to forget one's troubles)—and bruising himself with stones"—(bad books, sentimental jazz, dangerous films, vacancy of mind).

And above all, the demon of lying and of slavery. "If you are my disciple," Christ says, "you shall know the truth and the truth shall make you free. But the man who commits sin is the slave of sin and he has for his father the devil. The devil is a liar and the father of lies."

Who can describe the dreadful entanglement of sins, the dizzy slope down which the sinner feels himself slipping, the frightful complications of evil, the series of humiliations and degradations which follow in its train. The sinner is bound to his sin and by his sin. He is caught, tied, ensnared, bound. He sets out to lead a double existence, he makes for himself a double conscience, a double face, a double accountability. He feels like a spectator at what he has become capable of doing, he feels himself pulled about, maneuvered, managed like a puppet in hands that are tyrannical and pitiless.

To the extent that you have no experience of the power of sin, of its strength, of its domination over the world, to the extent that you ignore sin, just so much do you ignore the redemption. If you do not believe in the devil, the chances are that you do not really believe in God.

Unless we are aware of our weakness, of our capacity for blindness and forgetfulness, unless we have felt ourselves dominated by that "strong one" who fetters us and whom we cannot drive away by ourselves, we cannot begin to conceive or to desire redemption. We shall not cry out for a Redeemer, nor call for One stronger than we to deliver us and let us know once again the joy of liberty, of peace and innocence, the happiness of living in the truth. Then we shall again become capable of prayer, capable of relishing the Gospel, capable of desiring to receive communion. We shall enter into the beatitude with which our Gospel of today terminates: "Blessed are those who are capable of listening to the Word of God and putting it into practice!"

THE FOURTH SUNDAY IN LENT

"Make the men sit down." (John 6:1–15)

Today, just as it was two thousand years ago, at the approach of the Pasch, Christ sees immense crowds coming to Him. They are hungry and He has compassion on them. He calls them and He desires their hearts.

140

And today, as then, the provisions, the resources of the Church seem ridiculous. In those days, the Apostles had five loaves and two fishes for five thousand people. What are our hosts, what are our paschal communions, how can they appease the hunger of the world? The hunger of the body? The hunger of the mind? The hunger of the heart? The absolute famine of faith, hope, fraternity, and love? How can anyone think of feeding the whole world with that?

But, have you noticed the condition that Jesus lays down before He performs that miracle? Before everything else, He asks of them an act of confidence, a gesture of abandonment, of giving themselves into His hands. He tells them: "Everybody sit down!"

Be sure that you understand—He has asked of them, naturally, that which cost them the most.

As long as they were standing, they were independent, there was still a chance for them to go and find food by themselves. They might meet a friend, or a peddler with provisions, they might find an inn, or they could go away.

But the moment they were seated, they renounced their self-sufficiency, their freedom to take care of themselves. They placed themselves in His hands. They were bound, committed, handed over, like hosts on the paten at the Offertory.

When they were told to sit down, I imagine that many hesitated. He was asking of them that which they least desired to give. They were anxious, disturbed, tormented by hunger, and He wanted them to be calm, to sit down, to abandon themselves to Him, to trust Him.

By obeying, they put their lives into His hands. Bread is what sustains life. He who gives away his bread, gives away his life. The moment was of such solemnity that each one felt in some confused way that this was just what His proposal meant.

They hesitated a long time. His demand tore at their hearts, and uneasiness, fear, and pride struggled with each other. Should they give Him their confidence? Were they to believe that He was capable of feeding them?

What would we have done were we in their place? How should we feel, if, some day, we found ourselves for the first time in a situation where we had to say in all sincerity: "Give us this day our daily bread"? Would not we be tempted to try to provide for ourselves rather than have recourse to God? Is it not a terrifying thing to have to face the fact that we can have recourse to no one but God?

At last, some few sat down. It was an intense act of faith. With closed eyes and a supreme effort, they had given away their lives. Then others followed them, with beating hearts, conquered, overcome. One might see large groups, moving about, bumping into one another, then finally deciding and abandoning themselves. And then came an extraordinary moment, a miraculous moment, when the five thousand were at last seated and five thousand men had, all together, made an act of faith and of love.

And when the bread began to be passed around and each one had received as much as he wanted and there was still some left over, I do not think that anyone was surprised. The real miracle took place at the beginning. The true miracle was over. The greatest miracle was what Jesus had obtained from them—the miracle of their faith and love.

And this applies to us, too. Before our Easter communion, in order that it may be a multiplication of bread equal to the needs of the world, in order that it may work a miracle, in order that it may be a miracle, the same condition is imposed upon us, the same requirement is made of us—do we believe in Him? Do we believe that Christ is capable of satisfying our hunger? Do we believe that He has sufficient life Himself to give life to us? Before every miracle He asks us: "Do you believe in me? Do you believe that I can change your life, fill your life, renew your life? Do you believe that I am powerful enough, loving enough, so that you, with my help, may live a life that is very different from the one that you have lived up to now, the life that you have lived without me?" /

And if we are sincere, I believe that these questions will leave us very hesitant and undecided. We want to believe, we would like to believe, but we do not live by faith. Faith is inherent in the soul and the soul is continually fighting against it, rejecting it, refusing to trust to it.

Faith is natural to the mind. No one ever asks a question without some beginning of faith. To ask a question is an act of faith because one believes that there is an answer.

If the skeptics and the agnostics really believed, as they say they do, that the world is an absurdity, why do they ask so many questions? What good is there in formulating all those agonizing questions if no reply is possible? The world could very well be a frightful chaos, an absurd collection of electrons in movement, without order, in which we distinguish nothing. It is certainly the most probable hypothesis if God did not exist. Why should the world be intelligible if there is no intelligible Creator? Why should it be even questionable?

Whoever asks a question performs the act of a child—an act of faith. Is it not children who ask the most questions? They are so sure, the poor little things, that we are able to explain everything to them. They abound in faith.

When scholars seek the explanation of phenomena which seem to contradict their hypotheses, when they consecrate their lives to discovering new laws of science, they make an act of faith in the intelligibility of the world. There is more real faith in the laboratories than in our many churches on Sundays. For many scholars, these laws of science are placed in the universe very much in the same way that fathers and mothers hide Easter eggs for their children. Just enough so that they may have the pleasure of hunting for them, and not too many, so that they may have the joy of finding them.

And that faith which is so naïve, so ingenuous, so unconscious

143

of itself, is amply rewarded. See what magnificent inventions have crowned those patient and confident researches. Indeed, in the domain of the material, in physics, in chemistry, in electricity, in mathematics, our times are times of faith, certain that every thing can be explained, that it all makes sense, and that it can be discovered.

But, in the domain of the moral, the religious, where there is question of things absolutely essential, like "What is the meaning of our life? Why are you living? Who has need of you? Who wants you? To whom would it matter if you disappeared? Where, then, are you going and is it worth the trouble to go at all?" At questions like these, everyone gives up. In this domain no explanation is possible. But if an accident occurs, some failure, some sorrow or some great catastrophe, they bow their heads, let their arms fall to their sides, and say: "It is fate. It is destiny. If there were a God, these things would never happen."

In this vital domain, the possibility of intelligence is renounced. Here, man ceases to be a scholar, he ceases to be scientific, he ceases to ask questions in the belief that there is an answer. He ceases to hunt patiently, in the darkness, for an answer that will be a guiding light.

And all the while, faith is the most natural, the most indispensable movement of the heart. We have faith in everything except in God.

You confide your health to a dentist, to a doctor, or to a surgeon. You do not ask to see their diploma, nor ask how they made out in their final examinations. You do not ask them to treat several patients while you look on so that you may judge their mode of operating. Not at all. You trust yourself to them. You offer yourself. You leave yourself entirely in their hands. They treat you badly, they charge you dearly, they fix you up more or less, and you thank them effusively. "So-and-So has saved my life!" "How do you know?" "Because he told me so." "You are a brave man! I wish I had such faith."

144

Where is your money? (If you have any.) With a broker? A banker? Is it still there? Did you go to see about it this morning? Did you call him on the telephone? Sometimes these deposits evaporate.

No, you do nothing of the kind. You have confidence. Life would not be possible without it. We must trust other people.

And if your money were with God? Everyone feels uneasy. No one cares to think of that. God as a banker? He would refund 100 per cent. That is a little too good to be true. That is no investment for a father of a family. That is a risk which we will not take.

And what about your life? You confide it to the first chauffeur, to the first bus driver who comes along. You stop a taxi. You climb into a bus. You do not ask to see the license of the driver, his police record, his insurance policy. You do not ask him to exhibit his skill in driving so that you may judge of his ability. Not at all. You climb aboard, you take a seat, you trust yourself, you abandon yourself. And yet, how many auto accidents there are!

But we never confide ourselves to God. With Him, we are always trying to take the steering wheel out of His hands. We feel that we can direct our ways much better than He can. But as soon as our life takes a sudden or unexpected turn, we send up cries of distress, like ill-treated children.

Imagine a family going for a trip by car and all the children mistrusting their father, warning him of the dangers, crying out at every crossroad: "Look out! There is someone on a bicycle! Do you see that truck? Don't turn to the left!" Such a trip would be a nightmare. Yet, that is what we are forever doing with God. Faith is inherent to the soul and the soul never ceases to combat it.

We always have our reasons, and such good reasons, for not believing. Faith will always be an act above our natural strength. It is a grace to which we must correspond, an obscurity that we

145

must bear with. Faith is the ability to bear with one's doubts. It is having light enough to bear a margin of obscurity.

Many people imagine that they have lost their faith as soon as they meet with some difficulty. "I have an objection, a doubt, I have lost my faith." Not at all! It is precisely when you meet with a difficulty in believing that the moment has arrived to make a real act of faith. As long as you do not experience any doubt, just so long are your natural ideas in accordance with those of God. In this case it becomes impossible to tell whether you believe in God or in yourself. If you have excellent proofs of the existence of God, who knows whether you believe in God or in your proofs?

But, from the moment that you begin to question, from the moment that religious ideas contradict your own ideas, from the moment that you no longer agree spontaneously with God, from that very moment, perhaps for the first time in your life, you have the occasion to make a real act of faith, to prefer the ideas of God to your own, to place yourself in His hands. Faith is a doubt overcome and not a natural, or traditional, certitude.

We shall never have any evidence of our faith, but we know that we have, in reality, all the interior certitude that is necessary, and what we lack is not faith but the courage to act in conformity with our faith, to decide to live it.

The religious life, the life of faith, is its own proof.

A life of prayer and of generosity makes the presence and the intervention of the object of our faith more and more evident to us.

It is not the arguments of apologetics that strengthen and justify a devout and religious life, but contact with the nourishing Presence of God.

And, on the contrary, the abandonment of prayer, the relaxing of our religious practices, a life of sensual egoism enfeebles, and finally kills, that spiritual life in which it is so hard to believe when one no longer possesses it.

146

The Fathers of the Church tell us that the spiritual life and the carnal life are two opposites. The carnal life consists of eating, drinking, and sleeping, and when one lacks these things, one desires them vehemently. When they are obtained, one is soon satisfied. But, on the other hand, when one does not live a spiritual life, one has no desire for it. It seems like something completely unreal and one considers it in much the same way as a deaf person considers those who listen to a concert. What do they find in it? Why do they look so ecstatic? They must have lost all sense of reality.

But, when one comes to know the spiritual life, one tastes it, desires it, and wants to know more of it. It is a realization of those words of Christ: "To him that has, shall be given and he shall abound. But he that has not, that which he has shall be taken from him."

The fervent constantly recognize, in a thousand ways, the presence and the intervention of their God—in the joy which follows a good deed, in the strength given them by prayer, in a good inspiration, in a combination of circumstances which could crush them, and which, on the contrary, mercifully ministers to their good.

Everything, the complete explanation of which can be nothing but supernatural, all these things are but signs and proofs to him who knows the character of God, and he easily recognizes them as such.

The lukewarm beg for miracles in the only order in which they are interested, that is, the material. These God does not readily grant, for He fears to interest them still more in things material. After He had multiplied the loaves, Jesus had to flee because they wanted to make Him king. He told them: "You follow me, not because you have seen a miracle (and in the miracle have recognized the continual presence and goodness of God), but because you have eaten of the bread and are satisfied!" It was not a matter of faith but of food.

A miracle is but a translation, in the physical order, of the innumerable interventions of God in the moral order. The gross and uncultivated have need, in order to read the writing of God, that the divine text be translated into their mother tongue, the only language that they know—the material. But attentive and religious souls understand, and are able to follow, the text in the original language.

Truly, the more we pray, the more often we communicate, the more deeply we love God and our fellow-men, the more we shall be convinced of the reality and of the abiding presence of the object of our faith.

Yes, for us also, the Word has been made flesh. He lives amongst us. He speaks to us, He nourishes us. And we can also see His glory—in the miracles, in the marvels, in the great things that He can do in the faith, in the poverty, and in the complete confidence of His servants and His handmaidens.

PASSION SUNDAY

"He who is of God, hears the Word of God."   (John 8:46–59)

There is nothing more tragic than the dialogue between Jesus and the Jews as given by St. John. This tenacious incomprehension, implacable resistance, total insensibility to God who is speaking to them, who is calling them, astonishes us. It ought rather to frighten us because that is our own attitude. It is both revelation and prophecy of our own deafness and blindness towards God.

"He who is of God hears the Word of God!" And we who believe ourselves to be "of God," do we hear Him speak? Does His Word mean anything to us?

God speaks to us. He comes to speak to us in the Gospel of

today. Who feels himself called upon, drawn, nourished by this Gospel? What part of it have you retained in your memory? What spiritual provision are you going to take away with you to sustain you during the coming week?

Who can recall a word that struck him and which he will mediate upon?

Alas! We must admit that, in general, God has hardly finished speaking when we have completely forgotten what He said. God is always speaking. He is revelation because He is Love, and love speaks, love reveals itself, and God has never ceased to be revelation because He has never ceased to be love. He enlightens every man who comes into this world. For us, too, the light shines in our darkness. The darkness is to blame for not accepting it. Have you ever realized that you could never have more light than you have today? God has made a supreme effort. He has given His Son and sent His Spirit. There is only one possible way in which we can make progress towards the light, and that is to raise the shade which we have pulled down in order to protect ourselves against it.

God speaks and we do not listen to Him. God speaks and we have the strange power of reducing Him to silence. It is a joy for God to reveal Himself to us, but His closest presence remains always a hidden presence to us; His cry, His loudest call, seems to us like silence, for it has not yet happened that anyone has heard without listening.

The reason why we do not hear is not hard to find. It is denounced everywhere in the Gospel. It is because we are rich.

Rich, not because we have money, that is certain, but rich in the sense that we think that we have no need of God, we are satisfied with ourselves, with what we know, with our religious practices, so that we want nothing more, we need nothing from God.

Who has come here this Sunday, hungry, hungry for a word, a light, nourishment? Who is expecting his daily bread? Who is there whose very existence depends upon the need that he feels for God?

My brethren, there is no greater sin than that of expecting nothing from God. To love a being is to expect much from him, to hope in him always. If a husband no longer expects anything from his wife, if a wife no longer hopes for anything from her husband, if parents no longer believe in the infinite possibilities for good that there is in their children, and if children no longer find love in the hearts of their parents, then they no longer love one another, they no longer believe in one another.

If you no longer expect anything from God, it is because you have no faith in Him and do not love Him.

The Pharisees, to whom Christ was so outspoken, were like this. They felt very sure of themselves, they were completely satisfied with their knowledge and their observance of religion. They felt that they had nothing more to learn, and they listened to the teaching of Christ only for the purpose of catching Him in some error. They knew better than He the things that He had come to reveal to them. They were rich. They gloried in their heritage and in their religious traditions. ("We are Christians and have been for generations.") ("That is what we have always done in our home.") They had Abraham for their father—taking refuge in their family tree.

But Abraham, so Christ told them, was a poor man. He heard the Word of God, he believed it, he left his country, the land of his fathers and their religion. He allowed himself to be uprooted, to be started on a journey by the Word of God (while his people, and ourselves like them, make use of it to avoid the least change!), and Abraham rejoiced.

Who among ourselves is poor like Abraham? Who among us rejoices, even for a moment, upon hearing the word of God? And who among us, if he feels that it is meant for him, will allow himself to be affected by it, will allow himself to be questioned by it, or will make any change?

150

Happy are the poor! The Kingdom of heaven belongs to them. And only to them. There will be no entry for us into the Kingdom of God unless we are poor. Only a poor person knows God and hears God. "Father, I give you thanks that you have hidden these things from the wise and prudent (these are the rich) and revealed them to little ones"—to the poor.

Poverty is not the summing up of the spiritual life, it is not a final virtue. It is really the initial virtue, —if you are not poor, you have no faith.

For faith has always been a call to detachment. Go, leave your country, go forth from the land of your fathers. And Abraham, the father of believers, set out, not knowing where he was going.

One sign of the fundamental importance of poverty is the fact that as soon as a lukewarm Christian is converted to a more fervent life, as soon as a Christian home makes an effort to rise above its religious mediocrity, the problem of poverty must be solved. They are uneasy and seek ways in which they can become poor.

Woe to the rich! For the rich man lives in the midst of deceit. The rich man believes that he can do without God. He places his confidence in his possessions. He does away with Providence. He thinks that his wealth dispenses with God. He hopes to steer his own life, using his own resources, and has no need of having any recourse to God. Someone has said that many Christians look upon God as the aviator looks upon his parachute—there, in case of need, but one hopes that he will not be forced to use it. Think what it would mean if we were ever placed in a situation where we would be obliged to say with absolute truth: "Give us this day our daily bread." If we could no longer count upon any other source, what anxiety would be ours and what a calamity it would seem to us!

The rich man regards himself as God. He is a fool, Christ says. He is senseless and stupid even though he be clever and calculating in money matters. Recall that rich man in the Gospel whose

151

farm had produced unusually good crops. (He had made a fortune on the stock market.) He said to himself: "What shall I do? I do not know where to store my harvest. (He was already embarrassed by his investments.) Then he says: "I will tear down my barns, I will build bigger ones, and in them I will store my wheat and my goods. And I shall say to my soul: Rejoice, for you have stored up enough to last for years. Rest! Eat! Drink! Celebrate!" But God said to him: "You fool! This night do they require your soul. And whose will be all those things which you have prepared? What does it profit a man to gain the whole world if he loses his soul?"

Woe to the rich! He cuts himself off from God, and he also cuts himself off from his fellow-creatures. One does not become, nor does one remain, rich without having to refuse to share with others. Our possessions keep God at a distance, and, if we want to keep them, we must keep our fellow-men at a distance. Otherwise we shall not have them long.

Take Lazarus and the rich man. What was the sin of the rich man? The Gospel does not say that he stole the money that he had, nor that he had robbed Lazarus. Neither had he exploited him by employing him to do hard work about the house for "starvation wages," "since he employed him only out of charity"! No, it simply says that he did not see Lazarus. Nor will he see him for all eternity. The space between them can never be crossed. The rich man will never obtain throughout all eternity that which the poor man did not obtain from him. That distance which he maintained between himself and the poor man, he maintained, in reality, between himself and God. For the Kingdom of God is for the poor, and he who will have nothing to do with the poor has nothing to do with God.

The complaint that Christ made against money is that it creates division between men. The man who is attached to money damages the work of God, that is, the community of humanity. He violates the two great commandments: he fails to recognize

152

God as his Father, and man as his brother. And that is why "no man can serve two masters. It is impossible to serve God and Mammon."

Woe to the rich! He lives in slavery. His possessions enfetter him. He is bound by what he holds. He is possessed by what he possesses. It is easier for a camel to pass through the eye of a needle than for a rich man to enter the Kingdom of God. This eye of a needle was a gate in Jerusalem through which a camel could pass only on condition of being relieved of his burden. As for a camel, it asks for nothing better than to be unburdened, but a rich man! Just try to relieve him of his goods, lighten his worries, deprive him of his interests? Impossible!

Happily, that which is impossible to men is possible to God. God can make even a rich man poor in spirit. Happy the man who has a soul that is poor!

Please, do not think that this happiness is for later on. It is now that he will be happy. The Kingdom of God *is* his, Christ says. He does not say "will be." Very often, this present beatitude is reversed, as if Christ said: "You will be as happy in the future as you are miserable in the present." In that case, then let us be as miserable as possible! And, logically, let us leave the miserable in their misery so as not to deprive them of their coming beatitude!

Neither has Christ said: "Impoverish one another." (Which we do, without any counsel on His part.) He has said: "Love, help, and then enrich one another!" Which, alas, we scarcely ever do.

Happy the poor! From now on he lives in the truth. The poor man knows that he is completely dependent upon God. He knows that all human things are limited. He knows that, alone, he is incapable of fulfilling his destiny, that he can never be equal to his task, that even to love those to whom he is most closely bound, to be faithful to them and to work for them, he has need of nothing less than all the love which God possesses, that it may fertilize the sterility and fill the void in his own heart.

Also he knows that he has a Father in heaven, upon whom he depends, and that this Father watches over him and requires that he have confidence in Him.

That confidence does not do away with work nor a reasonable amount of foresight. It excludes only that worry which gnaws, paralyzes, or enfevers. The poor man knows that the first gift of God, the first manifestation of Providence, is the gift which was made to him in his capacity for work. And even should he lose this, he still has a Father.

The poor man is fraternal. He is open-handed with others. He shares. He knows that our possessions are those of a family and for the use of all of its members. The poor man is not one who has nothing, but one who puts what he has to good use. A poor household is not one where there is not so much as a penny, but one where everyone who comes feels at home. You are poor if you keep your house open to everyone, if you know how to "receive." To give is often the act of a rich person. One gives from above to below. But to receive belongs to the poor. You are poor if everyone knows that it is a pleasure for you to have him come to see you, if you are humble enough and open enough to realize that everyone has something to teach you and something to give.

The poor man is free. His goods are never left to be confiscated, he uses them. He places them at the service of mankind. He does not indulge in that sickly preoccupation of "setting aside" and of believing that only what is in "reserve" is secure. Things are meant to be used. To spend wisely is the act of a poor man. To deprive oneself in order to hoard is the act of one who is rich.

In this technical age, we have more need for the poor who know how to make intelligent use of our resources and our machines, than for the poor who make a renunciation of these. Each epoch must invent its own form of poverty. In the Middle Ages one despoiled oneself of one's goods all at once. One

154

became poor. But is that true charity and a real act of benevolence? At the present time, the truly poor man is he who, regardless of what he may own, uses it efficaciously for the betterment of his contemporaries.

The poor man knows a better joy than that of being rich. He knows that it is better to give than to receive. That is but the discovery of a value of a higher kind which gives us the spirit of poverty. Woe to him who has need of being rich in order to be happy!

I have seen ordinary workmen whose souls were those of poor men. They refused promotion or an increase in salary in order that they might remain militant Christians. They had found wealth of another kind. There were others who refused to work overtime in order to be free to occupy themselves with their own concerns, in order to have the time and the leisure to live like men.

And I have also seen, much less often, it is true, doctors, lawyers, store-keepers, and industrialists refuse clients or refuse to undertake additional business in order that they might have that time to give to their wives and children, or to prayer, or to manage some work of charity, or to visit the poor.

No one can serve God and money.

It requires nothing less than everything in order to allow yourself to do without God. You will be borne along in that foolish course so that you will be completely delivered over to work, to gaining money, to worry about profit, and this is what nearly all of our contemporaries have done. And they generally make this a virtuous alibi for not having time for prayer, time to give to the education of their children, time to be men. You will never have enough so that you can dispense with God, and you will cry out in revolt if any one pretends to relieve you of the slightest portion of that armor which is supposed to guarantee you against chance, as you designate Divine Providence.

There are those who see nothing in this world but material

155

goods, and they never find them sufficient to guarantee them the independence and security that they desire. But there are others who raise their eyes to the face of the Giver of these material things, and there they see such goodness and tenderness that they are always content. They have a father. With an assurance and a confidence which the rich never know, they say: "Our Father!"

THE SECOND SUNDAY IN PASSION TIME

The Passion

Lent is drawing to a close, Holy Week is beginning, and the Passion of Jesus recommences. Jesus goes once again to be crucified. Jesus is going to suffer again. Jesus suffers again among us. What role have you chosen to play?

The Gospel is not a legend. Nor is it merely a history of the past. It is a prophecy. It foretells what is happening and what will happen eternally in the world. It is a living and actual revelation which unveils for us the true significance of what is happening under our very eyes. The Gospel depicts for us the life of God among men. God is ever living among men. Jesus is with us all days, even to the consummation of the world. Jesus is our contemporary, and the Gospel tells us what is happening today between Him and ourselves, —how Jesus treats us and how we treat Him. You are described in the Gospel, you are foreseen therein, even named, and it is only necessary that you open the book and you will recognize yourself immediately.

The Passion begins. This year the same roles, the same actors, are mobilized as in the year 33 after Christ.

Let's see. First, there are the millions and millions of the indifferent, the easy-going, those who give consent by silence. There are those who wash their hands, those who never budge as

156

long as the blows fall upon someone else, those who have no
opinion on these disputed questions, those who let things go their
way, and without whom many things would never be done, for
the wickedness of the few finds security in the cowardice of the
many.

Before how many injustices and dramas have you shown this
criminal indifference?

Then there are the thousands of escapists, the people who,
when things get difficult, are like St. Peter and "know not the
man." Oh yes, they have listened to his sermons, one sees them
participating in processions, they are enthusiastic about miracles,
they will go far in order to witness a miracle, they have been to
Lourdes, to Rome, to Fatima. But now, when there is trouble,
when things go wrong, when there is bloodshed and the Cross,
now when there is no miracle, when it is up to us to be ourselves
miracles of fidelity, of faith, and of love, they will have nothing
more to do with Him, they no longer know this man, they act as
if they never knew Him.

Some thousands of executioners also. These are never wanting
and they are always the same. There is the brute with his whip,
his electricity, his bath, the educated man with his sarcasms, the
functionary with his rules and regulations, and the simpleton
with his curiosity.

And always the same sorrowful victim, infinitely patient and
loving, who turns upon us his eyes, gives us a look of tenderness,
of questioning, of expectancy, and of reproach. There are more
victims now than ever before. There are good people suffering,
innocent ones being persecuted, thousands of abandoned children, hundreds of thousands on government relief, untold thousands more of migrant workers. But why go so far? In your own
home, close to you, is there not someone who suffers, someone
who weeps, are there not people who are cold and hungry, who
are sick, who have lost a loved one by death, who are lonely, in
pain or enduring shame and humiliation? There they are, wait-

ing, looking for you. Who will be Veronica? Who will be Simon the Cyrenean? Come, the parts are being distributed and time is running out. There is something for each. Impossible to be overlooked. Who would like to be John? Who wants to be Peter? And does anyone want to be Judas?

What an extraordinary opportunity is ours! There is Jesus, living and suffering in our midst all over again. And we have been warned, we are aware of what is going on, we have been informed, we have been given the key to this terrible tragedy, the true names of the actors have been whispered to us and the true meaning of the drama. Come now, there is nothing left to do but to begin our parts, to get into the drama. What joy! We can choose our own roles, we can be for Jesus whatever we wish, we can be in the midst of that enormous crowd of enemies, or merely indifferent spectators, as His watchful servants, with attentive hearts, showing love in our faces, offering marks of compassion, and deep adoration. Come! And we do not come. Not because we lack faith, but because we lack courage.

"But," you will say, "the Passion is no longer possible! I cannot believe it! That once again God should be struck in the face, abandoned, wounded, despised, we would never do such a thing! Never would we allow that!"

Alas! When you no longer believe that Christ is in your neighbor, that you are not dealing with Him, then the Passion is repeated.

If your life were to come to an end today, on what would you be judged? And what is your attitude towards whom? What would be said to you? "Withdraw from me, you cursed, into everlasting fire, for I was hungry and you did not give me to eat; I was thirsty and you refused me a drink; I was naked and you did not clothe me; I was a stranger, a foundling, and you did not take me in; I was sick and you did not care for me; I was a prisoner, and you took no interest in me, you had no desire to help me."

And we shall say to Him: "But Lord, when have we ever seen you hungry or thirsty? When were you sick or in prison?" We shall know very well at that moment that Jesus has been among us and that we have always known in some obscure way what we were doing. We shall know that the Gospel was true and that our condemnation is due to our not knowing how to live the truth which it revealed. We have passed our life with the pleasant image of Jesus enthroned in heaven or soaring above the clouds from whence He shall come one day as a triumphant Judge. And here He is, beside us, waiting for us, rubbing elbows with us, humiliated, hidden in the bread, naked in the wine, despised in the most insignificant of men, so close to us that our glance passes over Him when we look for Him.

Hence, there is only one Passion, and I should believe that it is so and should act in accordance with this belief. I must believe that this is actually happening, that the Passion is taking place before my very eyes all over again. This means to accept the fact that the Passion must come into my life, too, and that I must live it. There will be tragedy in my life as in every life into which great love enters and overthrows the comfort and tranquillity of our easy-going habits. Such a love obliges us to make a response, to make a choice, to take a side, either for or against, to be with him or against him, to give our name, to declare our party.

We shall be like those people who are living peacefully in the rear and then, suddenly, are transported to the front, suddenly obliged to take part in something that is beyond their control. Then, for the first time, they know themselves, they see themselves truly. They learn what is in man, how simple it is to die. They learn the sincerity of actions and of words, solidarity in misfortune, fraternity, and love. And it is hard for them to believe that they once were people in the rear, people with some importance and a right to complain, calculating and quarrelsome, boastful and lazy, thoughtless and giving orders.

It is then that we shall come to know our real selves and to see

159

how far we have gone, wearing the mask of religious life and practicing the etiquette of piety. Until now we have not really believed in God, but rather in those who have spoken to us about God, those who have described Him for us and commentated upon Him. But when we live through our own passion and carry our own cross, loving while we suffer, then we shall really come in contact with God. We can then say to our instructors in religion what the Samaritans said to the woman: "Now we no longer believe because of what you told us. We have heard Him ourselves and we know that He is the Saviour of the world." And we also, in the partaking of His sufferings, in association with Him in the redemption, we recognize the truth and we know that Jesus will be in agony until the end of the world, that Jesus is always suffering, and that this suffering is saving the world. We know also that it has paid the price for us, as well, and that we are truly saved.

We shall begin to know a new life, new depths in our hearts will be opened and our souls will be alive with faith, piety, tenderness, and compassion. For the first time in our lives, perhaps, we shall find happiness in suffering, and be glad to aid and to accompany our Saviour. It is a joy to suffer together with those we love, it is a joy to feel oneself living in the truth, it is a joy to be a member of the immense fraternity of the humble and of those who suffer and to climb Calvary with them, bearing our own cross. That cross is no longer the shameful and intolerable burden that one makes every effort to forget, to hide, to reject. It is the sign that we are chosen, it is what permits us to be there, it is what makes us less unworthy to walk with the saints, the just, and all those with faith and fire in their hearts who redeem the world together with Jesus. We shall be like Simon the Cyrenean. At first, he was stunned and humiliated by being obliged to carry the cross. He was rebellious and had no wish to carry that cross. But, little by little, his attention was caught by the man in front of him, who went on in silence, this patient companion, who

160

never turned round and whose silence began to impress him. He studied that other man, his patience which nothing could disturb, his extraordinary capacity for suffering, his sweetness, his attentive charity in consoling those who wept, in rewarding those who helped him, in pardoning those who ill-treated him. He felt the power of his strength and sweetness envelop himself. It penetrated his being and he longed to draw closer to Him. He began by seeing only the cross and he ended by seeing only Jesus and nothing in the world could make him wish not to be there.

The Blessed Virgin herself suffered intensely the day that Simeon told her that a sword of sorrow would one day pierce her heart.

After that she waited. She did not understand, but she remembered and meditated upon those words, turning them over in her heart all the while that she lived with Jesus, and was occupied with caring for His needs. The only moments that she dreaded were those in which she was separated from Him. Every other moment, no matter what it might bring, was a joy to her because He was with her. Then, when the day came that she found herself beneath a large cross on which her Son was dying, she understood at last that this was the sword that she had so much feared and which she now embraced with passionate love in order that she might not be separated from Him.

And this is our religion. This is Christianity. It means to learn that there is no greater joy than suffering accepted with love.

EASTER SUNDAY (I)

It is a difficult, but delightful, task to endeavor to fill your hearts with the joy of Easter. It is not such an easy matter to make your hearts thrill with the happiness that sounds in the ringing of the bells and the chanting of the Alleluias on this beautiful day,

161

because they have become hardened and indifferent. We are so rebellious when it comes to joy. Our hearts are as if closed, and even hostile to it. It seems as though all the progress we have made over a number of years is no longer to believe in happiness and no longer to expect to find joy. We have made a virtue of our vices. Because we have become pessimistic, we conclude that we have become reasonable. We know about war, we can discourse indefinitely on the dangers of communism, the increase in taxes, the possibility of depression, but we smile incredulously when anyone tries to persuade us that real happiness does exist. We have come to regard it as a virtue no longer to believe in God, and we cling to what we regard as our dearest possession, the most certain of our experiences—not to allow ourselves to be carried away by that painful thing which has already caused us so much suffering—hope.

It is quite true that it is impossible for man to be perfectly happy. I agree that it is extremely difficult, with your cares, with the bereavements that have come to you, with the deceptions that you have encountered, to believe that you can be made over, begin your life anew, and find in it a new happiness. And, notwithstanding all this, what is impossible to man is very easy for God. For only God can do that impossible thing, —make you happy.

How do you expect God to manifest Himself if you allow Him to do for you only those things which you can do for yourself? To do the impossible is God's prerogative, and His alone. It is His signature. Your greatest sin is not to expect anything from God, and by this very fact you refuse God the means of manifesting Himself in you. To the extent that you have closed your life to happiness, you have closed it to God. All the regions of your soul which you have refused to permit joy to enter, you have refused to God. We must accept this impossible thing—that happiness can come again, that it will lift all the mountains off your heart, that it will enable you to enjoy the

162

purest, newest, strongest joy because God in you can become God once more. And that is precisely what happens at Easter, that is what we have been preparing for during the long weeks of Lent and during the terrible days of Holy Week. These have revealed to us how much God is interested in us, how much God wishes to intervene in our lives, how much God wants to have a place in our existence, and that God's love is such that, if we will consent to believe, He cannot do otherwise than take possession of our being and bring about this complete renewal. It is just this that is revealed to us by the Passion, that God loves us, loves us passionately, and that He wishes to transform us and save us. I am going to say it in another way so that you may understand it better. The Passion reveals to us our terrific power over God. You know what it is to have power over another. When someone loves us, we have great power over them, either to make them happy or to make them suffer. Recall when you were children the power you had over your parents, how the least word that you said to them, how a little flower given to your mother, even a smile, could bring joy to their hearts.

It is a joyous thing to be loved, to be a fiancé, to have such power over another that the least little thing done for the loved one can be counted on to give pleasure, increase his happiness, and enable us to share each other's joy. It is a joy to use this power, a joy to use it to give joy, but, alas! we are so made that, very often, we like to use it to cause suffering, or only because we like to feel our power, or for the mere pleasure of exercising it. How much children can make their parents suffer! Recall how we pretended that we were not hungry simply because we knew that they so much wanted us to eat. We pretended not to love them because we knew very well what pressure we exerted over their hearts.

And there is a worse manner of abusing this power. Because we are so sure that we possess it, we act as if we were indifferent, distant, strangers—as though our parents no longer existed, as

163

though we were not their children and have forgotten to show our love. How deeply we regret this when the day comes when we can no longer show them any love.

And so the Passion is a revelation of the great power that we have over God. He has delivered Himself to us, we have Him at our disposal. We can do what we like with Him. His hand, His "holy and venerable hands," one might take hold of them, as lovers do, in joyous familiarity, and they did take hold of His hand, but it was to pierce it with a nail. His face, one might take it between one's hands, as a mother takes the face of her little one between her hands, to caress him, to make him smile, or to smile upon him. We took His face but it was in order to strike it. He gave His heart to us, and we pierced it with a lance. One could do anything to Him, strip off His clothing—anything that one might do to someone who loves us and is given into our hands.

And still, when one thinks of it, what a source of joy there is in all this. What does all this mean if not to show us that we also have the power to make Him rejoice. Since He loves us, He shows us in this manner how responsive He is to our love. To please Him, we can do all that others have done, all that we ourselves have done, to make Him suffer. We can take His hands in the most audacious familiarity and kiss them, venerate them. We, too, like Veronica, can take His face in our hands in order to wipe it, to console Him. And we can give joy to His heart. What joy, what audacity, what folly of love ought not the example of His executioners encourage within us. When we see all that they have done to make Him suffer, we should rival them in our zeal to make Him happy.

Up to the present we have loved God with a love that seems to be discouraged, tired out, a love that does not dare to call attention to itself, which does not believe that it is pleasing, which has not the audacity to believe that it can give joy. We come before Him, and, overcome by His silence, we leave in a hurry. We very soon find that we have had enough of this solitary sort of thing. But what the Cross teaches us and what the Easter Resurrection brings before us is that God is tender, simple, like a child, infinitely sensitive to our marks of affection, just as He was infinitely vulnerable to our cruelty. He has no prejudices against us, He is gay and finds joy in our affection for Him. What astonishment in all this for us! God is infinitely better than we had believed, in our eyes He grows to His true stature. God breaks through the narrow envelope in which our prejudices, our hostilities, and our deceptions have enclosed Him. God becomes really God, the true God, He who reveals Himself to be so much better than we ever believed, so capable of making us happy and filling us with enthusiasm. Before this true God, the pessimists and those who believe that they have foreseen everything are the ones who are most astonished. Those who thought that they were free from all illusions recognize that they were deceived and that the greatest truth in all the world and the one virtue that they have most neglected is that of hope.

We have been thinking ourselves to be orphans. An orphan is naturally sad. He goes about his duties sorrowfully, he has no one to be made happy, no one to love him, no one who feels honored by his success, no one to whom he can show affection. Orphans are very often spoiled. As they have nothing, they have need of everything. They find that everything in this world of theirs is a gift, and they never find these gifts sufficient to furnish them with the security that they require. They never regard themselves as rich enough, beautiful enough, strong enough, pure enough, because they are always too much alone. But what a change if they discover that they have a father, if they find their true father. Then they begin to be themselves, they discover their true selves. Boys and girls alike, it is the same if they are united once more to their father. They were like lost persons, but now they have recovered their security when they can be encircled by the arms of their father. They no longer have any need for the gifts that were necessary before this. They no longer need to be rich, nor

strong, nor beautiful. To be somebody's own child is all they
need. To have a father suffices. Gifts mean nothing now. They
lift their eyes to the face of the giver and read in it such goodness
and such joy that it satisfies every desire.

That is the joy of Easter, to have recovered our Father, our
God. It is to have come to know what He is and what He has
always been and that we have never truly known Him. To come
before God, to kneel or to sit, and to laugh with joy at the
thought that we have made Him glad, that is the joy of Easter.

EASTER SUNDAY (II)

The Feast of Our Resurrection

To be a Christian is to believe in the Resurrection of Christ.

We are not Christians because we believe in sin, in the Cross,
in suffering and death, but because we believe in pardon, in joy,
in liberation, in the Resurrection, and in life.

The heart of our faith is the hope that every trial becomes an
increase in grace, that every sorrow will become a joy, every
death a resurrection, and even that every fault may become a
happy fault.

All this makes our religion something supernatural.

We live as though crushed by the weight of a stone; each of us
dwells in a tomb from which we despair of ever coming forth;
each of us bears an identical and crushing burden, identical in
that it is above our strength; each of us has become accustomed
and is resigned to our darkness and our slavery. "Who will roll
away the stone?" Easter is that almost sad experience that the
stone has been rolled away and now we must accustom ourselves
to the light of day.

Christianity is light, joy, and resurrection. And the Christian is a man who believes, who lets himself be invaded and transformed by that liberation which comes from an Other.

And it is so tempting to resist. To believe in joy is almost like consenting to renounce oneself. Our sadness is the measure of our attachment to ourselves, to our experience, to our doubts and mistrust, to our sorrows. And our joy is the measure of our attachment to God, to confidence, to hope, and to faith. All that we have closed off from happiness, we have closed off from God. All those areas in which we have resigned ourselves to know only frustration and bitterness, are areas from which God is excluded. In our lives God holds the same place as joy.

The sentiment of our solitude is the dimension of all that in us which has not been spiritualized, of all that has escaped from faith and love, of all that we jealously reserve for ourselves.

For there is nothing that we hug to our hearts so closely as sadness.

Look at these Christians. They multiply the number of their crucifixes, and who among them ever kneels to pray before the Risen Christ?

The Fathers of the Church say that there is only one means of curing sadness, and that is not to love it!

We must offer God the sacrifice of being happy! To believe in Him is to believe that He is capable of making us happy. It is to say to Him: "You have loved me enough, you have suffered enough for me and from me, you have so proven your love that I ought to give you this return at the very least—to see me happy!"

God can do that impossible thing in us, —make us happy and let us know a life that we would wish to continue for all eternity.

For, for many of us, there is great question, not of our faith in the Resurrection, but of our desire for a resurrection.

And before asking if we desire a resurrection, it should first be asked if we desire to live.

Before our belief in the Resurrection, it is essential that we be born to a life that can become eternal. Who is born to such a life? Who feels that he has it?

That which will be resurrected is not our little egoistic life which is so mournful and blind. It would be a chastisement far more than a recompense to prolong such a life.

God alone can endure an eternity of life. God alone loves so much that an endless life causes Him no fear. Only God can open to us a life that is so full of love and generosity that we shall desire it forever.

Faith in the Resurrection has its source in true love alone. Christ will give us this love which shall never fade. "Faith and hope will pass, but charity shall remain." Whom do we love so much that we desire to live with that person forever? What have we that we value so highly that we want to make it eternal? Is there a being, a work, a state of soul, or are there moments in your life so good, so happy, so full of love, that you would like to make them immortal?

Our faith, and even our hope of resurrection, both of ourselves and of others, strictly depends upon our capacity to love. Our potentiality of redemption, our potentiality of resurrection, is directly related to the strength of our love.

Is there so much love in us that we experience a need to rise and a need to people eternity with the presence of an innumerable multitude whom we would like to bring there?

Here is the question that Christ puts to us this Easter morning. "Do you believe that I am the Resurrection and the Life? Do you believe that I can bring back from the dead this corpse that is yourself and the others that surround you? Do you believe that I can show you a life that you will want to live eternally?"

For the essential thing is not to rise in ten, twenty, thirty, or fifty years from now, but to live and to arise right now.

For, in order that we may experience a life of love and of faith, we must die as quickly as possible to our doubts, our sorrows, our resentments, and our complaints, and then we shall rise at once.

Easter means that we can rise from the dead, that the Resurrection does exist and will take place, not only in the future but also in the present. It can be the experience of each one of us and we can bear witness to it.

Instead of asking you if you believe in the Resurrection of Christ, I should ask you if you believe in your own resurrection and if you have experienced it.

Have you ever risen from the dead?

A Christian does not believe in a future life but in life eternal. If it be eternal, it has already begun and we are now living it.

Nor does he believe in a future resurrection. We are already risen, or are on the way to our resurrection. Eternal life has begun and it begins only with death and resurrection.

There can be no Easter for us unless we are willing to die in a portion of ourselves in which we are only too much alive, —in our agitations, our fears, our interests, our egoisms. And also if we do not consent to rise in a portion of ourselves in which we are but too dead, —that is, to rise to peace, to faith and hope, to pardon, to love, and to joy.

There can be no feast of Easter without a true confession, and what is a confession if it means not to die to ourselves, to our own wills, to our sad, weak, poor, and ugly wills which are our sins, and rise to the will of Christ, which is love, hope, renewal, and tenderness.

There is no feast of Easter without the Easter communion, and what is an Easter communion but a leaving of one's dwelling place, one's habits, one's bread, and one's life in order to taste another bread, another life, —a bread of justice, of sincerity and sharing with others, —a life of love, of faith and fraternity.

An Easter like this means to leave one's old life and take up a new one, a life in which one finds oneself living the life and the love of the Father.

Shame on the religion which has no witnesses but those of the long past!

169

Shame on the religion which knows no resurrection but that of 2,000 years ago!

We need witnesses in this present day. We want people who have passed through death and experienced a resurrection, people who can assure the world that it is possible to die and to rise again.

That is the message that the world is waiting to receive from us.

How do you expect it to understand the Resurrection of Christ except by seeing our own? There is only one unassailable proof that Christ is risen, and that is to show that He is now living, and that His love, too, is still alive, and that means that there must be persons and there must be communities that live His life and love one another with His love.

St. Augustine tells us that on the night of the paschal vigil the pagans themselves could not sleep. At daybreak they met the neophytes in the streets, on their way home from the church, wearing their white baptismal robes and transfigured with joy. "On seeing this apparition," he tells us, "they thought that they saw Christ."

The only face that Christ now has to show to our contemporaries is our own. They will be convinced and converted by what they see in us, and in our communities. "Where two or three are gathered together in my name—in my love—I am there in the midst of them."

It is up to us to prove the Resurrection of Christ. We ourselves are the proof that Christ is risen.

May the world, with its violence, its doubts, and its despair, which seeks to feel the wounds of Christ as a proof of His presence and His love, find us with open heart and open hands, with joyous and affectionate welcome. May it bring to mind the gentle reproach of Christ: "Because now you have seen, Thomas, you have believed."

THE FIRST SUNDAY AFTER EASTER

Thomas, the Hopeless

"My Lord and my God!"   (John 20:19–31)

Today Easter comes to a close. It is the last day of the Octave of Easter, the last occasion, the last chance to take part in the joy of Easter, to be converted and to give expression to our faith in the Resurrection.

The Church has chosen for this means the Patron saint who is most like us, whose resemblance to ourselves is close enough to convince us—St. Thomas, the distrustful, the stubborn, the incredulous, he who has grumbled all along that he would not give in, that he is no "easy mark," the outstanding pessimist, one of those who are suspicious when things look too good.

Thomas is truly a modern man, an existentialist, who believes only what he can touch, a man who will not be taken in by illusions, a courageous pessimist who can face misfortune but who dares not believe in happiness. To him, the worst is always the surest.

The character of Thomas is sketched in several places in the Gospel and always in the same terms. At the resurrection of Lazarus, a messenger comes and tells Jesus: "Lord, he whom you love is sick." (This prayer is so discreet and so confident. It asks nothing. It informs, and then waits.) The disciples are anxious about the risk that exists in Judea. Jesus reassures them in a mysterious sentence, but one which tells them that there is no danger. "Then Thomas, called Didymus, said to his fellow-disciples, Let us also go, that we may die with Him!"

Certainly, this is no confession of faith but of despair. Thomas

171

flatly contradicts the Saviour. His courage is limited to dying. It does not go so far as to have confidence. This is the same pessimism which will make him reject the announcement of the Resurrection with so much energy.

Here is another dialogue. Jesus is speaking: "When I go and prepare a place for you, I will come again and will take you to myself, that where I am you may be also. You know where I am going and you know the way." Thomas said to Him: "Lord, we do not know where you are going; how, then, can we know the way?"

It is by this stupid intervention that he interrupts the extraordinary music of the discourse after the Last Supper. It is the only thing that he says the whole evening. And Jesus answers him in a manner that is both mysterious and transparent: "I am the Way and the Truth and the Life." Thomas now knows less than he did before and grumbles to himself in his corner: "With such precise directions, we won't go far!"

And above all, there is his final declaration of stubbornness: "Unless I see in His hands the print of the nails, and unless I put my finger into the place of the nails, and unless I place my hand into His side, I will not believe!"

What strikes us about Thomas, what makes him so fraternal to us, so much a contemporary, is, first of all, the violence of his revolt. There is a hardness in the conditions that he lays down for his surrender. Such hardness comes only from great suffering. It is because he suffered more than the others that he would not run the risk of allowing himself to hope. Thomas is, doubtless, the one who suffered most because of the Passion and probably had the deepest regrets that he did not die as well as his Master. So he found only one stone on which to rest his head, and that was despair. It was something firm. It would not be easily taken away from him.

And have we not also tried often to believe, and the only

172

result has been to expose ourselves to cruel disappointments? At such times, one is tempted to say to oneself: "That's enough. Let's give up. It is easier to be dead than it is to live." Such was the condition of Thomas, —sorrow pushed to the point of exasperation.

Modern men are also courageous, capable of facing suffering and death. They know how to kill themselves, but on condition that their action affirms their disbelief in the causes for which they die. How many heroes of the war make apologies for having shown themselves the most generous by being the most skeptical, the most cynical, the most withdrawn of all. We fear to open up to hope and to happiness, we are afraid to open, even a little, our armor of distrust and resignation, lest we be unprotected. This does us great harm later on.

A modern man risks his life several times every day. He crosses the street without looking, he jumps from the bus while it is still in motion, he imprudently tries to pass ahead of another car on the highway, he gaily takes his chances between two imminent dangers. But never does he offer himself. He will risk his life for a mere nothing, but there is no one to whom he can offer it. When, on Sunday, he at last comes to Mass, to make (so he says) the offering of his whole being, he comes with empty hands. The modern fad is to pretend to believe in nothing and yet to fulfill one's duties. In this there is something both beautiful and puerile. He who pretends that he no longer hopes, really hopes not to hope. He who pretends to believe nothing, really believes that he believes nothing. He who affirms that everything is uncertain, makes an affirmation that he believes to be certain. He who says that he is free from illusions, is really filled with illusions.

We are living at a wonderful time. There has never been an age when there was so little faith, so much atheism, so much despair, so much that is negative. But neither has there been a

173

time when people have suffered so much from their lack of faith, nor a time when they have taken human affairs so seriously, so tragically.

To suffer because there is no one to love is the mark of great love. To suffer because one is unable to believe nor to hope is the form that faith is taking in this our day. It is discreet, humble, tragic, searing, but so sincere, so loyal, and so pure.

Happily, the Lord understood Thomas. Only our Lord knew that it was because of his suffering that he acted as he did. Only the Lord would admit that, in order to cure Thomas, it would first be necessary to console him.

Have you remarked how Thomas's requirements are concrete, positive, almost materialistic? "If I do not see with my own eyes the hole of the nails, and if I do not put my finger into His hands and my hand into His side." Another trait by which he resembles us. That demand to see and to touch, that fear of being duped. How consoling it is, it seems to me, to find oneself so accurately foreseen, announced, and expressed. It is the same with ourselves. Our spiritual life will never change if we find no satisfaction in it. It will never become what it ought to be—passionate, enthusiastic, alive—if there is nothing in it that corresponds to our appetite to see and to touch the divine.

The response of God to this requirement is astonishing, unheard of, disarming. That which Thomas had laid down as a foolish challenge, a bit of defiance, in his passionate resistance to believe what he heard, to all that Jesus submits. He yields Himself to Thomas's conditions with the most tender docility. "Come, Thomas, put your finger, put your hand . . . and be not incredulous but believe." The Lord let Himself be conquered by Thomas. He seems to have abandoned, for his sake, the plan of action that He followed in regard to all the others. For Thomas only, did He make this change. But, by acting thus, He won Thomas.

Thomas had resisted the authority of the entire apostolic college. This makes of him the first Protestant. (Note that, if he had been a conformist, if he had joined the others in order not to be singular, he would have become a very mediocre Catholic. He would never have said "My Lord and my God!") He has been led by an unusual way. (It is by becoming a Protestant that he prepares to become a fervent Catholic.) The Apostles were so angered by the stubbornness of Thomas that they might have used force to oblige him to believe. But the Lord loved Thomas. He knew that when Thomas showed himself so intractable it was because he was so unhappy, that he had suffered more than the others from the desolation of the Cross, and that he was more generous than the rest. ("Come! Let us go and die with Him!")

Then Jesus drew Thomas into the shelter of His mantle and spoke to his heart. "All right, Thomas, do what you will. Put your finger . . . put your hand . . ." And Thomas was completely overcome, for he never had any idea that his demand would be heard. His challenge had really been a refusal, a means of enclosing himself within his doubts, of excluding that band of irritating believers. Of excommunicating himself.

The Lord, by His gentleness, had reconciled Thomas without delay. Thomas placed his finger in those luminous wounds. He felt the wound of the nails, the wound of the lance, the living proof of all the love with which he, Thomas, had been loved. He felt, he touched, he became satisfied, and knelt in tears before his Lord and his God.

Then, come with him, you who share his doubts. Feel, touch, put your finger into His hand and your hand into His side. Be convinced. It is true. It is really He. And you are the one whom He has so loved.

When Thomas saw the Lord before him, all illumined with joyous tenderness, shining with peace and love, he suddenly became aware that he had always known that Jesus was risen. He always knew that it would be this way. He had had enough experience, he had lived with Jesus long enough to know that he ought to wait for just this, that, with Jesus, things like this were always happening, always something good, something delightful, something unbelievable.

(He ought to have believed the others. In refusing to do so, he had but mortified himself, made a martyr of himself, in order to protect himself from what might be too much of a shock. He suffered at the same time from a desire to believe and a fear that, if he did, he might be mistaken.)

There could have been no worse punishment for Thomas than to obtain what he had demanded as a condition for his belief. He saw that he had ruined his chances and that he, too, would have to believe in the Lord. At bottom, he had no need of these proofs. In being so skeptical and hard, he had acted like a spoiled child who makes demands when he is only too sure of getting what he wants. When he said that he must see and must touch, when he resisted the others so peevishly, it was not from need of proof but from a desire of attention, to show his feelings, and to make a stir.

In the presence of the Lord he no longer had any desire to feel, and he would have given everything rather than have to put his finger and his hand into those wounds and to have avoided hearing that gentle reproach: "Because you have seen me, Thomas, you have believed. Blessed are they who have not seen but have believed." Even before Jesus said it, Thomas knew it when he looked at those others who had believed.

And when he put out his hand to touch those wounds it was through docility and repentance. He no longer acted like a person who would make a test, but who was making a pilgrimage. It was done. He surrendered. It was the most painful and the most humiliating thing that he could do. It was his reparation and his punishment.

(After such intimacy with Jesus, we see a revelation of his love. Thomas has been lifted to a height which none of the others has

176

attained. Dazzled and overpowered, he exclaims: "My Lord and my God!" He is the first to carry his belief that far. No other Apostle has as yet said to Jesus: "My God!" From this poor Thomas, unbelieving and violent, Jesus has drawn the most beautiful act of faith given in the Gospel. Jesus has loved him so much, treated him so gently, that He has drawn from that fault, that bitterness, that humiliation, a souvenir, a souvenir that is a cry of fidelity and of love.

Thomas felt sure that he did not believe. We, too, very often, have more faith in the depths of our hearts than we think. The proof is the fact that we feel so unhappy over our lack of faith. To suffer because we do not believe is already to believe. To suffer because one does not love, is love already. Blessed are those who suffer because of their incredulity. Nothing has so influenced the Lord as this desperate resistance to faith on the part of Thomas, when, in fact, he so much wanted to believe.

Happy those who have not seen and have believed. Notice that here is our opportunity, our joy, our privilege. We can still believe without obliging Jesus to show us Himself and let us touch Him. Let us be careful not to be so childish, so stubborn as was Thomas. Do not ask for proofs lest, perhaps, they be given to us, and we be obliged, like Thomas, to make our Lent all over again, to meet once more the nails, the wounds, the suffering, before we meet our Lord where He awaits us, the Risen Christ.

Jesus will not refuse us anything. If we persist in our request, if we insist, if we childishly exaggerate our obstinacy and our bitterness, if we cry out to Him to let us see and touch Him, He will do it. We shall see Him and we shall touch Him. He will not be less favorable to us than He was to Thomas. Some day we shall be convinced. The day will come when we can no longer deny the happiness, the love, and the presence of God. And that day we shall learn what we have known all along, that our greatest sin was to pretend that we did not see it.

Let us pray to St. Thomas that he will enable us to avoid his humiliation, and wiser than he was, let us offer to God the only gift that we can offer Him here below, that of believing in Him a little while before we see Him.

THE SECOND SUNDAY AFTER EASTER

The Good Shepherd

"I know my sheep and my sheep know me." (John 10:11–16)

God behaves towards us like a shepherd. He is our Pastor, devoted and affectionate, our Master who takes care of us, our Father who suffers for us and with us when He sees us go astray and suffer because of it.

The intimacy which our Lord desires should be between Himself and us is total, an exchange of confidence and love which will make us live completely in one another, —He is us and we in Him. He longs to be known by us as completely as He knows us, —as His Father knows Him and as He knows His Father.

Such condescension seems to us absurd. And it also frightens us.

Even in our family life, it is so rare to let oneself be fully known and it is regarded even as something dangerous.

Who dares to say: "I know my wife as my wife knows me. I know my husband as my husband knows me. I know my children as my children know me. I know my parents as my parents know me."

What screens there are even in the most closely united families! What reserved domains! What silences! How many things one does not say, how many things one no longer speaks about, things about which it seems better to keep silence, things which it is impossible to say. It would do more harm, it would make

178

things worse, because one would not be understood. How many lies in a single day! And while we think we are doing good, what a pit we dig between ourselves and those we love best! What a comedy we are constantly playing!

It requires extraordinary love to enable one to become transparent. One must be sure of being loved unconditionally in return before giving one's entire confidence to another, before one dares to tell him everything, before letting him know us as we are, with our miseries, our hateful vices, and that strange remnant of innocence about which we are more ashamed to reveal than all the rest.

But can we abandon ourselves like that to our Lord?

Undoubtedly. We know very well that the Lord knows us through and through. But that very knowledge causes us, in general, more fear than joy. We have learned from our catechism that God knows all and sees all, and we have come to feel that He spies upon us and condemns us, instead of thinking that His eyes follow us in order to help us, to compassionate us, and to be with us in the evil that we do as well as in the evils to which we submit.

But, on our side, how do we come to know the Lord? How do we become His friends and share His confidence? How shall we be introduced into His intimacy, be delighted and warmed by His tenderness and His friendship for each one of us? Such a state of affairs would change our whole life, consume our time, our interests, and our liberty.

And yet, if we do not know Him like this, we are not His sheep. "My sheep know me. They hear my voice and they follow me."

Is there anyone who is resigned to not being His sheep? Is there anyone who chooses not to know Him?

But where shall we know Him? How shall we know Him when we have not seen Him, nor have we heard Him, but only heard others speak, and so remotely, of Him?

179

Since the feast of Easter, we ought to know Him better. We should know Him by what He has given, by the fact that He has given His life for us.

And each Sunday, each Mass teaches us and repeats over and over again, that we know Him in that He breaks bread for us, that He gives us His flesh to eat.

The Mass of today shows us that His disciples themselves had no better means of knowing Him. "The disciples recognized the Lord in the breaking of the bread." At the Last Supper, as at Emmaus, there happened just the same thing that will happen in the midst of us within a few minutes. At the center of the table someone rose, took bread, blessed it, broke it, and gave it to each one, saying: "Take and eat, this is my body, delivered for you."

Understand this well. Bread is what sustains life. Without bread, there will be an end to life. He who gives his bread, gives his life.

Christ give us His bread, which is His Body, in order to show us that He gives His life. From this we are to learn that He loves us to the extent of giving His life for us, to dying willingly for it-does-not-matter-whom among us. For He is like the father, or the mother, of a family who spends his life—who gives His life—for his children.

How do parents make themselves known to their children?

When does the family gather together? When do they learn to know and to love one another and to be happy together?

This is easy to answer, especially on Sunday. At the table, at meals, at those good family meals, at those home-like meals. Those meals that the father is spending his life to earn, to provide. All those hours of toil that the father has spent, often out of sight and away from home, all those hours reach their fruition at the table, in the service, the food, the decoration, all are transformed into a good dinner that is appetizing and savory.

And those meals the mother is giving her life to prepare, to foresee, to make pleasant, to organize the surroundings and create the proper atmosphere. How many hours of her life are passed in making those purchases, in that work, in those calculations? "What shall I give them for dinner?" That humble, daily question really means: "How am I going to make them happy today? How am I going to show them again today, once more, on this day, that I love them?"

Yes, the life of love is just that. The life of your mothers has been spent in those cares and in that work. She was once a young girl, bright, lively, full of plans for the future, full of possibilities and dreams, and now her life, to a great extent, can be resumed in those meals into which she put her whole heart.

All of you, young men and women, who are preparing and desiring a life of love, who think that you are in love, think also of the humble, severe, and lowly outcome of all these legitimate exaltations of youth. Are you capable of loving your husband, your wife, your children enough so that you find your happiness in serving them?

It is very true that the love of parents shows itself and is eaten at the family meal. It is there that we see how much our parents love us. We learn to know them, and quietly learn to love them as they have taught us to love. At the family meals we speak, we exchange, each brings his own thought or something that he has learned, all is in common, there is no reserve. And it was at the end of a meal that Jesus said: "Now I will no longer call you servants but friends, because everything that I have learned from my Father I have made known to you in my turn. I have confided everything to you. I have told you all."

And in the family, too, in the family above all, one is recognized in the breaking of the bread.

Again, when the family is dispersed, when the bonds have been broken, if anyone wishes to bring the family together again, it is always at a meal.

Those family dinners, not always very gay, but that is because

181

there is not always a great deal of love. There is not always much animation and life, but that is because love is not always as alive as it should be. But, in a family where there is love for one another, is there anything more enjoyable than meal-time?

Yes, the breaking of bread is the sign of love and the gift of life.

At each one of your meals you eat and drink the love and the life of your parents. All of you children whom I see before me, you are as big as the love which has nourished you. You have grown in proportion to the love which has surrounded you. And because there is much more love reserved for you in the heart of your parents, you will certainly grow and continue to develop. One does not grow up well unless one is greatly loved.

Jesus also has wished to make Himself known to us in the breaking of bread. Jesus has also wished to invite us to His table so that, little by little, we may become accustomed to Him, learn to know Him, learn to believe that He loves us when we see Him daily sharing with us His Bread and His Life.

How many meals did we have to share before we became aware of the love of our parents? How many meals taken thoughtlessly, greedily, with caprice—"I don't like that"—before we became aware of the work that it had cost our father, and we showed our joy and gratitude for so much love?

How many communions will be required before we become conscious of Christ's love for us, His patience, His devotedness? And to the consciousness of our immense ingratitude and negligence? For the Bread is His Body which He gives us, and He has won the power to give it to us daily by dying for us on the Cross.

But we know nothing, we never think of it. And the priest, the priest first of all, the priest who replaces Him and who celebrates, is still learning.

But Christ continues to invite us—and there will be but one among us to accept His invitation and respond to His appeal.

182

And if there is only one among you who receives communion, the Blood of Christ will not be lost and Jesus will rejoice to have a child at His table.

It is then that the words of the Communion of today come to mind: "I am the Good Shepherd, alleluia. I know my sheep, and now, at last, my sheep have learned of my love and they know me. Alleluia, alleluia."

THE THIRD SUNDAY AFTER EASTER

The Little While

"A little while and you shall see me again." (John 16:16–22)

"In a little while you shall not see me, and again in a little while you shall see me, because I go to the Father."

A Gospel of farewells, sad, and yet comforting, mysterious and at the same time enlightening, with predictions of persecutions and sufferings, all clothed in such tenderness.

What does our Saviour mean? The Apostles, like ourselves, murmur and question. This "short time" of our waiting and our sorrows, —how long will it last?

Until the Resurrection? But at this time Christ had not yet ascended to the Father. Until Pentecost? But the persecutions announced by Jesus did not really begin for the Apostles until after the coming of the Holy Spirit. Until the end of the world? The glorious return of Christ? Until a new humanity had been brought to birth by the Church?

But this delay is terribly long. How could the Saviour speak of a "little while" when 2,000 years have already passed and who knows how many more will pass before His return? Of course, for each of us, this life is but a short time. We do not live very long. Our Lord tells us: "You will suffer, but it is only for a short time. Soon you will be consoled. You will soon know that you have suffered but a short time in comparison with the eternity of your joy."

You are not separated from Him and from your loved ones but for a short time. Soon you will meet each other and nothing shall ever separate you again.

You are rich for but a short time. Do not become attached to your goods. They will pass and you will be delivered from them quite as rapidly as from your ills.

But there is still a better interpretation of these words of Christ.

Jesus does not wish that we wait for Him so long a time. Even the little while of our lifetime is too long for His impatience to see us again and to make us happy.

In the Communion of today's Mass we are told that there are relays along the route to the great Return, that there are occasional halts, and meeting places, times for rest and relaxation. Each communion is a stage in our journey. Each communion is a rendezvous.

The short while is no longer than the interval between two communions. Along the path of our life we have need for just the courage necessary to await the communion of the morrow. "And again in a little while you shall see me."

THE FOURTH SUNDAY AFTER EASTER

"It is good for you that I go."   (John 16:5–14)

In today's reading from John there is the most astonishing sentence in the whole Gospel. It is the most paradoxical, the most unbelievable, the most provocative of sentences. Have you noticed it?

"It is good for you that I go away."

Our Lord said that to His Apostles to whom His presence was their life. Imagine what it would be to have Jesus, to be able to hear Him, to see Him, to touch Him, to live in His radiance, in that zone of power which came from Him. ("Everyone tried to touch Him because virtue went out from Him and healed all.") To be able on every occasion to take refuge beside Jesus, to throw oneself at His feet, to embrace His knees, what marvellous security there would be in that! The whole world, all one's surroundings, seemed uncertain, inconsistent, dangerous, but close to Jesus, there would be peace and one would be invulnerable and happy.

Think how attractive Jesus was, what an exalting adventure it was to walk beside Him. Everything would be seen in a new light—people, things, ideas would disclose new truths. All would be illuminated with wonderful clearness, a brightness that did not dazzle. At last someone could speak to us about God as no one had ever done before. At last God became alive, near, young, tender, just, favorable, loving, and active. This is something entirely new, and yet, each one feels that this is just what he has been waiting for all the time, that God could never be otherwise, that God would not be God if He were less good or less beautiful than Jesus revealed Him to be.

All along His path vocations and friendships came into being which transformed lives. He filled the whole world with joy. Those who were fishing (and you know how absorbing that can be!) received fish, the wedding guests were given wine, the sick were cured. Justice, truth, goodness, compassion poured forth from His Heart and renewed the world. For the first time, one really knew what it was to be alive.

And now He announces that He is going to leave them.

And He adds: "It is to your advantage that I go."

The Apostles were thunderstruck. They were silent. This is the first time in the Gospel that a mysterious announcement was not met by a stupid question. They were completely overcome.

And ourselves? One has but to look at us, to see us, in order to

185

know that it is good that He went away! One has but to see our inertia, our laziness, our incredulity, or our tepidity.

But we would have been very different if He were here! If He had spoken to us. We would not have allowed ourselves to drag along like this, we would have become energetic, animated, we would certainly have been changed, even unrecognizable, if He were here, if He had spoken to us, if we but believed that He were here, if we but believed that He were speaking to us.

But, be careful! The same thing happened to those who did not believe in Him as happens to us all the time. They immediately forgot what He had said. They found His words hard, obscure, paradoxical, and they ceased to listen to Him. They went their way, unaffected. They justified themselves by saying that He exaggerated. Who did He think He was?

Many of those who heard Him did not understand. Many of those who saw Him did not recognize Him. Many of those who touched Him were not cured.

From that time to this, one must listen to Him in the right way, that is, with dispositions of entreaty, of openness, of desire, and of respect, and one must listen to Him with faith. We must see Him in the right way, touch Him in the right way, like that woman, alone in the midst of the crowd that jostled around Jesus. She touched Him in the right way, she touched only the fringe of His garment but she did so with faith. All touched Him, all jostled against Him, but only one was cured because that one had faith. The rest were passed over.

Truly, those times were very much like our own. The days of His presence by faith are now.

At the present day there is far more faith in the world than there was in the lifetime of Jesus. Recall how He converted only a few, very few remained faithful to Him; recall how He was betrayed and abandoned even by His own disciples. He has infinitely more followers now. He is infinitely better understood now. He has more people around Him in a single large city today than He ever had when on earth. There are more sick assembled at Lourdes in one year than were ever brought to Him during the whole of His life. Two thousand years ago they thought to stifle the spread of Christianity by killing Him alone, but Christians are still persecuted, imprisoned, executed in all parts of the world and the end has not yet come.

Now, perhaps, we will consent to listen to His words: "It is good for you that I go away." It is necessary that I send to you a Spirit who will dispose you to listen, a Master who will repeat until you have understood, a great Educator who will be the Spirit in the Church who will never cease to instruct you, to repeat my words and penetrate you with them. "He will bring to your mind all that I have said." It is the Holy Spirit in the Church who repeats these things. God has invented a remedy that is suited to our inattention, to our dullness and hardness of heart. The Church repeats every word of Christ's, and even more, she reënacts His behavior. Thanks to the Church, Christ is still living. He recommences His life before you each year at Christmas, Easter, Ascension, and Pentecost. Each Sunday of the year He is born anew among us; for us also the Word becomes flesh and establishes His dwelling in our midst. He speaks to us in the Epistle and in the Gospel. He invites us to touch Him in holy communion and He pardons us in the confessional.

You have not, as yet, understood His birth? You do not, as yet, truly believe in His pardon? You do not understand His words and they mean nothing to you? You do not know, as yet, that He loves you enough to die for you, to trust Himself to you for your whole life? Patience! Keep on hoping! He is about to begin again today at this Mass. He will begin again tomorrow and every day. His patience is stronger than all our resistance. His fidelity surpasses our caprice. His love prevents and calls forth ours. We shall finish by being allowed to touch Him. For, after all, it is He who wishes to touch us far more than we wish to be touched and cured by Him.

Such is the work of the Holy Spirit in the Church and in our own souls. Let us rejoice that there is in us Someone who cares for us, who leads us, who never leaves us in peace, the Spirit that Jesus sends us.

Happily, our salvation does not depend upon our own clear-sightedness, our own shrewdness, our perseverance, our fidelity, nor upon our intellectual penetration, nor upon our strength of character. Salvation is for the poor and the little ones. God is in charge of us. Salvation would never have been offered to anyone if it were not offered to men and women like ourselves. God will never permit discouragement to keep Him from dwelling within us, from testing us, from calling us. How can we doubt, then, that the day will come when He will succeed in piercing through our shell and entering our heart?

THE ASCENSION OF OUR LORD (I)

"You men of Galilee, why do you stand there looking up to heaven?" (Acts 1:1–11)

The feast of the Ascension is the one which best proves to us that our religion is something supernatural, and shows us how much it goes beyond human resources, how much of it is incomprehensible and mysterious.

Do you really find that the Ascension of our Lord is a feast? Are you really able to rejoice over this feast? Do you see clearly what value for us there is in His departure? Who among us rejoices over the loss of his father or his mother, or the mere disappearance of a friend? How can we have the heart to rejoice over the disappearance of Christ? Ah! We see very well what we are losing as Christ goes up to heaven but what are we going to gain? The time before the Ascension is, for the greater number

188

of Christians, the golden age of Christianity, that of the sensible presence of Christ among us, the good time to which they go back in imagination with ease and delight and for which they feel a longing which they regard as the best proof of their sincerity in matters of religion. At that blessed epoch of the world the Word was made flesh and lived among us. The angels came and went between heaven and earth. The Holy Spirit was a radiant Dove, the Father a voice from heaven, the Son an infant wrapped in swaddling bands, an adolescent, about whom no one knew the mystery, a man of God, and virtue went out from Him at every word, every gesture, every look. Ah! For once the old dream of humanity was realized, for once religion was down to our level. Ah! If we had only lived in those days! If we had only seen those crowds gather round Him, those crowds which caused Zacchaeus to climb his sycamore tree, and towards which the lame and the blind turned their steps, uttering loud cries. If we had but met that glance which would have purified our glances. If we had but heard those words which effected what they said, which would have detached us from our goods if they had said to us: "Happy the poor!" —which would have softened our hatreds when they said: "Happy the meek!" —which would have liberated us from our lusts: "Happy the pure!"

Alas! Those times are past. Our delight in God went up to heaven when He did. Christ has become invisible and ourselves, we have become insensible. Christ has mounted to the skies and we have fallen back to the earth. We are but flesh and blood, we have taken our revenge for His apparent withdrawal, since He no longer has a body, a face, there is nothing left of Him to touch our hearts, to excite our feelings, or to make any impression upon us.

Let us be sincere. If we were permitted to choose, who among us would not vote for the time before the Ascension? Who does not long for it? Does it not seem to you that we are waiting for such a thing in order to begin a truly fervent spiritual life which

189

will produce fruit? In which God will come closer to us? In which He will manifest Himself more clearly? In our own hearts, we all believe ourselves to be well disposed, we ask for nothing better than to believe, to love, to attach ourselves to the Lord and to follow His will. But it is He who fails us. It is on His side that there is something wanting. Religion ought to change, it ought to come nearer to us so that it may speak to our heart and to our senses. Truly, if we were sincere, we could not help but give utterance to the same complaint as did the Apostles: "Lord, will you not restore the kingdom of Israel? Then we are not going to live together here below? Then the time will never come when we can rest and be happy here below with you?"

But, unfortunately, people are not sincere. Everybody dresses up in borrowed sentiments. All make believe that they believe and the result is that no one believes anymore. Christianity, for too many well-meaning persons, is to pretend. For some, it means to pretend to be a little sad; for some, it means to pretend to be gay, but always with a deep and distressing certainty that nothing will ever change. They have, so they think, swallowed all the dogmas of religion with the salt of their baptism; once and for always, they have learned the entire catechism by heart; and they are able to recite the creed. And do you think that that means that you believe in it? Not at all. Dogmas are assimilated slowly and in proportion to our growth in the spiritual life—just as in infancy we were fed milk until we became capable of digesting other foods. At one time in our life, it was the Real Presence that became clear to us; at another, confession (and do we even now believe in the remission of sins?); at another time, it was the Trinity (and that was probably when we became parents); later, as we increased in age, perhaps for the first time the idea of our own death came to us, and we came to realize that this body, in which we had enjoyed so much happiness, would fail us, and we began to understand what is meant by "I await the resurrection of the dead."

190

So it is with the Ascension. Nothing is falser than to imagine that you really believe in it; nothing is more artificial than to rejoice without having taken into account the immense sacrifice that it demands; nothing is more pharisaic than to think that, in regard to this dogma, it is sufficient to celebrate it, that there is no need to learn to live it with pain and sorrow and thus to merit it.

How much I prefer to all that, the sincere boorishness, the avowed hardness of heart of the Apostles. How much more at my ease I am with these rustics who, at least, say that they never understand any of these things. How they comfort us after all those pious comedies, those affected and devout airs. How our slowness to believe becomes natural, and, if you understand me, reassuring when their incredible opacity, their hardened resistance to the spiritual, their positive imperviousness to the divine is expressed with such candor.

They had the best professor of religion that there was in the world. (Compare Him, mentally, with yours.) They had lived three years with Him without interruption, they had witnessed all His miracles, heard all His lessons, and seen all His way of life. And now, you recall? —they understood nothing. They questioned Him about the most transparent parables. They gave a base interpretation to His most spiritual doctrines, and tried to make use of Him, believing that they were honoring Him. Recall how scandalized they were by the Passion. Jesus had foretold it to them. He had put them on their guard. He even went so far as to prophesy their behavior so that they might find in their cowardice itself a motive for believing in Him. Nothing succeeded. How difficult they found it to believe in His Resurrection, how slow they were to give in, how stubborn in their despair, how blind at the time of His manifestations. And the mere mention of His Ascension filled them with consternation. Their last word to the Risen Christ, on the point of going up into heaven, was the childish complaint: "Lord, then you are not going to reëstablish the Kingdom?" And there they were, gazing upward with opened mouths, as all their hopes went upward with their Master. "You men of Galilee, why do you stand there, looking up to heaven . . . ?"

How good it is to think that they, at least, did not pretend to understand, pretend to believe, pretend to rejoice. They were sincere. They showed themselves as they actually were, and that is why religion was able to take hold of them and set them apart forever. The Christians of the present day seem like charming acrobats in comparison with these slow and heavy Apostles. But every step that they made was true, was real, and their faith was as sincere as was their incredulity.

For the Ascension was of infinite profit to them, as often is the case with great suffering and separations. Later, we come to look upon them as beneficial and liberating. It was not until after the Ascension that they began to center their thoughts on the divinity of the Saviour. They were attached to Him by the bonds of a human friendship, then by their admiration for, and their confidence in, that power of His for which they could find no name. But they never seemed to know who was in their midst until they saw Him going back to heaven, the place that was His true home.

Above all, they discovered, much to their stupefaction, that the Lord was more attentive to their prayers and heard them better now that He was with His Father. Everything that they asked in His name they obtained. They were continually putting this marvel to the proof. The treasures of heaven lay open and they had but to take them for the benefit of those to whom the Lord sent them. The earth was never more filled with the divine than after Christ left it. Never before had they felt Him to be so really present, so strong, so comforting. Everywhere that they went, He helped them, confirming their words by the miracles that accompanied them.

They then understood that the Saviour, who had not left the

bosom of the Father in coming down from heaven, did not leave them in going back to heaven. The moment that they thought they had lost Him was the very moment in which they really received Him and recognized Him for the first time.

That is why they never expressed any regret over having lost the physical presence of Christ. They never experienced that homesickness for "the days of His flesh" which are, for us, the test of Christian fidelity. They never complained of the absence of God. On the contrary, they said what, to our ears, are scandalous words: "If I have known Christ according to the flesh, now I no longer know Him according to the flesh." They now knew Christ only according to the spirit. And St. Ignatius has proclaimed: "Celestial things are much more illuminating than terrestrial things. Even our Lord Jesus Christ is more clearly manifested since He has ascended to the Father."

This is the thing that we shall have to learn by our own experience, slowly, patiently, progressively, and here our greatest danger lies in wanting to go too fast. Our dogmas and our liturgy make it possible for us to enjoy the fruit of twenty centuries of research. Do not let us think that, like mendicants, we can enjoy that for which we have not toiled in our turn. Let us tell Christ of our sadness at His disappearance, our anxiety as we see Him leave our visible universe, our longing for a kingdom where He and ourselves may be able to live side by side. And when we have partaken of the weakness of the Apostles, then we shall be able to partake of their experience of Christ's strength. During this time before Pentecost, let us pray to Christ and ask Him to let us know the fidelity with which He hears us, to show to each one of us that it is advantageous for us that He has gone, since He is ever interceding for us with the Father. By His Ascension, He has made us trustees of all the treasures which His victory has won, and He has confided to us the task of being His witnesses and representatives here below. Think of the Apostles who were prepared for their task by so many lessons, miracles, graces, and prayers. Let us ask our Lord to provide us with the same preparation. Let us say to Him that, if He desires to make us His witnesses before other men, let Him first make us witnesses of the great things that His grace can effect in the lowliness of us, His servants.

THE ASCENSION OF OUR LORD (II)

"Lord, may this world pass, and may your Kingdom come!"

The feast that we shall try to celebrate together in today's Mass reveals to us our destiny and how the world will end, —by an Ascension.

What do most people do when they go to see a film or begin to read a book? They begin by the end. They go to see, or they find out, how it is going to finish. If they do not do this, they run the risk of being too anxious, of not having the courage to bear the vicissitudes, the suspense, the momentary setbacks of their heroes.

Why is it that you have none of this curiosity for the romance of your own life? How will it end? What is going to happen at the end? Does not that interest you just a little? And the history of the world, what will it achieve? How is all this going to finish? Don't you ask yourself this question quite often?

The Mass of today tells you, —by an Ascension.

One day we shall all find ourselves together again in heaven. All of you who are here, with all your neighbors, will be reunited, on the last day, just as you are now. (Only I hope that we shall be more numerous!) Your presence each Sunday, together at Mass, prefigures, prophesies, announces, and prepares for this great final reassembly about our Lord and for which you are training yourselves again today. In a few moments we shall all be

separated, our daily life brings dispersion, but that is only temporary, this separation will come to an end when, for the last time,
we mount to the altar of God in our final ascension.

Our Lord has gone up to heaven only that He might open the
doors for us, "to prepare a place for you," He has expressly told
us. And just as we all assist today at this feast of the Ascension,
just as the two angels in the Epistle which we just read have told
us, so we shall see Him come back again to take us with Him.

All that happens here below is provisional. Beware of judging
a work which is hardly begun. Too often we lose heart after the
first chapters, after the first pages of a novel. Some trouble comes
to us; an accident, a failure, some misfortune, and we abandon
our course, we close our eyes, hide our faces, and we say: "It is
not possible that God exists and at the same time permits this. It
is not possible to believe that God directs our lives, and then
turns them upside down like this." It is true that sometimes this is
terrible, but wait, be patient just a little, do not pass judgment
until you have seen the end. If the hero does not meet with some
danger, if, for a moment, his adversaries do not seem to be
triumphant, how is he to show his courage and make use of his
resources and his talents? Very well. You are the hero in your life
story, and, happily, you are often in danger, all is not easy for
you, you meet with failures. But nothing is concluded as yet.
Patience! Have you not been told often enough that, after the
Passion and Calvary, comes the Resurrection and the
Ascension?

Be sure of this: all sadness is only temporary. You are unhappy but it is only for a short time.

Why have I prayed and not been heard? Because God, who
inspired and encouraged your prayer, is waiting to give you much
more and much better than you would have dared to ask. Why
am I sick and infirm? Because you will soon be cured forever.
Why am I sorrowing over the death of those I love, why does life
separate me from those who alone made my life worth living?

195

Because you will soon be reunited and nothing more will ever deprive you of their presence.

And also, do not forget that joy, all union, insofar as it exists in this world only, is also transitory. You children know that you cannot promise yourselves that you will always have your parents with you. And you parents know that you cannot keep your little ones always with you. The same is true for husband and wife. And also for all who love each other. There is only one place where there can be no separation and that place is not here below. Let us try to keep our appointment!

And it is the same with your possessions. Are you rich? You will be so for only a short time! Yes indeed, it will pass. Either you will lose your money or you will give it away. In any case, you will not take it with you unless you have placed it in that famous bank of heaven which returns 100 per cent, but which has so few clients.

Your houses, your goods, your families, —ah! if we but understood that we ought to go to God with all the strength of the attachment that we bear towards them! He alone is able to keep them for us, to return them to us, and to reunite us!

All that is not offered to God is lost.

All that you retain for yourself alone, and by your own strength, shall slip out of your hands, often even before you have it in your grasp. One day your hands will open to let go of things, but today you can as yet open them in order to offer them to God.

All that you hold dear, all that you have that is precious, would you run the risk of not putting them under the care and protection of God?

When a little child is born to you, when you hold a tiny baby in your arms, do you keep that little one all to yourself? Do you believe yourself sufficient to protect that child's life and assure his future happiness? Not at all. You hasten to offer him to God, to consecrate and to prepare that soul for eternal life. You are not

196

satisfied with the frail and hazardous existence which you have transmitted to him. Your desire is that by baptism he should live the same life as God, and you want to be sure that you will never lose him but be with him throughout all eternity in heaven.

When a young boy and girl love each other they know well that their merely human love is too feeble a thing, too earthly and too profane to keep all its promises. So they come to offer themselves, to consecrate their love, and they receive from God the promise of eternal life, that they will not be separated even by death, that they will be spouses for all eternity.

And when you are about to lose someone whom you love, you hasten to call the priest and you have him anoint and mark him with the sign of God which is to be your means of recognizing one another. You have him communicate a last time as if to appoint for him a rendezvous where you will meet him again, united to Christ, each time that you receive communion. The first Christians went so far as to place a Host in the mouth of the dead so as to be the surer that he would rise again, and in the hope that this "viaticum" would enable them to recognize each other more quickly and more surely on the great day of the General Ascension.

We ourselves know well that, when we communicate, we receive the food of immortality. Because of our communion, something of Christ becomes living within us. Only those will live eternally, only those among you will survive, who have been marked, nourished, vivified with Christ by each of your communions. Only Christ is living eternally and only Christ has ascended to heaven. Only those among us will live and will ascend who have become living through Christ, those who have been offered to Him, those who have become His in their lives, in their affections, and in their possessions.

At the Mass today, as at every Mass, the priest takes what you offer Him, a little bread from your earth, your offering which represents an offering of yourself, —your work, your life—, and he makes it pass from this world to the world of God. He consecrates it and makes of it living bread, capable of giving life. He makes of it the beginning and the means of living an eternal life. At each Mass, a little of this world passes into the other world. At each Mass, a little of earth ascends to heaven. At each Mass, the Christians are invited to choose, to elevate themselves, to ascend, to detach themselves a little from the earth, to decide: Do they really want to pass on into the next world? Do they want to begin their passage now?

Undoubtedly, at such a proposition, many of you will grasp hold of your chairs in order to assure yourselves that no such thing is going to happen. But what are you going to hold on to when it comes time to die? Have you not by now seen enough of your dear ones pass on to the other world? Have you the courage to remain here alone? And remain where? "Where your treasure is, there also is your heart." To what are we attached? What is it that keeps us far from God? Are not those whom we have loved the most already with Him, and, thanks to Him, they are not separated from us?

The first Christians, after they had communicated, knelt down and said this prayer which has been found in a very old book: "Lord, now let this world pass away, and may your Kingdom come!"

They had taken part in the Mass, they had communicated so sincerely, they had so truly "passed" to the other side, they found themselves so close to God, and God seemed so good to them— think of it—communion was so good, that they longed not to have to go back to their daily life but to remain in this new world to which they had ascended, that they hoped and sighed after the great and final assemblage of all their friends close to God without being obliged ever again to separate.

At this Mass of the Ascension, on this feast (and we call the Ascension a feast!), many among you are going to communicate in a few moments. You are going to prefigure, to anticipate that day when the whole world will communicate. You are going to attempt to live this prayer which, when said with sincerity, will be granted: "Lord, now let this world pass away, and may your Kingdom come!"

SUNDAY AFTER THE ASCENSION

Witnesses of the Resurrection

"You shall be my witnesses."   (John 15:26–27)

"You shall be my witnesses," says Christ. "It is you who will give testimony of me."

Since the day of His Ascension, Christ has only one way in which it is possible for Him to appear to men, and that is through us. The only countenance which He can show to our contemporaries to call them to Himself and to convert them is ours, our parochial societies, our Christian families, our fraternal organizations.

There is, in this, our day, a very striking contrast. The elite are converted to the faith and the masses are falling away from it.

The explanation is simple, yet terrible. At the present time, one is able to discover the true teaching of the Church and become a convert by self-instruction, by study, and by reading books which deal with religion and discovering the proof of the Church's doctrines. Only those who have education and a certain amount of leisure can do this. The masses, the ordinary people, must content themselves with looking on, with seeing the upper classes, and it is quite certain that they will not be led to make the great sacrifices a conversion entails, for no other result than the privilege of resembling ourselves.

We read in the Acts that: "The Apostles rendered powerful testimony to the Resurrection of Christ."

How do you think that they did it? Did they ascend the pulpit and preach eloquently? Did they make faultless demonstrations? Doubtless, they did make use of these means, but, read the following line: "There was no one in need among them." There, surely, is a powerful witness to the Resurrection of Christ.

If these first Christians brought about such upheavals, so great a transformation in the structure of their Christian society that there was no one among them who lacked bread, who lacked friendship, who lacked welcome, consolation, and sympathy, then truly this was a most extraordinary state of affairs. They witnessed to the teaching of Christ. There was among them such love and such joy that it could be explained only by the fact that Christ had risen and was living again in their midst.

How does one become a witness to the Resurrection of Christ? How do you prove to those around you that Christ is truly risen? By documents? By philosophical proofs? Do you take those who question you to the nearest library and show them the documents relating to the sources of Christianity?

There is one proof that He is living and that is ourselves. That is that we, the Christian community, live with such love, with such understanding, with such joy, that everyone will want to join us and be unable to explain our conduct without admitting that Christ has come back and is living among us.

Christian joy, the joy of being brothers and loving one another as such, is a powerful testimony to the Resurrection of Christ. Christ has given us this order: "If you love me, you would rejoice . . . I will that my joy may be in you and that your joy may be perfect."

What have you done with His joy?

Christ teaches us that this is a great means of carrying on the apostolate. That is what should distinguish us from the world. "Yet in a little while you will no longer see me. But I will see you again and your hearts shall rejoice and your joy no man shall take from you."

200

It is a strange thing, but we are not in accord with that joy. The greater number of Christians are far more disposed to afflict themselves with Christ than to rejoice with Him.

Take Lent as an example. People understand Lent and take part in it. When we begin those forty days which we consecrate to penance, to compassion, and to mortification, Christianity, on the whole, is aroused.

But compare that fidelity with the inertia which, in general, follows Easter.

After Easter, we begin another forty days, the forty days of penance in Lent is followed by forty days—and even fifty days—(until Pentecost, because this is more important and more difficult), in an effort to arouse us to become joyous.

You have made the Way of the Cross? But have you made the Way of Joy? The Church invites us to stations of joy which ought to be as much frequented as the Stations of the Cross. Each recital of the apparitions of Christ, each Mass, each feast of paschal time ought to fill us with joy, and continue to do so indefinitely, so that we become conquered by the joy of Christ, partake of His Resurrection, and become filled with that extraordinary sentiment, Christian Joy.

Too often, after Easter, our spiritual life goes on a vacation, the Easter vacation. Christ is risen . . . He is now happy . . . He is safe . . . Pensioned off for services rendered.

And from then on we are no longer interested. We cannot do anything more for Him. Our life continues here below. As for Him, He is enjoying beatitude.

Now there is something hard and egoistic in consenting to be afflicted with a friend when he is in trouble and refusing to rejoice with him when his trouble ceases. We leave him just at the moment when we could give him the satisfaction of sharing his joy with us. Just as though we were professional sufferers, or specialists for funerals. (And certain people treat us as though they considered us to be this.) We are quite willing to be on

201

hand when things go wrong, but as soon as it is time to rejoice
we are no longer interested, no longer concerned.

The explanation of this attitude is not a pretty one. In sadness,
we seek ourselves and we find ourselves. Our naturally pessimistic temperament is in accord with tragic events. We each have
good reasons of our own to be sad on our own behalf which
permit us to feel pity for ourselves while seeming to be pitying
another. We each have a little reserve of personal tears to shed
on any pretext.

But to take part in the joy of another, to rejoice in the
happiness of another, that requires a disinterestedness, a kindness
of heart, and a detachment from self which, as a general thing, is
beyond us.

After Lent comes the much greater mortification, the much
greater renunciation, that which prepares for all the others and
which will prove how sincere they are, —the sacrifice of being
happy. Not the sacrifice of being unhappy! Give God the joy of
seeing us happy because of Him. Say to Him: "You have done
enough for us, you have loved us enough and suffered for us
enough. Let me give you this recompense, —that of seeing me
happy. To live so much with Him, to be so closely bound to Him,
that when we look into ourselves we shall find that what is most
active in our lives is His Joy.

We cling to our sadness with tenacity, as though it gives us the
right to withdraw, to become hardened, to snuff out the joy of
others. A Father of the Church has said that there is only one
way to cure oneself of sadness and that is not to love it.

The true love, the true faith, the true disinterestedness and
detachment to which Lent ought to lead us is that we consent to
be happy.

Who among us prays before an image of the Risen Christ?
Every one of us has in our houses a crucifix. For us, Christ means
a crucifix. Has anyone thought of brightening his home with a
representation of the Resurrection of Christ? If you know only
the Cross, you have not yet come to Easter, the Pasch, you have

not yet made the passage from death to life. Your religion does not keep on going to its term. It is a religion of suffering, of turning in upon self, of sadness. It is not the religion of Christ which is the religion of the Resurrection, of openness to God and to others, a religion of joy.

Without doubt, the joy of the Christian is not an easy state of contentment, a naïve satisfaction with oneself and with others. It is an overcoming of sadness. Christian joy is expressed in all the Beatitudes. "Happy the poor, the Kingdom of God is theirs! Happy those who mourn! Happy those who hunger and thirst for justice! Happy the persecuted!"

But not at all! You keep only the little half—"you ought to be happy."

But make no mistake. If you are happy because all goes well with you, then you are not calling attention to God, you do not testify to anything, you are not announcing anything out of the ordinary. And if you are an unhappy poor person, unhappy in your unhappiness, you do not teach me anything new. I understand you, but you do not astonish me. We are all like that.

But if you are a happy poor person, a happy unhappy person, if you are happy in being misunderstood and persecuted, then surely that is because you have come in contact with One who has given you the grace to bear your misfortune, with One who is so good, so loving, so affectionate that He enables you to be joyous in the midst of persecution.

Then, indeed, you render true testimony to God. Then you perform an extraordinary deed, —you are filled with His Joy.

"But," you will say, "it is impossible for me to be happy! It is easy for you to speak. I am married, I have a wife, or I have a husband, I have children, or I have parents. I have work that is impossible, my surroundings are impossible, and my character is impossible."

Really, if you do not ask of God what is impossible, you do not give Him an opportunity to show that He is God.

If you ask of Him only what is possible, you are asking of Him what you can and ought to do for yourself. God is pleased to do that which is beyond our power. God manifests Himself in realizing the impossible, in showing to all the world that He is capable of doing what to us is impossible.

In reality, every part of ourselves that we have closed to happiness is closed to God. All those zones of our being to which we have refused to let joy, hope, confidence, friendship enter, are zones from which we have excluded God. God has exactly the same place in our lives that we give to happiness and joy. They are the measure of our belief in God.

Too many Christians follow the religion of the Cross. They witness to the absence of God. They mount guard beside the empty tomb. They pay homage to themselves for not having, like other men, filled their lives with money, distractions, and pleasures. There they are, —severe, somber, bitter, —witnesses to the absence of their God.

But our religion is not the religion of absence. It is the religion of the Presence of God. No one is a Christian until he can say that he has met God, that his belief in Him is great enough so that, no matter what may happen, he is sure, absolutely confident in His love.

The Apostles never regretted the absence of Jesus in the flesh. They knew Him better now, they understood Him better since He was present among them in His Spirit. They were filled, they were overflowing with the Spirit, and it became something contagious. They were constantly receiving inspirations from His Spirit of Love and they gave proof of it to everyone by this miracle: "There was no one in want among them."

Would anyone who came into our Christian assemblies, or who saw us as we enter and leave the church, feel that shock of surprise which is caused by a person who believes in the Resurrection of Christ and bears witness to it? Would he notice our friendliness, our welcome, our smiles, our attention to one another, a certain courtesy and regard which can be understood only by the fact that the Risen Christ is the source of our union with one another?

This present world will never be converted to God if it does not meet with a true Church. Our world will never be brought to believe by reasoning, by proofs, or by demonstrations. The modern world is like St. Thomas, the Apostle, it wants to see, to touch, it wants to verify words by deeds, principles by effects. The modern world is too realistic, it has seen too much of deception, too much of failure, it is too distrustful. Faith must prove itself by its works and Christianity by this miracle—does it make us capable of loving one another?

The world is seeking a real Church. It is looking for open hands and open hearts, a welcome that is affectionate, indulgent, generous, and cordial. Then, like St. Thomas, it, too, will fall on its knees and confess the resurrection of Christ, because it will have encountered Christians in whom the Love and Joy of Christ will be fully manifested.

PENTECOST SUNDAY (I)

"The Spirit of the Lord fills the world."

Today no one has the right to be anything but optimistic. Today no one has the right to hesitate in being joyous. Today no one is a Christian who does not cry out, who does not weep, who does not exult for joy. How can anyone believe that God is given to us, that God is communicated to us, that we have God in our hearts, in our hands, on our lips, and not be enthusiastic? Can God come so close to us and not stir us deeply?

He who speaks of God and does not do so passionately, speaks unworthily. Today, God charges each one of us to speak of Him, to declare Him, to announce Him. We are the ones whom He sends forth today, as He sent the Apostles from the Cenacle, where He had them locked up, and whom He now pushes out the door, into the street, to astound the world by this great, this unbelievable good news, that we are no longer orphans. He has returned, He is within us. We have been invaded by a Spirit of strength and wisdom, by a Spirit of joy and of faith. He has manifested Himself to us. After a little while, He has come back to see us, and our heart is filled with joy. Oh, how our heart rejoices, and our joy no one shall take from us!

We have but to stop for a moment, but to consider a moment, and a Spirit of adoption gives testimony to our spirit that we are the children of God, a Spirit of adoption cries out: "Father, Father, I love you! Father, I believe in you! Father, I have placed all my hope in you!" And the Father Himself loves us and bends over us to tell us: "And you, you are my beloved son, my beloved daughter, in whom I am well pleased."

Today the ruling and vivifying Spirit takes possession of the universe and fills it prodigally with His gifts. "In those days I will pour out my Spirit on all flesh; your sons and your daughters shall prophesy, your old men shall dream dreams and your young men shall see visions."

This is what faith tells us, that the Spirit is the one reality that counts. The rest are but shadow and illusion and we shall have the evidence of it one day. We shall know what the gift of God was and that the Spirit has conducted all things. Ah, let us open our souls, let us learn to know and to love this Creator Spirit who moved above the waters. The earth was void and empty when the Spirit of God created it and, for the first time, renewed the face of the earth. He it was who raised up thousands of representations, images, and resemblances of God. God was unknown, invisible, an obscure light, whom no one had ever seen. It is the Spirit who has manifested God in the created world, who has made God joyously, warmly visible in creating this world all about us so full of forms and figures, of beings with intelligence, instinct, laws,

—these things, these animals, and these plants all formed and filled with His spirit. It is He who by a breath over clay brought forth a man, made to the image and likeness of God and who has peopled this earth with the dear presence and the lovely faces of our friends.

It is He who has spoken by the prophets, those poor men, drawn from the midst of men, with unclean lips and stuttering tongues, timid hearts ready to give way to fear, pessimists, stubbornly seeking to hide from the mission to which God was sending them. With His burning coal, He touched their lips and they burned. Let but His inspiration touch them and they could no longer keep from speaking, no longer hold back the words, they could no longer keep silence regarding the Name they had sworn never to utter. *Qui locutus est per prophetas!* Who spoke by the prophets!

And the most beautiful, the greatest work of the Spirit is the Incarnation. No longer is He dealing with a rude man who resists Him and who must be constrained to obey. The lightest, gentlest ray of divine grace touched with respect a Virgin of fifteen years. Here were the placid waters which awakened and moved, docile to the least breath of the Wind. Here was a heart, the most delicate, the purest, the most sensitive of all hearts listening with fidelity to the Spirit. And once she had understood the message, without hesitation or trouble, the response came from the depths of her being, the response was pronounced in such a way that it showed to what depth God dwelt within her and possessed her whole being. She has said yes, she has consented and conceived the Word. She bore Him, the Word of God! No prophet has ever spoken as she has. How well she has spoken in her silence, how well has she announced Him, how well has she revealed to the world the message with which God charged her!

Just as we ought to be, ought to believe, and ought to live, so with her. She was inhabited, peopled, nourished, filled with God.

207

She knew, she believed, and she never denied this invasion of God into His creature, nor the indwelling of the Spirit of the Father and the Son who come to make their habitation with those who love them. She was far more the Spouse of the Holy Spirit than she was the Mother of Jesus, and her carnal maternity, her parentage of flesh and blood would have been useless to her if she had not unceasingly received, kept, and meditated in her heart the inspirations of the Holy Spirit. Beginning with her, the signal was given, slowly the almighty force of the Spirit supplied the impulse, started movements, supplied inspirations. Elizabeth felt the infant leap in her womb, and she uttered her inspired cry: "Blessed are you who believed." Zachary, the incredulous, prophesied; Simeon is led to the Temple by the Spirit, and for the first time a man no longer fears to die, because he believes in another light and has held in his arms another life.

The Jesus Himself, filled with the Spirit at His baptism, begins that dizzy course along which He was urged by the great breath, the great audacity of the Spirit. The Spirit shines out in all the actions of Jesus, in all His words and deeds. At last, there is a man filled with God, an enthusiast of God, a Son of God. At last, a man speaks the truth, searches the heart and reins, penetrates into consciences and reveals the truth. At last, a man does good, repairs evil, cures, consoles, strengthens. At last, a man loves the Father, is solicitous for His glory, honors Him "so that the world may know that I love my Father and that I obey the command that He has given me."

And He had so much faith and so much confidence in the Spirit that, wishing to found the vastest and the most durable Kingdom in all the world, and knowing Himself to be alone, without reliable friends, knowing that, at His departure, humanly speaking, all would be lost, He chose to begin by having Himself killed, such was His confidence, such was His faith in what the Spirit could, and would, do.

This is why Jesus has been glorified, —Resurrection, Ascension, Pentecost. The Spirit is poured out, the water has gushed out, floods of grace flow over the world. The Church is born and spreads with the rapidity of lightning. What thunder, what great wind unchains the voice of the Spirit. Thousands upon thousands of men, docile hereafter to His inspirations, instruments of His impetuous activity, preach the truth, strengthen the humble, enrich the poor, cure, lift up, and save. No longer do they speak in parables, it is the flaming truth that they cast into the hearts of men and which is a greater miracle than to cure the blind or lift up the paralytic. Souls are brought back to life, cleansed, animated, rejuvenated. The eyes of the soul are opened to a better light. Everything becomes possible at this time, and each is invited to throw off the mountains of impurity, of feebleness, and of incredulity which weigh him down and to walk upon the waters.

It is a joy to think that this all-powerful Spirit is at work everywhere in the entire world. Believers and unbelievers, faithful and unfaithful, no one escapes from His consolations and His graces. Everywhere, in every heart, He works, He stimulates, He arouses, He inspires. There is not a movement of true love, of pure tenderness, of goodness, of gentleness, of true strength which does not point out His action. It is His presence which gives us fecundity, freshness, suavity, interior humility, for all this flows from His grace. The Church teaches us that we do not perform a single act of true faith, of true hope, or of true love or repentance without being inspired to do so by Him. If we set out to pray, ah, let us rejoice! He it is who has suggested it. It is a sign that we are already heard even before we begin to pray, since it is He who has attracted us and won our consent to accept a gift which God has wished to give us from all eternity. We, too, are the dwelling place of the Spirit and ever receiving stimulation from Him. Ah! If only we could learn to consult Him living within us, to observe His activity in others and within our own souls. Then we would truly be what our Lord desires us to be,

—His witnesses. As He has borne witness to the Father, so shall we bear witness to His Spirit, we shall proclaim His works.

Yes, we have seen Him at work in others. In that child who was confirmed but yesterday, and who knows that he will become a priest by a certitude which goes beyond all human knowledge; in that young man of twenty who has accepted death; in that mother at the bedside of her dying infant, who accepts this death and thanks God for having allowed her to have him for just a few hours; in that young woman whose heart shrinks within her whenever she comes upon a woman with a baby, or when she chances to see a marriage in the church, but who is giving herself to God without a second's hesitation; and in that poor sinner who crouches, vanquished, upon the bench within the confessional and whom the fiery Spirit leaves no repose until he has avowed his faults, gasping in a struggle in which he defends himself so poorly against this great grace.

Ah yes, the Spirit works, He never ceases to act in this world. But He is also at work in us, mediocre and inattentive though we are. He travels by obscure paths, He undermines resistances, overturns obstacles, fills up the depressions, overthrows all the fences that we have thought we could erect to oppose Him, and even in our own humble little life, what great things may He not do when He takes possession of us?

PENTECOST SUNDAY (II)

The Spirit of God enables us to savor and to comprehend the things of God.

It is always Pentecost. We must be terribly distracted if we do not notice it. We readily express our longing for the early days of the Church which we think so wonderful. But, for example, the Council brought to Rome 3,000 bishops of all races, colors, peoples, states, languages, and latitudes. Never has there been in the history of the world, nor that of the Church, a like Pentecost.

You all have the chance of being witnesses of this, and yet, it is very probable that you will be entirely unconscious of what is going on around you.

In reality, the history of the world is nothing more than the development of the first Pentecost, and it will end when all peoples, gathered together in one faith, will all sing together the marvels that God has wrought among them.

In our own lives also, there was a Pentecost. At the time of our confirmation, each of us received the Holy Spirit, and since then we have not said a single prayer which was not inspired by Him, we have not received a single communion without Him urging us to do so, we have not made a single confession without Him suggesting that we repent and amend our lives, and at times, what difficulties and delays there were before we finally knelt in the confessional!

How is it that we are so blind? How is it that so many of us practically ignore the Holy Spirit, never pray to Him, and are astonished when someone tells us that it is He who has inspired us and conducted us in all that was worth while in our life as Christians?

For we must remember the beautiful words of our Lord, His beautiful promises: "I will not leave you orphans. It is good for you that I go. I will come back to you. The world will not see me any longer but you shall see me. I will manifest myself to you. You shall rejoice and no man will take your joy from you!" These words, these promises sound in our ears more like condemnations and reproaches.

Jesus promises us a Consoler, a Guide, a Support, who will be to us as He was to His disciples who could always have recourse to Him whenever they wanted to. They could consult Him. They could question Him. And Jesus tells us that we have at our

211

disposal a like presence, a like favor. And we regard ourselves as orphans, alone, blind, abandoned!

Is not this that famous sin against the Holy Spirit which will not be pardoned? Those whom neither the action, nor the presence, of the Holy Spirit has ever touched, moved, transformed, —there will be no salvation for them. Heaven has nothing more to give them.

Let us try to convince ourselves. If the Holy Spirit in us is so little noticed, if He scarcely filters into our being instead of flowing like a stream, the fault can be but our own, never God's.

God is not sparing in His gifts. "He does not give the Spirit grudgingly," says St. John. Has He not given abundant proof of this in His Passion, wherein He spared nothing to achieve our salvation?

God will never change. God could not be better, in our regard, than He is. From all eternity you have been before this God who has revealed Himself and communicated Himself to us. There is, then, but one sole chance of salvation for all of us, —to change, to profit by the time that is left to us, to use what is left of our life to modify an attitude which makes of us reprobates, those "unmindful of God" for all eternity, to learn to taste, as soon as possible, that "the Lord is sweet," to pray to the Holy Spirit to give us "the taste for the things of God," to awaken us, to accustom us to that divine tenderness which is going to be our happiness throughout all eternity and to which we are so utterly insensible during our period of earthly apprenticeship which will soon come to an end.

The great obstacle to all this is the devil.

Yes, the history of the world, and above all your own history, that of your life, is a struggle between the Holy Spirit and Satan.

Two great forces are at work in the world and in you, too, the Spirit of God and the spirit of evil.

212

The Spirit of God enables us to understand and to relish the things of God, the words of God. Under His influence, they "speak" to us, they take possession of us, they lift us up and even send us out with joy to bear their message to others.

Satan smothers them, persuades us that there is nothing to understand, nothing to seek, nothing to learn, and that we are Christians solely for our own benefit.

In this way he makes 80 per cent of all Christians inert, useless, half-hearted. Because they think that they have found God, they no longer search for Him (and this is the indication that they ignore Him). Because they believe that they know their religion, they make no effort to learn anything more. Because they believe that they believe, they no longer believe at all and do not realize it. They never pray,—they "practice"!

Is there a more evident proof of the existence of Satan than that indescribable numbness that has taken possession of the very ones who fill our churches on Sundays?

Let us look into our own lives. We all believe in God but we do not cling to Him. We believe that He is the best and most beneficent of beings, we believe that He will be our happiness throughout eternity, and, nevertheless, we have not the least desire to consecrate to Him even one quarter of an hour of our time.

Do you want to catch Satan in the act? Resolve to go and pray for an hour in the Church. He will begin to howl.

It is the Holy Spirit who invites you, who urges you, who inspires you to come and place yourself at the disposition of God so that God may, at long last, be able, just for once, to do in you and for you what He would like to do always—strengthen you, enlighten you, pacify you, gladden you, —and which you never give Him time to accomplish.

However, the Holy Spirit never makes a proposition but there is a counter-proposition on the part of Satan.

You have hardly thought of going to church to pray when

213

your mind becomes filled with a thousand good, solid, excellent reasons why you should not give time to prayer, even virtuous reasons why you had better put it off until later and, just now, do something else.

If you set out, an innumerable multitude of things which are urgent and require attention will come to your mind. You will find yourself becoming unusually obliging and ready to be of service, forgotten promises will suddenly be remembered, menial tasks that have always been shunned will suddenly become welcome if they but furnish a pretext for not going to pray.

At the door of the church, just by chance, of course, you will meet someone. You will be affable and sociable and will stay there a long time. You will find a thousand things to say and all very interesting in order to delay your entry into the church. Every Sunday, when I come to the church, I find the steps crowded. For a second or two, I have the impression that there will be many people at Mass. I enter and find the interior of the church completely empty. Just a little breathing space before we enter. God has plenty of time!

But let us continue with our experience. You will scarcely be one minute in your pew before you will feel the greatest desire to leave it. We are always pressed for time when we come to church.

But suppose we persevere in spite of all this and we try to pray. But if we have been able to stop our car, Satan will keep the engine going. He excites our memory and our imagination, he arouses in us so much interior twittering and chattering that it seems as if we are surrounded by birds. He unfolds before our eyes the past and the future. He jumps around like . . . like a devil in a holy water pot. He cries as loudly as possible in order to drown the voice of God.

For he knows that when we pray, God becomes a danger to him. God works in us, and if ever it happens that we stay, that we

214

persevere in our prayer, and listen to Him, there will take place in our souls that calm that Jesus brought about after the storm upon the sea. We will begin to understand what He can do in us when we trust in Him. We shall learn anew that we have a Father, that we are loved, that He dwells within us and animates us, that we can place our confidence in Him and that we are even capable of communicating this to others, —and we shall rise from our knees transformed.

What the devil hangs between God and ourselves is not an iron curtain—he has not that much power—but only a curtain of nerves. He is constantly weaving around us a veil of impulsiveness, of nervousness, of agitation, of worry, of tension, which is easily torn down but to which we have become so accustomed that it seems like an integral part of ourselves. At last, we reach the stage where we can no longer live without noise, without music, without agitation, without taking a drink, —all in order carefully to keep between God and ourselves this obstacle which we regard as a liberation.

Is not that a masterpiece of Satan?

God does not cry out loudly. He speaks softly but each of His words is active and productive. Satan howls like a loudspeaker. He deafens, and when he stops for a second, one feels empty and sick.

It is the calm waters that are docile to the least breath of wind. If our soul were calm, if we had formed the habit of prayer, if we had learned to make the sacrifice of our first impressions, if interior mortification controlled the movements of our heart, our tongue, our activity, we would continually feel the breath of the Holy Spirit passing over us.

For if the unbelievable activity of Satan in us and around us is a real prodigy—and should convert us—, the work of the Holy Spirit is a much greater marvel.

Do you know that, at the Council of Trent, the Church defined

215

that, without the inspiration and the help of the Holy Spirit, no one can truly pray, make a sincere confession, or a true act of charity? It is He who has inspired you to come to Mass to-day—do not think that you have come here by yourselves—and certainly He had to use all His power, all His attraction, to succeed in getting you here.

If, during the course of this Mass, there comes to your heart a prayer, rejoice, exult, recognize that it is the Holy Spirit working in you, that He is striving to establish His dominion over you, and if you continue to listen to Him you will soon learn what He wishes to say to you, to give you, and how He has already heard your prayer.

And if, by some extraordinary movement of grace, He should remind you that it would be well for you to go to confession, remember that it is the Holy Spirit Himself who is calling you. And if, as you usually do, you refuse Him, it is the Holy Spirit who will let you know that He is pained by your resistance. (Do not sadden the Spirit!) Is it not true that every time you have refused some act of loyalty, generosity, pardon which He has suggested to you, He has reproached you for it and filled your heart with bitter remorse?

And the most extraordinary thing of all is that, in spite of the zeal and ingeniousness of Satan, in spite of our heaviness, our inertia, our resistance, the Holy Spirit has made Christians of us, that we have been baptized, confirmed, and receive the Eucharist.

If we are here this Pentecost Sunday, that is a miracle of the Holy Spirit. And if it should happen that we thank Him, recognizing this as His gift, and if during this Mass we allow some true prayer to be born in our hearts, our poor little Sunday assembly will not be very different from the first Church on Pentecost where they marvelled at the great things which God had accomplished in the poverty of His servants.

216

FEAST OF THE HOLY TRINITY

"For from Him and through Him and to Him are all things." (Romans 11:33–36)

If someone were to ask you what you thought was the principal dogma of the Christian religion, the most vital and the most important truth of the Catholic faith, what would you answer?

And if I tell you, in advance, that it is the dogma of the Holy Trinity whose feast we are celebrating today, you will have the impression that here is a truth that is weighty and hard to understand, something we are all ready to acknowledge if it be imposed by faith, but still, something that is far from having any direct influence upon our lives. And yet, in revealing to us the mystery of the Holy Trinity, God has shown us that He lives a life that is the nearest and the most like to our own. In this mystery He shows us that He lives a family life, a life in which He is entirely given, in which He communicates Himself in His entirety to another, in whom He takes delight. God has revealed that His life is one of giving and loving, the joy of loving and of being loved.

God is a Father, and when we say that we think: "Yes, God is a little like my own father." This is to put things backwards. Our earthly father is the one who is a little like a Father, he is the one who has some resemblance to the One who created him and by whom he has been charged to manifest, in our regard, the paternal goodness which is proper to the One who is truly Father.

How true that is! Our fathers are but images and reflections of Him from whom all paternity on earth and in heaven takes its name. They are father in part, but they are also many other

217

things. They are men of affairs, men of their profession, of their marriage, of their pleasures and their occupations, and they also belong to themselves. Only the Father is only a father. To His Son, He gives Himself completely and perfectly. "All that is yours is mine," Jesus says, "and all that is mine is yours. His life is entirely one of giving and His one aim is to diffuse Himself. Yes, it is very beautiful to be a father here below, to give oneself with generosity to another, to put an end to egoism because one no longer seeks oneself, but if you could only know Him who is completely Father, in whom there is not a particle of self-seeking of any kind, who is entirely given to another, whose whole pleasure is in another, to whom He communicates Himself perfectly."

And that is why He has a perfect Son, because He has given Him all. His Son has received everything from Him and He contemplates Himself perfectly in that Son. And this is what explains the predilection of the Father for large families. In them He meets with a generosity in paternity which recalls the divine gift, the perfect gift. This is the way that God is a Father, and if we would make this fact more a part of our lives, what security, what complete abandonment we would enjoy! To remember that the Father is the source of all good, an unfailing source, immortal, infinite, of all that exists in this world, and that these things are a signal proof and testimony to the fatherly goodness of God. To remember that all comes to us from Him and that all is well in spite of terrifying appearances because all this comes from Him. To remember in the midst of the noise, the wind, the agitation that ever surrounds us, the cries of fear that we hear about us and in which we are tempted to join, that all goes well because it is the Father who is in control and we are in His paternal care.

God is Son. The Father, in loving Himself, in diffusing Himself, forms a pure image of Himself. God of God, Light of Light, true God of true God, equal to His Father, yet in a dependence of exquisite modesty and respect which constitutes the charm of the Son. It is He who manifests the Father, who recounts, who never ceases to publish the glory of the One who has given Him everything, He has come into the world to show us what a Father deserves that His Son should do for Him. "In order that the world may know that I love the Father and that I obey the commands which He has given to me . . ."

God is Spirit. And in order that we may comprehend this He makes us have recourse to this same truth, that the realities of our human existence are images and figures of the divine reality. Our Lord saw the families here on earth, all the people who love each other, filial love, paternal love, the love of friends for each other. He said: "That is beautiful. They love, but they do not love enough. Father, that they may be one as you in me and I in them, that they may be one like us." And He thus revealed that Spirit of union, the family spirit in the Divine Family, where the gift of the Father to the Son and the gift of the Son to the Father is such a reality that it is a Divine Person, the Spirit of Love, the Gift. So, in our earthly families, parents and children are united in one same family spirit by a reciprocity of affection, by an exchange of love which descends from the parents to the children in tenderness and goodness, and goes back unceasingly from the children to the parents in gratitude, confidence, respect, and abandonment. The more this gift is mutual, the more it is vital, the more it is sincere, the more the family spirit is enlivened, the more the family is happy. The great drama, the great tragedy in each family, is anything whatever that creates division, that causes separation in their mutual gift, their reciprocal affection. Happy those families in which one feels something sacred and mysterious between its members and where one cannot but feel that here is an image and a resemblance to another Family in which Three Persons are perfectly one, perfectly transparent to each other, so well do they know and love each other.

And this is the underlying motive for performing all our

219

actions and receiving all our sacraments in the name of the Holy Trinity, that is to say, in the name of the Spirit of Love and of union who must inspire us in order that we may do here below something worth while and in order that, no matter where we may be working, we may edify a nation, a society, a group, a class, a family, so that therein may be manifested and publicized the infinite mercy which the Trinity has shown to us in enabling us to imitate them and make them live among us by our loving one another.

FEAST OF CORPUS CHRISTI

"My flesh is meat indeed, and my blood is drink indeed." (John 6:56–59)

We Christians must seem to others like very strange creatures. They hear that we are so strict, so rigorous, enemies of the flesh, eager to mortify the body. And here we are, celebrating the feast day of a Body. We are filled with joy, we sing with rapture of a Body. We are ravished, elated with tenderness for the dear Body of Jesus Christ. We adore it, we incense it, we shall carry this Body in triumphant procession today as the dearest thing in all the world, all our consolation and our salvation.

Nevertheless, we know well, quite well, much better than others, because of our own experience, and theirs, too, how the body can torment, soil, trouble, and degrade. We all know—don't we?—what suspicious kind of thoughts it arouses, what regrettable desires, what lamentable curiosities, what stupid desires, desires that are unyielding, shameful, selfish. We also know to what depths the lazy man, the empty heart, the idle hands can fall, —the sorrows our bodies can cause us. "O Lord," cries one sorely tried soul, "give me the power to look upon my body and into my heart without disgust!"

Doubtless, it is because of this, this deep despair, this overwhelming shame, that God, the most loving, the tenderest, the most audacious of beings, has willed, in becoming incarnate, to give to us, to entrust to us, and to satisfy us forever by a Body. He has willed that His Body should be a great feast, a banquet, an occasion of pure joy and chaste delight, the loveliest and the most purifying of feasts. Up to the time of Christ, religion was something hard, something complicated, something abstract. What good to us is a religion of the brain, this God before whom we must work out some ideas before we can think of Him, whom we must invent before we can believe in Him, and whom we must study before we can know? God wishes religion to be simple. He has made a religion for simple people. He has placed religion on our level, within the reach of our hands, within the reach of our lips. This is the Incarnation.

The revelation of God, the manifestation of God, the new and eternal covenant consists in that which our eyes have seen, our ears have heard, and our hands have touched, Himself, the Word of Life.

And the Incarnation is going on all the time. It continues in the sacraments. The sacraments, they are the Body, they are the flesh, they are the voice of Jesus, extended, perpetuated on through the ages down to us. The Incarnation, this is God who enters into us through all our senses. It is God whom one eats and drinks. It is God who comes into our being by the easiest way, the most ordinary way, the way most frequented, most in proportion to our capacities and to our tastes. These people who are so simple, so poor, God has willed to enrich them with a joyous prodigality. He Himself has wished to load with gifts those to whom no one else has ever given anything. What joy to be able, like Simeon, to hold in one's hands that which is the best in all the world. God is there, the most active, the most operative, the most loving of beings. He has become the nearest, the most accessible, the most really present. God has become someone whom we can touch, someone we can cling to, to whom the Curé of Ars said: "Ah! If I were to know that I should be damned,

221

separated from you for all eternity, I would never release
you!"

God has become someone whom we can love and kiss, beside
whom we can sit, upon whom we can lean and find comfort in
the security of love, to whom we can open our mouth and our
heart. Here is the whole work of our sanctification—to eat and
to drink divine food. Here is our God before us, to whom you can
ceaselessly lift your eyes and lower them—lift them in order to
see Him better, lower them in order to know Him better—turn
away your eyes in order to experience the joyous surprise of
seeing Him still there, close them again in order to think over the
reasons for our happiness and to remind ourselves that He is
there. That which the woman in the Gospel was able to do for
just a second in the midst of the crowd: "If I but touch the fringe
of His mantle, I shall be cured!" —to our joy, confidence, and
hope, we can do at all times. We have the promise, the certitude,
of being able to do it again and again and again, and always.
What would not have been her joy, poor thing, if, instead of a
mere attempt, a taking a chance at touching Him, she had been
allowed, as we are, to have Jesus before her, or seated at her side,
for an hour, two hours, three hours—as long as she wished!

We all have this opportunity. It should be our joy, our exalta-
tion, our hope. As many Masses as we are able to hear: "This is
my Body," to see it, to touch it; so many feasts, so many prayers,
so many communions, so many confessions. What use are they?
Innumerable churches and chapels! Enter! Sit down! Fall on
your knees! Kiss the pavement, touch the communion rail, the
cloth, or only your pew; —that is He, that is His garment, that is
the covering of His Body, His dress. What a joy to think: "He is
there, my pilgrimage is at an end. I have nothing more to do. He
is there for eternity."

Come and see, come and touch, come and eat, come and sit
down before God. Come, all who are tormented, starving, brutal,
and violent because of your cravings which urge you on to rage
and disgust. Come and gratify your desires with a Body. It is

222

offered to you, delivered over to you. Eat, satisfy yourselves with it, dare to look upon it, dare to touch it, dare to take hold of this Body, and see how your own body grows peaceful, is purified, is softened, becomes light, delicate, tender, and pure.

Come, all you who live in isolation, you who are sick and in solitude, sad, pessimistic, without friends, without family, without love. Come and be comforted by a heart and a soul, that of Christ, and your own soul will again know indulgence, grace, goodness, patience, and tender affection.

Come and be filled with graces, those of you who have no faith, come and be nourished by the faith of Another, and, with surprise, you will find faith being born within you, a faith that does not come from yourself. Come, you who no longer have hope, come, eat, receive the hope of Another, and you will be astonished to find hope awaken within you. Come, you who are without charity, and you, too, will ask how it is that your heart is burning within you when He nourishes you.

For the Body which you eat is supernatural flesh, flesh that has been mortified, purified, glorified. It is risen and glorious, penetrated with light, filled with joy, filled with life. When you eat this Body, you eat the death and the life of Jesus. In you the mysteries of His Passion and His Cross are renewed. While you eat this Body, there dies in you all that should die, and all that ought to live is revived. You return bathed in God, penetrated with His grace, no longer alone. Even your solitude is no longer a solitude. It is shared with God. The Real Presence will be your real occupation. Every port of entry guarded, every weak spot under observation, a gentle, filial sentiment will spring up and will constantly remind you that you belong to God and that God belongs to you. One will be there who will fill every need of your being. You may read, work, speak with your friends, but, even in the midst of entertainment, a moment of recollection is all that will be needed, like the furtive clasp of a hand, in the midst of a crowd, a brief glance of love, unseen by those around, a secret sign and a miraculous security.

You will never be the same again. Another will be living in you. He will open your heart for Himself, for yourself, for others. What a marvel! What a surprise! You will find again in Him all those others whom you had thought that you had abandoned, all those whom you were loving so wrongly before, to whom you did so much that was evil, for whom you were so powerless to do the good that you would have liked to do, —your parents, your children, your husband or your wife, all those whom you love, and even the dead from whom you thought that you were separated. Here is where you will meet them all in a marvellous communion, and grace, like a river, will flow from you to them and from them back again to you.

As the bread which is on the altar is made from flour, which is itself made from grains of wheat that grew on many hillsides, and as the wine upon the altar is made from grapes that grew in various places and are now united in this one wine, so all those who communicate are gathered together in one single Body, the Body of the living Christ, the great Body of the children of God. And when you have become this Body, when you will have taken your place and live your life in the Body, then you will understand in your turn that this Body is to be offered again—given, delivered—to others, that you are this Body of which others are in need in order to be purified, consoled, and converted. You, too, will give to them this Body, and there will be born within you that love and generosity which He, first of all, has given to you by means of His Body.

FEAST OF THE MOST PRECIOUS BLOOD

"If we receive the testimony of men, the testimony of God is greater." (1 John 5:9)

Sometimes, in the streets, a crowd gathers. People run to see what it is all about. They elbow their way in, they stretch their necks.

There has been an accident. A circle has been formed of men who stand there, immovable, fascinated, curious, and horrified. On the ground lies someone whose blood is flowing from a wound. Just a moment ago, that person was attracting no attention, someone of no importance, —an old man, a woman, or, maybe, a child, —but the most insignificant of persons becomes something solemn, a sign, a symbol, a warning, simply because his blood is flowing. Nothing testifies like blood. Nothing arrests us, draws from us pity, fear, emotion, or anxiety as the testimony of blood. Life becomes suddenly a visible thing, we see it flow, we see it diminish and we see its loss. Those wounded on the stretchers, covered with thick bandages, muddy, depressed, mute, completely absorbed by one single thing, —that part of their body from which flows, or spurts, the blood, their poor blood, their life.

And those dead whom we may find, lying on the ground, stiff, and that large stain around them like the red paten upon which they offered their bodies, a body now emptied, the empty envelope of all that they have offered.

What mystery there is, then, in blood that it should affect us so, that it should have such meaning. No one knows until he sees it flowing, until there flows before his eyes blood that he loves, either his own or another's. Then one is well aware that it is life which is flowing, which is escaping with the blood. Who gives his blood, gives his life. He who has given his life has given all, and there is no greater love than this.

And to think that there are people who have done this for us. There are those, it is hard to imagine such a thing, who have done this foolish thing, this magnificent thing, for us. They have poured out their blood, they have given up their lives for us. There are men who have thought of us, proudly, affectionately, joyously perhaps. They gave all and they were sure that they were right. They were so sure, with a certitude that is incomprehensible and obscure, but total and triumphant, that their sacrifice would be useful to us, that their blood would flow upon us, that their lives would animate ours. None of those who died thus had the least doubt. And shall we, when we think of them, we whom by our lives, our laxity, our forgetfulness lie to them, shall we dare to say that they were wrong? Each of us, in his family, among his friends or those about him, has known some hero of the war, and now it takes an effort to recall a name, a face, to such an extent have we forgotten. We are not like that young Cardinal of fifteen years whom history tells was splashed across the face with the blood of one of the Medicis who was murdered at his side during a Renaissance banquet. For the rest of his life that Cardinal's face remained pale. The blood of so many of our dead has been splashed upon us during our youth and who is there among us who is marked by it for life?

How well all this makes us understand devotion to the dead, and the religion of redemptive Blood! How well we begin to understand that religion, in which we eat and drink of the sacrifice which has been offered!

Are these thoughts too sorrowful, too unpleasant? Is it possible that we can forget what another human being has done for us with all his heart, with all his soul, with all his strength? Is it possible, after this, that we can continue to live without him? But then, being what we are, it requires a supernatural force, a miracle, the intervention of God to bring together the living and the dead, the living who have given their lives for the dead that we are, and who do not live except by our communion with His Life?

Lord, how I thank you! This is truly what you have done. It is you who, by your sacrifice, have given meaning to sacrifice, who has demonstrated and enabled us to believe in the fecundity of sacrifice, that there is nothing to surpass it, that there is nothing more nourishing for our souls. You have wished to be the first to die defeated, breaking the heart of your mother before the dawn of victory, to die in sorrow and torture, giving a life for those who refused to accept it. And you have made this death a

226

perpetual redemption, a covenant that is always new, the beloved source of salvation, joy, purification, and peace. You have made the Sacrament of Consolation to spring from this sacrifice, the Food and Drink which has strengthened us all. And as you know us as we are, you have wished that this sacrifice should take place again each day before our eyes. You have made this a daily institution which equals our distractedness, our stupid indifference, our torpor. You have wished that it be repeated so many times so that, some day, we will no longer be insensible to it and no longer be able to keep from seeing what we do and understanding what you are doing. Upon each altar of the world, each day, within the fingers and by the words of the priest, there continues, and there is renewed, the testimony, the mystery, the awful appearance of Blood. Blood is offered every day; Blood is born every day, and is poured out; a life is given every day and a Body is drained of its Blood and given in sacrifice for us. We thank you for it and we acknowledge that it is you whom we need, you for whom we hunger and thirst, you whose absence, or our forgetfulness, degrades us, condemns us to a life that is too sad and too mediocre. We know well that we could not live any other life but yours, since you have given that life to us, but we would never have found the means of doing so if God had not created this bond between yourself and us, this source in which we can find each other.

Blood of heroes, you who have "filled up in your flesh what was wanting of the Passion of Christ," this day is also your feast and we drink of your blood, too, for if you shed your blood to complement the Passion, what joy for us to be able to drink it mingled with the Blood of Christ!

For this day we celebrate the feast of all the blood which humanity has shed down through the ages in testimony of God's love and of His Gift.

Sweat of Blood of Jesus in the Garden of Olives, anguish of the condemned on the eve of His execution, anguish of the

227

prisoner on the morning of his trial, anguish of the soldier when the zero hour comes, ah! we gather it all together, and give it our admiration, we tremble with respect before it, before all that fear which human beings have felt and which did not prevent them from doing their duty.

Flagellation of Jesus at the column in the pretorium, Blood which has gushed forth and run down the whole Body of Jesus, Body which has become but one wound, where each can recognize them as his wounds and kiss them with love.

Blood of the Crown of Thorns, long drops of warm, blinding Blood which flow with the tears down the cheeks of the Saviour, ah! we are indeed unhappy, Lord, but what are our tears compared to yours?

Blood of the Crucifixion, river of Blood from the hands and feet of the Saviour, hands of Jesus, so tender, so compassionate towards the sick, so purifying to sinners, so consoling to the afflicted, ah! they have not found a better use to which to put them, no way to make them more efficacious than to nail them, motionless and out of reach, stigmatized, like the hands of our dead. But, nevertheless, it is at this time that they have cured the most, strengthened the most, cleansed the most, and it is to them that all the chalices in the world are raised.

Blood which gushed from the heart and side of Jesus, that heart of Jesus which has so throbbed with tenderness, love, affection, and joy, they have found nothing better to do with it than to open it, to pierce it. But this Blood, now that it is shed, has become nourishment, and, upon the altars of the world, it is lifted up as a sign, a banner, calling: "Come and drink and slake your thirst, all you who thirst for love, who thirst for God, you who desire to believe in life, in sacrifice, in the redemption. Come, you who will never admit that any sacrifice is of any use, and that all those who have offered their lives did so unwisely, come, drink this Blood, slake your thirst. Mount the altar, take hold of this chalice, go with sure and audacious step. Take;

228

drink; it belongs to you, it is your blood; it has been given for you, it is waiting for you. And when you shall have taken the Blood, you will find that it is a spring, a river, flowing on to Life eternal. Attend to the voice of this Blood, —it speaks of love, of strength, of audacity, of faith, and of enthusiasm. It is ever flowing, ready to give itself, to pour itself out. Listen, follow the counsel of this Blood. And then you will appreciate your heritage, you will enter into your true family, you will be invested with your rights, and you will understand why it was worth while that men, and even God, should have shed so much blood for you.

THE SECOND SUNDAY AFTER PENTECOST

"The discourteous guests."   (Luke 14:16–24)

Between God and ourselves there is ever taking place a trial in which each of us participates, either as witness, plaintiff, or defendant.

Men say that God is silent, distant, impossible to contact.

And God, in the whole of revelation, assures us that He speaks, calls, solicits men, and that they do not pay attention to Him.

God tells us that He is Father, but that men have only one ambition and that is to emancipate themselves, to break away and to do without Him. God says that no matter how much men may hunger for Him, that is as nothing in comparison to the hunger that He has for men. And He invites to His table the sinners, the pagans, the savages, if His children refuse to come.

Everybody finds some excuse when there is question of God. Anything will do when we want to get rid of Him. Each one finds that his excuse is legitimate, that his motive is worth while.

229

It is only when we find that everyone is doing the same thing that we begin to comprehend that the one reason for all this is that we do not want Him.

We are always ready to go on a trip, an excursion, or for a feast or for some work. Those among us who are not overburdened consider themselves unhappy, and some get sick because they do not receive enough invitations to go out.

But, at God's invitation, no one is flattered, no one rejoices.

We always put off until later the time that we will occupy ourselves with Him. After I am married, after I build my house or make my fortune, when I no longer have to work, when I am no longer needed by my children, by my husband, by my profession, then I shall be able to give my time to God.

All this means that we are chasing God out of our real life, that we are refusing to sanctify our state of life, that we are pretending that the love of God and the existence that we are leading are incompatible.

Those who are delaying to return to God until they find leisure or make a change in their occupation are persons who are unwilling to change their hearts.

It is not leisure that takes us to God but the accomplishment of our duty.

THE THIRD SUNDAY AFTER PENTECOST

Christ and Sinners

"There will be more joy in heaven over one sinner who repents than over ninety-nine righteous persons who need no repentance." (Luke 15:1–10)

The Christian religion is for sinners. Only sinners are in their right place in the Church. Christ came but for them, and they alone are capable of understanding Him. That is why today's Gospel tells us that "they were all in the front row in order to hear Jesus."

We are Christians, not because we think ourselves better than others, nor because we are virtuous, honest, irreproachable, but most of all because we acknowledge that we are sinners.

We are not Christians because we occupy the first places, but because we take the last place (sincerely, not designedly, in order to be invited up front).

Religion is full of strange paradoxes. So many men believe themselves incapable of being Christians because they are impure, weak, backsliders. But the truth is that a far greater number will never be Christians because they think themselves to be just, honest, and pure.

Many Christians judge themselves to be hypocrites and give up religion because they still fall into sin. They lose their faith after they have lost their morals. They believe that they can no longer have a high idea of God because they can no longer have a high idea of themselves.

But I believe that those who are without religion (without knowing it) are the far greater number of Christians who do not believe themselves to be sinners. (You are going to ask: "And who is left?"). For the Redeemer came not for the just but to seek and save those who were lost. Those who are well have no need of a physician.

Nevertheless, the greater number of Christians believe themselves to be in that "happy medium." They say that they have never done anything very good, but neither have they done anything very bad. They go along in a comfortable mediocrity where they keep each other warm.

But there is nothing reassuring in all that. Our Lord has expressly said that He has not come for the "happy medium." He who claims to belong in that class automatically excludes himself from salvation.

How refreshing it would be if all the Christians who are present at a Sunday Mass would acknowledge that they are sinners and confess their unworthiness. What a relief it would be in the midst of this hypocrisy that smothers us!

Jesus enjoyed eating with sinners but He could not stand the lies of the Pharisees!

I think that this must be one of the chief reasons why people are so bored during Mass. They try to look as though they know that they are sinners and ought, therefore, to be a little sad. Or they pretend to be a little glad because they are forgiven. And the Mass is lost between these two hypocrisies.

There is joy in knowing oneself to be pardoned. The wonder lies in the discovery that God is so much better than ourselves.

For if God were to love us because of our virtues, we would soon lose His love because of our sins. But if He loves us for nothing of our own, He will love us always. It is He who is good, not we. We will never finish detaching ourselves from ourselves and of finding our delight in Him.

THE FIFTH SUNDAY AFTER PENTECOST

Fraternal Charity

"Go first and be reconciled with your brother." (Matthew 5:20–24)

Since the Incarnation (and the Incarnation is still going on. Christ is always man. He is always living among us, in each member of His Church, in the least of His brethren.) —since the Incarnation, the second commandment has become equal to the first.

The proof that we love God is that we love one another.

232

Christ has revealed that we shall have the same standing with God that we have with our neighbor. We are no nearer to God than we are to our neighbor. He who pretends to love God whom he does not see without loving his neighbor whom he does see, is a liar.

The love of God can contain many illusions and much imagination. But the love of our neighbor is very realistic. We know at once just how we stand with him. From this it follows that our social relations are, in fact, theological. Our love for our neighbor is our concrete way of entering into love for God. Our neighbor is Christ, within our reach, ready to receive our love. We do not love Him truly if we do not love Him there.

Christ has even wished to establish a sort of priority for the love of neighbor over the love of God. "If you are offering your gift at the altar, and there remember that your brother has something against you, leave your gift there before the altar and go; first be reconciled to your brother, and then come and offer your gift."

For the love of God is not sincere unless it includes the love of neighbor.

THE SEVENTH SUNDAY AFTER PENTECOST

The Tree and Its Fruits

"You will know them by their fruits." (Matthew 7:15–21)

This Gospel gives us a lesson in supernatural prudence. In order to judge a person, a movement, a doctrine, we must not let ourselves be guided by appearances, by declarations, by prestige, or by reputation. Look to the actions.

Doubtless, it would be well for us to make use of this criterion

233

as a guide in the midst of the theories, the masters, and the fashions that solicit the adhesion of us modern men and women. Let us not follow along too quickly, let us learn to keep cool heads and wait for their fruits, their actions, their results.

But, perhaps it would be still more advantageous to us not to employ this criterion solely to others, but to turn it upon ourselves, to use it to find out if we ourselves are good Christians, prophets and masters of the truth, to make sure, even, that we are in the right religion!

We, too, we are like trees ("I am the Vine," our Lord tells us, "you are the branches"), and are we producing good, useful fruits that are savory and beneficial to others? Do others come to us for what they need? Do they readily come to us for counsel? Do they turn to you when in need of some service? Do they follow your example? Do they like to have your company?

We, too, we are here in this church on this Sunday, and we say: "Lord! Lord!" (So far, so good. That is much better, of course, than not coming at all or coming and then going to sleep!) But that is not enough, if it does not lead us on to do the will of the Father, which is to show justice to all those who depend upon us, love to those who surround us, help to all those who are in need, to be sincere, faithful, and upright.

The danger in all religion lies in going through ceremonies, gestures, rites, and making no change whatever in one's daily life. There are those who feel that they are making their salvation certain by going to Mass on Sunday, performing their Easter duties, and listening to sermons. (And this last they find quite penitential.) But all this will avail them nothing when the day of Judgment comes. In the Gospel (Luke 13:26–27), to those who tried to justify themselves by saying to Him: "We ate and drank in your presence, and you taught in our streets," Christ replied with unusual severity: "I do not know where you come from; depart from me, all you workers of iniquity!"

The rites, the prayers, the sacraments, the religious practices are excellent if they change our life, if they lead us to actions, if they arouse in us such dispositions that, on leaving here, we will go and ask pardon for the evil that we have done, or we will perform the service that we have refused, or if we restore that which does not belong to us, or if we become reconciled to those whom we have been treating as if we did not know them.

The Mass, for example, is the sign and source of our union with God, but it is perhaps even more the sign and source of our union with our brethren. For Jesus Himself reminds us that if, at the moment of coming to place our gift on the altar, we recall that our brother has something against us, it is better to leave our offering there, to go out of the church and away from Mass, find our brother and be reconciled with him, and only then come back for the Offertory and the Eucharist.

For God gives us His love in order that we may use it, that is, pass it on to everyone else. The supreme desire of Christ is that we may not only be one with Him but that we may be one, that is, that we should love one another. He foretells that the world will be converted, not if we love God (everybody can make a pretense of that), but if we bring about that indubitable and rarest of miracles, —if we begin today, all of us, to love one another.

St. John declares with brutal plainness: He who pretends to love God, whom he sees not, and does not love his brother whom he sees, is a liar.

He who pretends to be united to Christ, whom he does not see, but refuses to be united to his brother whom he sees, is a liar.

It is so easy to fall into illusions about God. He keeps silence, He lets things go along, He effaces Himself. But His creatures do not let things go along! It is impossible to imagine them according to our fancies. And they are not silent, not they! Or, if they are silent, their face is more eloquent than their words! They judge us by our fruits and they leave us in no doubt about their taste!

235

It is quite in vain that we have been present at Mass if, on leaving, we do not love more than we did when we came in. What good is there in our assembling here every week, to make the gestures of union, of communion, to implore God's graces if we are quite determined beforehand that nothing in our hearts nor in our conduct will be changed when we leave?

The one sign that your assistance at Mass today has been fruitful is that, on leaving, you feel nearer to one another, and you do the things that prove it. Has it ever occurred to you to invite to your home for dinner one of those with whom you have just shared the Lord's Supper?

The purpose of communion is to unite you to God, but also to others. He who receives Christ, necessarily receives with Him all those who belong to Him, —His members. When you communicate you find again, united to Christ, all those whom you have lost and who are united to Him in heaven. But you also take into your heart all those whom the grace of Christ has drawn together and sustains. In swallowing Christ, you must swallow all your brethren, too. He who nourishes a grudge towards a single person is not able to communicate. How can you divide Christ between yourself and that other person? Christ loves you but He also loves the other. You cannot oblige Him to choose. You are the one to make a choice between loving Him in His entirety, with all His members, with that other person, or else to remain away from communion!

Christ gives us the example to follow. He shares with us His bread. Has that taught us to share ours? Christ made Himself known "in the breaking of the bread." Do we make ourselves known as Christians in breaking our bread with those who have none?

We make all the gestures, all the rites, all the appearances of sharing, all the ceremonies of communion. We eat the same bread, we are at the same table, we pass the same plate. And we stop there. Once back in our own homes, each eats his own meal.

236

At least, those who have one. As for those who have not, no one bothers about them. God for us all, but each one for himself. That is the motto of too many Christians.

It happened to me once to suggest to some children that, after communion one morning, we should put together all the provisions that they had brought from home for their breakfast and dinner, for we were going out on a picnic. You should have seen their faces, the anxiety that followed my invitation, their ill-humor, and their terror at the thought of being separated from the goodies they had intended for themselves and were now being asked to offer to others. Each closed his hands over his box like a cat grasping its prey.

They had just received communion and they did so quite often, but no communion had yet taught them or given them any idea of sharing. Christ shares, but not us. We make use of the sacrifice of Christ to economize on our own. We let the rite dispense us from the truth. Once the ceremony of communion is terminated, we are finished with it. Having offered sacrifice to fraternal demonstrations, we now feel freer to return to our natural egoism! However, our communions must be judged by their fruit.

We go to confession, but our confessions do us no good unless they teach us to pardon those who may have offended us. There is one thing which God cannot pardon us, and that is our refusal to pardon in our turn. Our pardon has not been a thorough one if it has not taught us to pardon also. We have not received our pardon as we ought if we do not transmit it. We do not know God's love if we do not love our brothers. On leaving the confessional, we should feel impelled to embrace the whole world in order to share with everyone the superabundance of grace which we have been given, to pour out upon them the pardon which inundated our soul with such gratuitous generosity.

Christ wants a religion in spirit and in truth, not in words and appearances. The fruits which we bear ought to testify to the

237

excellence of the divine life which we hope to live. Our conduct ought to correspond to our faith. Our love for men ought to prove our love for God.

We are no nearer to God than we are to our neighbor. Are you close to your neighbor? Are you on good terms with your neighbor and in sympathy with him? Your neighbor here at Mass? Your neighbor at table? Your neighbor in the street? Your neighbor at work? On the train or on the bus? You have no more genuine love for God than you have for your neighbors.

The first time that someone tells us that we are no nearer to God than we are to our neighbors, we feel a shock. Up to now I thought myself very close to God even though my life was solitary and very individualistic. I often think of God, perhaps far more often than I think of other people. I have desires for God, I have bursts of piety, a collection of sentiments which I call my interior life, but if I do not love God any more than I am interested in my neighbors, truly that is terrible. There is no doubt that I do not love God very much.

This notion upsets everything. I had set my sights on the infinite and now I must come down to earth. I have been saying to the Lord: "You are my God and my All! Whatever I have belongs to you. Let me come and be with you in heaven!" And He tells me: "I was hungry and you did not give me to eat. I was sick and you did not take care of me. I have been in prison so long and you have never visited me!"

We have been living in peaceful intimacy with God, saying: "Lord, Lord!" and now we are being hustled about and directed to our brethren.

But some day, instead of condemning us, those same words will console us. Perhaps a day will come when we will begin to be uneasy about our poor prayers, our lukewarm communions, our routine Masses, and we shall ask ourselves: "Where is my love for God?"

But if, at this time, we can see about us a family that is happy and united, our house open and accessible, our neighbors friendly and reliable, our surroundings either at home or at work more pleasant and fraternal because we are there, if we see in every man a brother, if we cannot see misery without trying to relieve it, if we feel so close to others, so involved in their affairs, so touched by their sorrows and their joys, then we can say to ourselves reassuringly: "I cannot be so far from God as I have been tempted to fear, since I am so close to my fellow-men!"

THE TENTH SUNDAY AFTER PENTECOST

The Pharisee and the Publican

"O God, have mercy on me, a sinner!"   (Luke 18:9–14)

Which are you, —the Pharisee or the publican? And how do you know? By what signs do you recognize yourself?

The Pharisee is quite satisfied with himself. He relies upon a certain number of practices which he carefully observes in order to be sure of his worth and of his salvation. He goes to Mass every Sunday. He confesses and communicates when he should. He observes the Friday abstinence and is regularly dispensed from fasting. Christ wants religion to be in spirit and in truth and has given the commandment to love. The Pharisee has reduced it to some obligations, which, once accomplished, he is finished with God, just as he settles with his creditors, the income tax, or the traffic laws. His was the true religion and he used it as a means by which to judge others rather than to judge himself. He never regarded himself as a sinner, but was greatly astonished to see how many others were!

Perhaps, while I am describing the Pharisee, all the non-practicing Catholics, all the lukewarm, all the free-thinkers are rejoicing. They are saying to themselves with no little pride: "I am not like that. I am a publican. I do not go to Mass, I hardly ever communicate, I never go to confession, and I am no worse than all these Catholics who make such a show of their piety!"

In speaking like this, how is it that they do not see it themselves? They act like the worst of Pharisees, they praise themselves, they are satisfied with themselves, they give thanks that they are not like the others! They call themselves the last but it is because they want to consider themselves the first. They abase themselves but precisely for the purpose of exalting themselves.

The true publican is perhaps the man who says to himself: "I am a Pharisee." The man who knows that he is not worth much, that he spoils everything that he touches, that he has need of Christ not only that he may do good but also that he may avoid even the worst sins. His trust is in Christ, he accepts these humble means of confession, of communion, of hearing Mass, since it is Christ who counsels him to use them. He is even willing to be included with the Pharisees, and he prays for them but does not judge them.

He who pleases God is not the man who expects to be rewarded for his good disposition, but he who depends entirely upon the mercy of God, who knows that, by his very nature, he is a sinner, both publican and Pharisee at one and the same time, but that his Saviour is good enough and powerful enough to make him simply His child.

THE TWELFTH SUNDAY AFTER PENTECOST

The Good Samaritan

"Go and do likewise." (Luke 10:23–37)

In asking "Who, then, is my neighbor?" the doctor of the law presents a question of capital importance. Notice that he agrees with Jesus in everything except this one point. But this is a very important point since it separates them even unto death.

The exigency of the religion of Christ resides precisely in the unlimited extension of duties towards one's neighbor, and that neighbor is not merely a parent, a friend, an acquaintance, or even a compatriot. The neighbor has become everyone, even the most distant of men, the most undeveloped country, the enemy, the persecutor. In Christ we are all near to one another. This unity is very beautiful, but it is constraining, too. Peter was dumb at the mere idea of granting pardon seventy times. We have to be ready to love our neighbor to the full extent of the world population.

The way in which our Lord answers this question disconcerts us a little. We would have expected Him to define who our neighbor is. What He defines is the manner in which we can truly be a neighbor.

But the meaning is the same. Jesus really says: "The neighbor is no matter whom." He puts aside all restriction, every barrier, all social or religious distinction, —even religious distinction. This is the most anticlerical parable in the Gospel. To a priest, to a Levite, those "professionals" in religion, He very definitely prefers a Samaritan, that is, a heretic, a schismatic, a man who, to the Jews, is even worse than a pagan. For he alone is truly charitable.

Have you never had this surprising experience? Have you not often met with more heart, more readiness to be of service, more compassion from unbelievers, and even more from libertines and loose women than from Christians who may be orthodox but certainly are hard?

How are we to explain this scandal?

Would you say that these people are more spontaneous because they are more superficial? That they allow themselves to be moved to pity as easily as they allow themselves to be dragged into evil? Or that this surface generosity would disappear before

241

true sacrifice, a long-drawn-out fidelity, or a costly renunciation?

Perhaps, but this is not what our Lord seems to say. The Samaritan cared for the wounded man, lifted him up onto his mount while he followed on foot, was concerned about him, paid with his money and himself, and even promised future service.

Then, ought we not to conclude that these people who are so persuaded that they possess the truth very easily become hard of heart? We so often find that the "practicing" Catholic is a dead Christian and very tiresome, —for we are not called upon to practice religion but to live it! The proof of our orthodoxy is not in our catechism but in our conduct. Our real profession of faith is found in the exercise of our profession, whatever it may be, and our warm and cordial love for our neighbor is the very best proof that we love God sincerely.

THE FOURTEENTH SUNDAY AFTER PENTECOST

The Lilies of the Field

"The Gentiles seek all these things."   (Matthew 6:24–33)

Whenever the Gospel of Martha and Mary is read, there is always some irritation and discontent evinced by those who are mothers of families. They would all like to be Mary and they find that the supreme disgrace comes when Martha is blamed for her devotedness.

They forget to observe that Martha is blamed, not because she is active, but because she is agitated; not because she is working, but because she is incapable of allowing the Word of God to work within her; not because she is serving our Lord and her sister Mary, but because she cannot leave them in peace.

242

And so it is with the Gospel of today. It gives the same impression and is the cause of the same scandal among the mothers of families.

Their objections are quickly made. "Perfect! Wonderful idea! Let's not bother about anything anymore! Let us live like the birds of the air and like the lilies of the field! We want nothing better! And our pastors will do the rest!"

And all the while Christ asks of us the most natural thing in the world—our confidence.

Confidence, —what little children give above all else to their parents.

Confidence, —what students must give first of all to their teachers.

Confidence, —absolutely indispensable in social relations. Money itself is a matter of trust.

You have confidence in your parents, in your teachers, in your bank, in your friends. Then have confidence also in your God!

That will not interfere with your work. Quite the contrary!

The Gospel encourages work. Christ praises the servant whom his Master, upon his arrival, will find occupied (Luke 12:43). Woe to the idle! Woe to him who does not use his talents fruitfully!

The true faith is quite the contrary of passivity, and in the Christian there is none of the fatalist. It is fear that paralyzes and anxiety that gnaws. One never works better than when surrounded by a sense of confidence. Disquiet over the morrow spoils the work of today. "Sufficient for the day is the evil thereof." God is with you, in your life, today. He will still be there tomorrow. Count upon Him!

A nun, the spiritual daughter of one of my friends, said to him when he came to the convent: "O Father, how I missed you! I thought I was going to die and I was so afraid!"

"My daughter," he replied, "that was the proof that you were not going to die. If it had really been the hour of your death, the

243

Lord would have given you the grace to accept it peacefully because such a grace was necessary. But because you became anxious in thinking that you were going to die, you withdrew yourself from Divine Providence. The Lord gives you the graces you need for your actual life, not for your imagination."

This is the thing about which Christ protests, not about work, nor about foresight. It is necessary to look ahead and to work. But Christ wants us to be on our guard against worry. His objection is not to occupation, but to preoccupation!

"Martha, you are troubled about many things! You are anxious!" —"Do not be anxious about what you shall eat, or what you shall drink, or how you shall be clothed . . ." It is necessary to be occupied about these things but within reason, not with anxiety, because anxiety is the very thing that paralyzes action, that prevents us from doing what we should.

Have you noticed, in the parable of the talents, the reason why the wicked servant failed to use his talents gainfully? It was not laziness but fear. He was tormented by the thought of the return that he would have to make. His imagination pictured the scene for him. He saw his master with a severe and menacing face and he trembled. He thought so much about the future that he had no courage to face the present. So he did nothing.

Thus it is with the student who has too great a fear of failing in his examination. He cannot study. He sees before him the face of the examiner (he is an austere man), and his anxiety prevents him from working.

God has given you your ability to work. Make good use of it.

Chesterton has said: "Once a year, at Christmas time, we thank the little Jesus when we find candies in our stockings. We would do better to thank Him every morning for finding in them a good pair of legs!"

Every morning, when you wake up, you find a good pair of legs, a good pair of arms, and a good head (at least, I hope you

244

do). Here is the first gift of God, your tools for your work. But, should a day come when you lack these, you still have a Father. His goodness of today is the promise of His tenderness tomorrow.

But is not improvidence a duty?

No, not at all. Providence is your duty. God has given you a good head with which to think and to foresee, but with reasonableness. Do not expect an absolute security, for you will not find it. We must accept a certain necessary insecurity. You ought to try to provide security, but you cannot be absolutely sure of everything. We must not try to do away with Divine Providence. Even in regard to your children. It is very good to foresee their needs, but you must not try to withdraw them from Providence. We must not dispense with their Father in heaven. Love them, rear them well, educate them as much as possible, give them all the opportunity you can for their future. But, above all, let them learn the joy and the encouragement that there is in having such a Father and of putting in Him all their confidence after your own example.

THE FIFTEENTH SUNDAY AFTER PENTECOST (I)

The Resurrection at Naim

"Young man, I say to you, arise!"   (Luke 7:11–16)

The rationalists who judge this miracle to be impossible, and the account of it merely a legend, probably believe in it far more than the numberless Christians who read it with no reaction whatever.

This event completely changed the lives of those who were

there, they were obliged to believe in it, since they saw it take place, but the chances are that it will make no change whatever in our own lives.

For them, everything was changed. Life was no longer the same. Death had been called in question, and they had to admit the existence of a Being who was capable of changing the conditions of life, and the presence of another world which might, at any moment, force an entry into this one. At first they were astonished, and then very much embarrassed and ill at ease. They had lost their "reasonable" certitudes, normal conditions could no longer be depended upon, the limitations to which they had become resigned, and which they regarded as a prop, were no longer stable. Anything and everything became possible, might actually happen, and could even be asked for.

Faith is a disquieting thing, and if we can remain so peaceful and so indifferent to the reading of this Gospel of resurrection, it is a proof that our faith is also in need of being resuscitated.

We have all had deaths among our relatives and friends, and doubtless there is no one here who has not seen a dead person or at least knelt to pray a few seconds beside a coffin.

Did you ask for a miracle? Did you pray that that person would return to life?

Perhaps you find this question stupid. Yet, I think that such a prayer is natural. It is the first and simplest suggestion of faith.

When we kneel beside a corpse, we all know that he, or she, is not really dead. We know that the soul lives, thinks, loves, and sees us, we all know that even this body will revive one day and be transformed.

But, more than that, we know that there exists a God who raises the dead, a God who has conquered death and who has Himself risen from the dead, and who, at each of our communions, introduces into our bodies a germ of immortality.

Then why do we not believe in an immediate resurrection? Why do we not ask at once for what we believe? Why not ask

246

for what we are obliged to believe will take place at some distant time?

He who, beside the body of someone who is dear to him, is not tempted to ask that he may return to life, has a soul that is weighed down, paralyzed by a sad resignation.

It seems to me that such a request—primitive, violent, almost savage—would be the first impulse of faith, but without this impulse, there probably is no faith at all.

Of course, upon thought, we understand that this hope and this thought are a little too hasty. It is not to this life that we should bring back our dead. Of what use was it to the son of that widow to be returned to his mother? After a few years they would again be separated. The daughter of Jairus was awakened from her sleep, as Jesus put it, but one day she went to sleep again. Lazarus came forth living from the tomb, but there is no doubt that he returned to it sooner or later.

It does not enter into the plan of God to do away with death at this time. And there are better, far more beautiful resurrections than those of the body.

What the Church invites us to ask for others, and for ourselves, are spiritual resurrections; that God will give us His life, that we may truly live the life of God.

The resurrection that God is capable of bringing about within you is constant and immediate. It has the power to change you.

We are all dead in one part of our being; we are inert, indifferent, cold; we are all dead to a lively faith, a joyous hope, an active and generous love.

There are vast portions of our being into which we never descend for fear of what we shall find. Yes, souls also die, in their own way. There are dead souls, and the most horrible corpse is less hideous than some spiritual decompositions.

But God is capable of reviving the dead, the spiritually dead as well as the physically dead, and even the most rebellious of all, those who believe themselves to be still alive. God is able to change us. Faith means believing that God can make new men of us, a new being, like a new-born infant. "At my age," asks Nicodemus, "how can I be born again?" And Jesus reaffirms His statement: "Unless a man be born again, he shall not see the Kingdom of God."

The true atheist is not one who says that God does not exist. Such a one is rare and one may well ask if he is sincere. The real atheist is one who says that God cannot change him, that He will never change him, that it is too late, or that he is too old, —and they say this at fifteen as well as at sixty. The real atheist is he who denies the power of the Infinite, the power that there is in the grace of God to bring about a resurrection. Among us, they only are believers who know that all they need is a true prayer, a sincere confession, and even one single Word of God in order that they may be reborn and have all that they lost restored to them.

And, finally, there is a third degree of faith, and that is to believe and long for a resurrection, a transformation, of the entire world. This universe that surrounds us, these mountains, the sea, the sky, the animals, the trees, these are not foredoomed to destruction. It would be a sign of ingratitude, and a proof that we have little appreciation for the gifts of God, if we can resign ourselves so easily to their loss.

And above all, our human associations, with all that they have that is carnal and of the senses, our families, our friendships, those we love, —faith does not demand that we renounce them forever, but rather that we love them so much that we want them to last eternally.

Christ has not promised us a Paradise that is purely spiritual. His first concern, after He had risen, was to convince His disciples that He was not a spirit as they thought Him to be. "Touch me and see. A spirit has not flesh and bones as you see that I have." And He ate and drank with them in this new life to which He was drawing them.

248

We should love the world and other people so much that we draw them with us into eternity. Perhaps the end of the world will come in the way that the Gospel of today prophesies. What will happen then?

Christ was moved to pity on seeing this desolate widow beside her dead son. He could not resist this sorrow, this love of a woman for her child. He could not bear that they should be separated any longer. Did He think of another mother, standing beside her dead Son, and she, too, was a widow?

Perhaps the end of the world, the end of this world of death, of separation, and of tears may come when that day arrives in which we shall love everyone so much, when we shall be so united, when our solidarity shall be so perfect, when we shall be so attentive to one another, so full of tenderness towards them, that our Lord will be unable to endure the sight of our separation and our mourning.

And as He drew near to that widow and her son in order to give them again to one another, so, the day when we love each other enough, He will return and make our loves and our joys eternal.

Let us hasten to love one another so much that we merit His return! Let us hasten to love one another so much that He may never leave us!

In order to bring about the fulfillment of this prophecy, let us bear in mind that there is already in heaven a Mother who loves all her children so much, a Mother who suffers and weeps when they threaten to withdraw from her and to disappear, that we can confidently hope for the resurrection of everyone.

Yes, the final action of Christ the Redeemer when He shall appear upon the clouds of heaven is prophesied in this humble miracle of Naim. One day we shall hear the voice of the Son of man being addressed to each one of us. With irresistible authority He will say: "Young man, I say to you, arise!"

And He will give us to our Mother.

249

THE FIFTEENTH SUNDAY AFTER PENTECOST (II)

"When the Lord saw her, He had compassion on her." (Luke 7:11–16)

In the time of Christ, His miracles were proof of His mission and strengthened the faith of His followers. After two thousand years, for many embarrassed Christians, they have become trials. We believe them out of a sense of duty, because we have the faith. But it was not these miracles that gave it to us.

How are we going to believe that such things are possible? And then, why do they not occur nowadays? Cannot these prodigies be explained by the ignorance of those times which attributed to God all that surpassed their limited knowledge?

In the presence of a corpse, who among us believes in a resurrection, in the possibility of a resurrection every bit as real and joyful as that of the son of the widow of Naim? Is not our faith lacking in enthusiasm like that of Martha: "Yes, Lord, I know that he will rise on the last day"?

We reply that Christ did not work this miracle to upset the laws of nature and put an end to death.

A miracle is a sign, a means of teaching, the revelation of a lasting truth on the occasion of some passing thing. He who attaches himself to the prodigy in itself, ignores its signification. He who seeks to obtain a miracle is interested in himself rather than in what the miracle signifies.

Christ wishes us to learn that He is the Lord (and this is the first time that this title, belonging to divinity, is given to Him in the Gospel of St. Luke), the Master of life, and that those who trust in Him, even though dead, shall live.

There is a law of nature: man must die.

And there is a law of supernature, which does not contradict it but completes it: the death of a man is his rebirth. As the grain of wheat is sown in the earth in order to live again and bear fruit, so the dead are placed in the earth to rise again one day to a state that is infinitely superior.

The resurrection of the son of the widow of Naim is not this resurrection which has been promised to each of us. His resurrection was not final and made no change in his condition as a human being. His was not a glorified body. This miracle was only a sign of the Presence of the Lord and a revelation of His power in favor of sorrowing humanity.

THE SIXTEENTH SUNDAY AFTER PENTECOST

A Cure on Sunday?

"Then He took him and healed him, and let him go." (Luke 14:1–11)

Christ acted with the liberty of a son of God. Love God and your neighbor and do whatever this true love inspires.

The Pharisees, on the contrary, had invented a code of "dos" and "don'ts" that was so ingenious that it sufficed but to observe them to be beyond all criticism. No one asked about your heart, which might be hard as stone, nor your faith, which was probably extinct, but only about your observance of the rules.

This is the way that religion dies.

The great enemy of the Church is not hatred or persecution. These, on the contrary, are a stimulant and the occasion of renewal. Nor is it sin, for every sin can become *"felix culpa"*—a happy fault, thanks to the grace of repentance.

251

The real enemy is routine which insinuates itself without being noticed, and which dries up the heart and corrupts the best impulses. This it is which leads to prayer without respect, assistance at Mass without joy, without gratitude, and without profit. This it is which causes you to come to church with closed heart and leave in the same state as you entered.

This is the poison which killed the Jewish church. The Jewish religion had resisted all its adversaries—conquests, deportation, and exile. But it succumbed to routine. The Law became desicated, in spite of the prophets. The letter killed the spirit. There was nothing but contempt for good sense, pity, true love, to the point where they said of the Son of God: "We have a law, and according to that law He ought to die."

Are we sure that we are not being pursued by the same enemy?

It is so easy to reduce religion to some dogmas and a few rites. Take our way of sanctifying Sunday. The Jews had reached the point where, on the Sabbath, even a miracle, even a cure, even an act of charity was not permitted.

We have no hesitation about allowing ourselves pleasures that are stupid and completely pagan, but we scruple about allowing a woman to knit peacefully or a man to work quietly in his garden.

We swallow the camel and strain at the gnat.

The Day of the Lord has become, with the exception of some three quarters of an hour, a day to indulge our caprices and personal pleasures.

When the sanctification of Sunday is reduced to a Mass which has no relation whatever to the rest of the day, and to the avoidance of servile work, what is that but the letter of the law replacing its spirit?

The service of God, in spirit and in truth, is to make Sunday a day of love and joy, a day of greater charity, a day of prayer, of family reunion, and of gratitude to the Father of every family.

252

THE SEVENTEENTH SUNDAY AFTER PENTECOST

The First and Second Commandments

"On these two commandments depend all the law and the prophets." (Matthew 22:34–46)

The Pharisees brought up a vital question, but they did it in a state of mind so narrow, so cunning, and so full of hatred that they could not profit by the response. Christ closed their mouths but did not convert them. They were beaten and irritated.

Nevertheless, there is a relation which is essential and revealing between the two parts of the reply given by Jesus.

The Pharisees claimed that they loved God, but they did not love their neighbor, that is, the man, Jesus, who stood before them. Now, these two loves are indissolubly united.

Jesus embarrassed them by showing them that the Messiah, who, according to them, was a man, the Son of David, nevertheless bore a divine title, that of Lord.

How could a man be invested with an absolute value, a divine dignity?

The mystery of fraternal charity is bound up with the mystery of the Incarnation. God has become man. God communicates Himself to man and proposes to each one that he accept this participation in the divine life which is grace. Our duty to God and our duty to man can no longer be separated. It is the same life which unifies the Body of Christ.

The Pharisees thought that they were hating and condemning only a man, and, in reality, their choice meant the rejection of God.

Let us beware lest we one day discover that, in neglecting what

253

we thought was only a man, a sinner, a feeble and importunate old man, we were neglecting God.

THE EIGHTEENTH SUNDAY AFTER PENTECOST

The Miracle of Pardon

"Rise, take up your bed, and go home."   (Matthew 9:1–8)

Upon reading this account, one asks oneself whether the crowd understood the meaning, or whether they were more enthusiastic over the miracle of the cure rather than over the pardon.

And yet, the intention of Jesus is plain. He wished to affirm, He wished to have us believe that the Son of man, —that a man on earth has this unheard of, divine power, the power to pardon sins. The miracle of the cure is but a simple way of demonstrating the astounding message which was to be the first one given to the world by the Apostles, —"Your sins are forgiven!"

But we are so made, we, as well as the contemporaries of Jesus, that what is sensible and exterior strikes us more forcibly. We go more willingly to Lourdes to see a miracle than we go to make our confession. And, nevertheless, more miracles are worked in the first confessional you come upon than in the piscina of Lourdes. There, in the confessional, every day there are cures, unhoped for resurrections, a man there changes the sentences of the Last Judgment!

Yes, there is a man who is offering to recommence your life, no matter what age you may now have reached, a man makes you this proposition, —a scandalous one in the eyes of "reasonable" persons, —to make a new being of you, one who is happy and overflowing with joy. Who wants to accept? Who desires to begin anew to believe, to be young, to hope, to pardon everyone, and to be on good terms with all?

254

If here there were question of physical cures, cures of rheumatism, bronchitis, of varicose veins, how they would hasten to the confessional! What a file there would be!

But these cures concern our souls, so we put it off until later.

Besides, if our physical ills were cured, it would rarely mean a change in our lives. The true, the real change would be in making us loving, cordial, fraternal, attentive to others, yielding and devoted.

If the state of our soul were to become visible, if the monstrosity of our soul could be seen on our face, if our body were as deformed as our soul, we would rush to the confessional, we would not dare to appear in public.

No one, saints excepted, likes to go to confession. But it was very different in the time of Christ. Have you noticed in the Gospel how every pardon ended with a banquet? Zacchaeus, perched in his tree, made haste to prepare a supper; Matthew the publican closed his tax office, invited his colleagues, and made a feast; the father of the prodigal son killed the fatted calf; and it is not impossible that the paralytic, cured in today's Gospel, invited Jesus to come and celebrate with him.

It is not so nowadays, and you will rarely see your father, your husband, or your brother come back from church bringing his confessor with him to celebrate with the family the pardon which has made him happy.

And if we do go to confession, we do it with great discretion. We close ourselves in and take good care that none of our acquaintances know about it.

It was just the contrary in the time of Christ, and Jesus invited Himself quite gaily to the table of sinners before He Himself invited them to His own table in holy communion. Thanks to Him, all faults became "happy faults" because of the love with which He pardoned them. One must be God to pardon like that, to pardon so that the memory of the sin recalled only the love that was shown in the pardon.

It is a real suffering to hear the confessions of most people. It is so rare to be filled with respect and admiration before someone who speaks to God, who has faith! So often there are nothing but stupid avowals, an enumeration of sins which is nothing but a form, or of things which are not sins at all, like "I missed Mass on Sunday because I was sick"—something like a phonograph record, prepared in childhood, of insignificant faults which we will always commit, which we are quite resigned to commit, and which, in reality, would make no change in our lives if we did not commit them.

There are curious people who would like to know what mysteries are whispered in the confessional, and there are even some people who are dishonest enough to stay within earshot of the confessional. Poor things! If they but knew that the greater number of people say nothing, that they present for absolution the mask beneath which they have long ago learned to hide, rather than to show the wound which really is in need of cure.

Sometimes, when I can stand it no longer, I interrupt the penitent, I stop the record, and I ask: "If you had the opportunity to meet our Lord, if someone told you that He was passing by, that you could go to Him, what would you say to Him? What would you ask of Him? What cure, what miracle, what change in your life, would you beg of Him?"

Then these people begin to realize that they would not say to Him what they are bringing to confession, that all this is unimportant, that none of this tiresome twaddle would be of any use. Then sometimes there will come a word of real truth, an avowal from the heart, and a soul has freed itself and discovers, in so doing, what his real problem has been, what it is that is smothering his religious life. It can be that he has never accepted his life, his family, his financial status, some passing sickness or some life-long infirmity, his appearance, his spouse, or perhaps he has never forgiven God for some deception, some failure, some bereavement which He has permitted, and this stands between that soul and God like a wall and prevents all filial relations. The essential very seldom comes to confession, —our revolts, our discouragements, that depression which we nurse with pleasure, those temptations which we cultivate, which we play with regularly, resolved not to sin, but finding pleasure in caressing the possibility which gives spice to our existence. There are complaints with which we burden those around us, and above all, there is our indifference to others. There is our disgraceful want of faith and hope, which, even while we are going to confession, we know we will not change, that our life will go along in the future just as it has in the past. We await nothing, we hope for nothing from God. We are quite resigned to remaining just as mediocre, just as gloomy, just as poor as we ever were, and we do not want to change.

These are the things that we should say to the confessor in order to make a true and efficacious confession. The man in today's Gospel who was miraculously cured did not pretend that he was not paralyzed, he did not hide his condition but made a display of it before Christ. He allowed Him to see that he was powerless, unable to move. He did not complain of a slight dizziness, nor ask for the cure of a scratch, or the removal of a wart, nor did he ask Christ to make him beautiful. He made known his real distress and he was cured.

To the greater number of Christians who come to burden us with their sterile confessions, I think that Christ would say: "Be still. Stop searching your memory. Look at me. Do you believe in me? Do you believe that I love you? That I have suffered so much for you, loved and desired you so much, that I am not willing and able to forgive your sins and change your life? Do you believe that I am capable of renewing your life? Do you believe that you can live a new life because of me?"

And I think that after such questions we would be silent for a long time. We would be under the painful impression that what we have been trying to do is to give Christ the small coin of little sins, like pennies to a beggar, in order to be rid of Him, and all

257

the while He was waiting for us to hand over to Him our whole fortune of sins.

And even before a word was spoken, once we had seen our Lord, as soon as we had met Him, we would have known what was lacking to us. We had scarcely lifted our eyes to Jesus when we knew that He loved us, that He was looking for us, that He was always waiting for us, and that we had never believed, never truly believed, in His existence, nor in His love, and that all our trouble came from that. This is really our greatest sin, this is what we should confess more than anything else. When love for Christ is lacking, our lives are empty and we must fill them with something, even though that something is sin. We must occupy our time, we must fill that terrible void, we must do something, even commit sin, sins which we do not like, which we are not proud of, but what else is there to do, what else would there be in our lives, if there were no sins?

But if Jesus loves us so much, if that love transfigures and fills our life, if we can know that we are followed, supported, filled by such a love, then we have all that is necessary, we have no need of sin, it has become useless, we no longer desire it, and we find that we are much happier without it.

That is what confession is, —an interview with Jesus, a visit with Jesus, the extraordinary discovery that He loves us, and this discovery can change our whole life. The absolution can cure us of our sins only on condition that it gives us something better, that it reveals to us a love, a life, a joy much better than anything our sins can give us, and it thus enables us to do without them. If it fails in this, then we go back to our sinful ways as a matter of course.

It is the achievement of this understanding that the penitent has a right to expect, and it is to arrive at this that the priest ought to be of assistance in the confessional. The penitent should come to realize that in this sacrament is to be found a presence and a love which will detach him from his sins and assist him to free himself from them.

258

That is what God is telling us in confession, that He loves us, that He pardons us, that our repentance and His grace have made us once more His children. The words of absolution have no other meaning. The only message that the priest is charged to give us is: it is God who loves you, it is He who has brought you here, it is He who works patiently with your soul by His grace to give you the desire, the courage, the opportunity to go to confession. It is He who desires to pardon you far more than you desire to be pardoned, it is He who rejoices at your pardon much more than you in being pardoned. He never stops telling us, never stops repeating to us as many times as we may wish, as often as we have need to hear, that we are always His beloved children, and that, in spite of everything, He is pleased with us and still has great hopes for us. It is this love, it is the revelation of this tenderness and goodness, which slowly awakens like sentiments in us and makes us resemble Him.

He who is never pardoned is not loved.

He who is pardoned only a little is loved only a little.

But he who is often pardoned, and pardoned much, will one day come to love much because he will have learned that he is loved much.

That is the true motive for going to confession.

We do not go to confession because we want to. We would wait long for that! Nor do we go to confession because we like it. We would never go! But we should go because God is waiting there for us, because God desires to pardon us, because it is a pleasure for Him to have His son or His daughter come to Him to be cared for, to be healed, to be strengthened and encouraged.

And then something of that love, that tenderness, that joy will find its way into our hearts when we are pardoned and begin to learn how we are loved, and we begin to love Him in return.

That love is His love, for we are so poor that we cannot love God except with the love which He Himself gives us.

THE TWENTIETH SUNDAY AFTER PENTECOST

The Miracle of Faith

"Go, your son will live." (John 4:46–53)

Have you noticed in the Gospel that our Lord almost always begins by refusing the miracles that are asked of Him? We find in this a confirmation of our own experience. How many times our own prayers have, apparently, been refused!

But, have you also noticed that He always ends by granting the request of those who insist with great confidence?

Even the Blessed Virgin, at the wedding of Cana, began by receiving a refusal. "My hour is not yet come." But Mary is not discouraged as we are. Neither is she obstinate. She simply waited for Him to act, telling the servants: "Do whatever He tells you."

In the Gospel of today, how harshly this first response of Christ to this desperate father sounds to us: "Unless you see signs and wonders, you do not believe."

The man does not allow himself to be drawn into an argument. He repeats his request and in very touching words: "Lord, come down before my child dies."

But even then, Jesus does not grant him what he asks. He imposes upon him a very painful test. "Go, your son will live."

Notice this: To us who are acquainted with the story this sounds like a promise. But the officer had but one hope. He wanted to bring Jesus back with him and have Him lay His hand on the child. He wanted that virtue to come from Christ which had healed so many who had been able to touch Him. Now Jesus refuses to go back with him and he must return alone. He has not been answered in the way in which he desired, but rather in a manner which required far greater faith.

The officer felt the refusal. He dared not insist, and it was so hard to go back. Our Lord had good reason for acting in this manner, and the man left with no other hope than the few words that had been said to him. He had come, just as we come, with confidence in the goodness of the thing that he was asking for, and he left, as we should do, with confidence in the goodness of the One of whom he was asking it. Jesus transformed the man's faith by asking of him all that he was capable of giving.

The poor man set out on his return, not knowing whether he had made the worst mistake of his life or the most heroic of actions.

Thus, when his servants came to tell him that his son was living, his first question was what hour he had begun to improve—which shows us in what he was most interested. The important thing to him now was not that he had obtained what he had asked, but how he obtained it and from whom. The question was not concerned with the child, but with Jesus.

God never wishes to give us anything less than Himself. While He discourages any attempt on our part to dictate to Him what gifts to give us, nevertheless it is up to us to lay ourselves open to receive what His wisdom, His love, and His will offer us.

THE TWENTY-FIRST SUNDAY AFTER PENTECOST

Fraternal Pardon

"So also my heavenly Father will do to everyone of you if you do not forgive your brother from your heart." (Matthew 18:23–35)

Among the Apostles, as in every human community, numerous discussions, and even disputes, occurred. Our Lord suffered much because of this, and tried to pacify them. He went over this topic again and again in His instructions to them. "If, when you bring your gift to the altar, you remember that your brother has something against you, leave your gift there, leave the church, and go first and be reconciled with your brother. Then come and bring your gift to the altar." Or again: "If your brother has sinned against you, go and reprove him privately. If he listens to you, you will have gained your brother. If he will not listen to you, speak to the Church, and if he will not hear the Church, let him be to you as a pagan and a publican," that is to say, not as someone whom you ought not to love (we must love all men and even our enemies), but as someone who does not want to be loved, who does not want to be a friend. To those who do not ask pardon, not only is it impossible to give it to them (how can you give a thing to someone who will not receive it?), but it would be harmful to them if they are treated like real enemies, for this would dispense them from recognizing and repairing their faults, from correcting their behavior. To pardon is to accept one who repents, to reëstablish a friendship. As for those who refuse to repent, those who act as enemies, all we can do is to continue to love them and to pray for their conversion, to show them that they are not disliked and that we are always ready to grant them pardon whenever they sincerely desire to be one with us.

Peter had a lively character, impetuous and quarrelsome. Being desirous of pleasing Christ and believing that he had understood His teaching quite well, one day when he was feeling very good he asked: "Master, how many times should I pardon my brother? Would seven times be enough?" Jesus smiled at this naïve proposition: "Not seven times, Peter, but seventy times seven times."

Then Peter gave up the notion of counting. It meant that there was no end. He would have to pardon always.

And to help them to understand the severity of His commandment, Jesus told them this parable that we are going to read.

God is like a king who is about to take an account of his servants. One is brought to him who owes him 10,000 talents. Sixty millions in gold. A sum which not one of us ever possessed. The learned exegetes have made all sorts of guesses as to how he could have accumulated such a large sum. Perhaps the king was rich and negligent and the servant evil and dishonest. Even that seems a little unlikely. But it all becomes quite clear if we make the characters God and ourselves. Count up all that God has given you, each one of you. Each infant, at birth, is a millionaire. Yes, the poorest among you is one to whom God has given millions. But no one takes account of it, no one ever thinks of thanking Him for it—until the terrible day when he is called upon to render an account.

Think for a moment: your eyes, yes, your eyes, at what price do you estimate them? You know that there is an eye bank to which one can give his eyes so that they may be grafted on to some blind person. For how much would you sell your eyes? You will never be able to see anything again. What is your price? And your ears? To be walled up within yourself, never to hear anything, never to converse with others. Man or woman, what price will you take in exchange for your hearing? And your hands? Or your legs? Never to walk again. Surely, they will give you millions and you can buy yourself a Cadillac. But, without legs, would you be happy in an automobile?

And even in regard to those things which seem to have no value, because they cost nothing. The sun, for instance. How much will you give in exchange for never seeing the sun again? To be always closed in, never to see a tree, a flower, to breathe pure air. For how much will you sell all that?

And all these priceless things, worth far more than sixty millions, even in gold, we have stolen them from God. We have attributed them to ourselves, and we have used them and wasted them as if they did not belong to Him. And worse than that, we have made use of them to sin, like a fiancée who makes use of the gifts she receives from her lover, to carry on flirtations or to win friends and accomplices for her folly, or even to repay the partners of her debauchery.

This is so true that, when giving the last sacraments, the priest anoints with holy oil just those gifts which God has given you and which you have used to commit sin. He anoints the eyes and says: "May God forgive you all the sins you have committed with your eyes." He anoints the ears, the nostrils, the hands, and the feet. He consecrates—he re-consecrates—to God all these gifts of God which we have so misused. He affirms, for the first time, perhaps, at the close of our lives, that all these were God's gifts, which ought to have been consecrated to His service, used for His praise, and call forth our gratitude. We are exhorted to acknowledge that we have hardly ever used them except to sin, and to try to break away from Him.

All the evil that we have done knowingly, all the evil that we have done unknowingly (but what precautions we have taken in order not to know it), how many fine names given to our egoism and our avidity, how many fine pretexts given in order to cover up our wrong-doing, how much malice even in our good deeds! We never do good so joyously as when we have a bad motive for doing it.

So many promises not kept, so many good inspirations neglected, so many inefficacious good desires, brief moments of enthusiasm for good, followed by forgetfulness, long periods of indolence, and of total indifference to God and to others, our profound lack of faith, love, hope, and charity, —yes, we are, in truth, insolvent debtors, we are burdened with crushing debts without having the first penny with which to pay them. We are thoughtless and sacrilegious prodigals who have been blind to our waste of the gifts of God and there is nothing now but to hand us over to executioners who will take from us, for God, all that of which we have deprived Him.

But, because of a special grace from above, the guilty one has recognized his crime. By means of an extraordinary light, he has seen, while there is still time, the folly which he has committed. He throws himself at the feet of his master, and, prostrate before him, he begs in a manner that is both touching and naïve: "Have pity on me and I will repay you all."

And then comes the theatrical. The king not only remits the chastisement but also the entire debt. God is like that. God is a Father. He is quickly moved to compassion for His children. It is a joy for Him to give to them, but it is a still greater joy for Him to pardon. God is like a mother. When her sick child comes to throw himself into her arms, the mother considers nothing too much for his sake. "If we were not sinners, having more need of pardon than of bread, we would never know the depth of the heart of God."

St. Ambrose was commenting on Genesis, line by line, as was the custom in those days. He came to the verse: "God made man and then He rested."

"Look," he says, "this is strange. Just above I read: 'God made the heaven and the earth' but there was no mention of repose. 'God made the plants, the animals, the birds, the fish.' No repose. 'God made the angels,' creatures infinitely more perfect than men, and He took no rest. But 'God made man and then He rested.' Ah! I have found it. God had at last found someone to pardon. An animal is never pardoned because it cannot sin. An angel is never pardoned because he cannot repent. But man, that feeble, contradictory creature, who never does just exactly what he would like to do, and who does what he does not wish to do, man can repent. He can recognize that he was deceived and that he does not like the consequences of acts that he thought he liked. A man, God can pardon." With man, God has at last found someone towards whom He can show Himself completely Father, completely God. He has found someone whom He can take into His arms and console in spite of all the evil that he has done, as we console a child, after a crisis, for having been so naughty. And then God rested.

But what would happen if, scarcely pardoned, the servant in the parable, who has just been forgiven a debt of sixty millions, takes by the throat some unfortunate who owes him a very small sum, screams at him, demands payment, and then has him imprisoned? You will say: "That is not possible. No one could be so cruel."

Unfortunately, that is just what we do every day. We leave the confessional where God has forgiven our sins and we refuse to speak to So-and-So, we no longer invite such a one to our home, we will not take the first step towards a reconciliation with another, we will not compromise our dignity, our prestige, our interests.

They say that women pardon, but never forget. (What good is it to pardon if you do not forget the offense?) That men are so indifferent and egoistical that they forget all about it instead of pardoning. They are not interested in others long enough to bear a grudge.

God will not pardon that. He cannot pardon it because He cannot accept us unless we have love in our hearts.

Briefly, if we would be pardoned our innumerable offenses we must fulfill two conditions. The first is to admit the fact that we are sinners. It is a grace from God and it seems to be rarely received in spite of the frequency of one's confessions. The first sign of the presence of the Holy Spirit in the soul is her recognition of her culpability. As soon as St. Peter saw Christ, he cried out: "Depart from me, O Lord, for I am a sinful man!" The saints saw very clearly that they had many defects. But the greater part of those who are not saints judge themselves to be quite acceptable. They have neither killed anyone nor stolen anything. There are others who are worse than they are, they are of the "happy medium," and they are quite unaware of their sins.

266

There is a physical condition in which one is conscious of nothing. They may shout at you, pinch you, shake you, and you perceive nothing. This is called being in a coma. It is a very serious state and can lead to death. It usually immediately precedes death. From the spiritual point of view, there are innumerable souls in a state of coma. They are in need of a violent shaking to awaken them to reality, to make them wake up to the fact that they are really sinners.

When you come to confession you say: "Bless me, Father, for I have sinned." You do not say: "Father, punish me, for I have sinned," nor "reprimand me" or "condemn me." No. You say: "Father, I have come to receive enlightenment from God." Or: "Father, congratulate me for I have just been brought back to consciousness." Or: "Father, I have just had good luck. Rejoice with me, for God has given me this special grace. I have at last discovered that I have sinned; at last I have seen my sin; I have just discovered that I also have been favored by the mercy of God, for I am now aware that I am a sinner."

The second condition is that you must also pardon others.

You have not received your pardon properly if you do not know how to pass it on to others.

To refuse pardon to others is the sign that you do not appreciate your own pardon.

You refuse, you deny the pardon of God in refusing to grant pardon yourself.

God would not have created hell if men had imitated His mercy.

Or rather, it is man who has created hell. Hell is the place where one never pardons.

A thousand absolutions, a thousand extreme unctions are not capable of supplying for a pardon refused to another. They can never purify a heart that is without pity. All the sacraments are become sacrileges in an obstinate soul that refuses to others the grace that it seeks for itself.

But be of good heart, for we can do with God whatever we wish. We may dictate to God our own eternal sentence. We can determine the measure which God will use when He judges us, and it will be the same that we use in judging others.

But do not imagine that God will imitate us, and that it is our pardon which will determine His.

God is the first. God has the initiative. It is God who pardons us, and that living and vivifying pardon is communicated through us to others. It is God who works in us, solicits us, invades us, so that, in our turn, we become as father and mother to others, we become like God who pardons and whose joy in heaven is to pardon.

THE TWENTY-SECOND SUNDAY
AFTER PENTECOST

The Tax

"Render therefore to Caesar the things that are Caesar's, and to God the things that are God's." (Matthew 22:15–21)

The Pharisees were trying to draw Christ on to political ground. If they mixed up religion and politics, out of this troubled water they would fish something to condemn Christ and to serve their own personal interests by feigning either national or religious zeal, as the opportunity presented itself.

But Christ rose infinitely above their calculations and He removed the confusion which was common in His time, and not uncommon in our own, between the spiritual and the temporal, a confusion which made the Emperor a god and the policeman a priest.

"Render to Caesar that which belongs to Caesar." I will not

mix with politics, not I, the Christ, not I, the Church. But it does belong to you, the Christian, to take part in it, that is your responsibility. You are part of it. You must take part in it, for either you make the world of politics, or you submit to what others make it.

Fulfill your political obligations according to your personal choice. (If you are in favor of Caesar, give him his due. If you are against him, campaign against him at your own risk.)

And also fulfill your religious duties in accordance with your Catholic faith.

When you have rendered all that you owe to your family, to your customers, to your employer, and to your government, there will still remain much more to give God, for it is His.

Do not be one of those hypocrites who use their religion as an excuse for not fulfilling their duties to society, to their profession, to their family. Nor the contrary!

In fact, you will be much freer and much more disposed to serve God when you shall have given your services to your brethren.

THE TWENTY-FOURTH SUNDAY
AFTER PENTECOST

The "End" of the World

The twenty-fourth Sunday after Pentecost celebrates the end of a world of crimes, of darkness, of tears, and the coming of a new world.

The end of the world is a feast, whatever you may think, and St. Paul thanks God effusively for having rescued us from the empire of the demon and brought us into the Kingdom of His Son.

The whole Mass breathes a joyous hope, an atmosphere of spring, as the Gospel tells us, but which, for many Christians, it seems to contradict because of the sinister predictions which they believe are uttered by Christ.

Let us begin by a correct understanding of this Gospel.

The end of the world, that fearful catastrophe, has already taken place. The greater number of us perhaps have not noticed it, have not been told of it, but, nevertheless, the death of Christ marked the end of the world, the end of a world, the end of an era of the world.

All the signs of the "end of the world" were present at the death of Christ. The Prince of this world was overcome; the earth shook; the sun was darkened; the darkness covered the earth; the dead rose and were seen in Jerusalem; the veil of the Temple was rent; and the centurion, in the name of all mankind, struck his breast and exclaimed: "Truly, this was the Son of God!"

And the Resurrection of Christ has inaugurated a new world in which Christ exercises His power from the height of heaven. Thus it is as He predicted: "This generation"—to which He was speaking—"shall not pass away until all this shall be accomplished."

The death of Christ was that "desolating sacrilege" of which St. Matthew speaks; the Body of Christ, the true Temple, was profaned, unveiled, and it is this which justifies the words which Jesus spoke to the women of Jerusalem: "Weep for yourselves and for your children." Can you imagine any other crime "such as has not been since the beginning of the world until now, and never shall be"? Compared to this, what is the destruction of the Temple in Jerusalem in the year 70? That Temple was no longer acceptable to God, it had been destroyed more than once in the past, and Christ spoke of it so carelessly when He said: "Destroy this Temple, and I will rebuild it in three days." By this He showed that the only Temple worthy of consideration was Himself.

This is the trial capable of shaking the faith of the elect, and of the Apostles themselves, and which was happily repaired within three days.

Thus, the worst is behind us. The most terrible event in all the history of the world is passed. And it is a lack of intelligence and of faith to be still expecting it to occur and still to be in fear and trembling regarding it.

Actually, we are now in the glorious phase of the Kingdom of God, in a time filled with happiness and hope. The Risen Christ, as He foretold that He would, now sends His angels, and that means His messengers, His missionaries—yourselves—to assemble His elect from one end to the other of the world. This is the time of the Church, the time of irresistible expansion of the mission of Christ.

Doubtless, all is not completed, the world still knows some shocks. Humanity, that is, the entire world, still suffers the pains of childbirth described in the Apocalypse, but let us have a true idea of these convulsions which ought to arouse our hope.

The Apocalypse is the revelation of something hidden. Well, then, the harvest is the "apocalypse" of the grain of wheat, of that grain which the earth has long been nourishing, and which the ear has used all its power to lift up to the sun. Doubtless, the harvest is something of a catastrophe, since it means cutting down and destroying the plants, but is it not regarded more often as a time of celebration?

In the same way, the birth of a baby is an apocalypse. It means bringing to the light of day that which the mother has borne in her womb for months. And, in spite of the pain of childbirth, who is there that does not rejoice that a man is born into the world?

Thus the end of the world will be the revelation of all that we shall have willed, loved, created, prayed for, and which will come forth one day in spite of all the apparently triumphant opposition.

The end of the world is, then, for us Christians, something to

271

hope for. It is pagan to fear it and to consider our final decisive meeting with Christ as something to inspire terror.

Let us correct our ideas. The end of the world ought not to be a catastrophe but an accomplishment. The world will never be finished unless we bring it about. God will not annihilate this world which He has so loved, nor will He drop down from heaven a prefabricated paradise which He, in paternalistic fashion, will substitute for our universe, but He is constructing it every day with our help. The salvation of the world, like the first Paradise, like the deliverance from Egypt, like the conquest of the Promised Land, like our own individual salvation, will be *indivisibly* the work of man and the work of God.

Contemporary exegetes say that, in reality, the Gospel does not present the end of the world to us as a catastrophe. Jesus wished, on the contrary, to have His Apostles understand that the dramas at which they were assisting, the ruin of Jerusalem, and even His own death, did not mean that the end of the world had come.

We know the date of the end of time. It is to be found in Chapter 24 of St. Matthew: "When this Gospel of the Kingdom will be preached throughout the whole world, as a testimony to all nations, then the end will come."

This end is just the opposite of a catastrophe. It is a glorious and universal manifestation of Christ.

This prospect set the first Christians on fire with enthusiasm. They were all apostles in order to hasten the evangelization of the world and, in consequence, the return of their Lord. It was this hope that forced Paul out onto all the highways of the Empire.

Our perspectives are considerably enlarged, but our hope, our haste, and our enthusiasm should be the same.

The end of the world has come to be recognized as a long way off, not only by what we now know of the true dimensions of the world, but, above all, because we have only recently come to understand just what the evangelization of the world really comprises.

272

First of all, there must be a minimum of earthly goods in order to practice virtue, and a minimum of liberty and of culture in order that one take an interest in the message of salvation. A hungry stomach has no ears. The only message that is truly evangelical and which we can address to the two-thirds of mankind who are hungry is to share our bread with them. There is no liberation on a world-wide scale without a liberation that is social, economic, and political, and all those among you who are working for this liberation, no matter in what degree, can certify that it is a long-drawn-out work and one that requires courageous hope.

After this, we feel that it will be necessary that the Good News of Christ, if it is to be taken to all nations, will have to be expressed in the language of the people, in their culture, in their mentality, and in their usages. Is it not one of the solicitudes and one of the principal aims of the Council to make the Church truly Catholic by making each race, each people, each rite, and each tongue equally catholic with all the others?

The Church, which knew how to become a Jew with the Jews, a Greek with the Greeks, a Roman with the Romans, has not known, up to the present time, how to become an Arab with the Arabians, Indian with the Indians, Chinese with the Chinese, and Negro with the Negroes. Hence, these people receive a European message, or one that is Western, Latin, or Roman, but which is not truly catholic, which is not the Good News of the love which Christ bears them and the affectionate appeal which He addresses to them.

But, if the achievement, the successful completion, of this world is not to be until some distant date, all our efforts are even more seriously required. We have need of all the medical personnel, all the engineers, all the soldiers, all the workers, all the politicians, and all the scholars in order to make this world a better place, in order to make it a place where justice reigns, where men love one another, and where God can properly descend.

273

The end of the world will be our own work. We are responsible for the salvation of the world, and happy that servant whom his Master, when He comes, shall find occupied.

The modern drama is precisely this, that so many Christians, despairing of the world, cheerfully consign it to final destruction. When business is bad and the international horizon grows dark, they take refuge in this idea and find comfort in it when they could be doing something to make conditions better.

The paradox of the present day is that the various forms of atheism offer doctrines of salvation, passionately endeavoring to give direction and a future to the work of man and to his destiny, and they think it a duty to deny the existence of God because the Christians, while professing their faith in God (who will save them), are at the very same time completely given over to pessimism in regard to this world.

In both quarters there is ignorance of the true God, He who has so loved the world that He has sent His Son into the world to save it. May He send, each morning, His son (yourself) or His daughter (yourself) out into the world to work for its redemption.

THE ASSUMPTION
OF THE BLESSED VIRGIN MARY

"Blessed are you among women." (Luke 1:41–50)

Mary has been called the "eschatological icon of the Church." This means that she is the forerunner of what we shall all become. Like a true mother, she has gone before us. She calls to us, she helps us to come to her there where God has led her.

Her Immaculate Conception, for example, has not radically separated her from us. She has been conceived in the state which

274

we all reach by our baptism. She has been exempted from original sin from the first moment of her conception, —we have been washed of it a few days after our birth. She was, like us, under the condemnation of this universal culpability. Theologians say that "she has been exempted from original sin, but not from the obligation of contracting it," and this because of "the foreseen merits of Christ." She is, then, the first pardoned sinner, the first fruit of the redemption and of grace, the most beautiful of all the fruits of creation. Mary surpasses Eve, because God, who has marvellously created the dignity of human nature, has still more marvellously reformed it.

Mary is "ransomed" like us but in a particular way. And it is because she is thus "graced" that she is all gracious. From the time that she became old enough she realized that God had done all this for her without any merit on her part, and she was amazed at the great things that He had accomplished in the poverty of His servant, as she proclaims at the beginning of her Magnificat.

And in the same way, her Assumption is but the promise, the announcement of that which concerns us all, that our bodies are destined, like hers, to a resurrection and to life eternal.

Heavenly happiness will be for her and for us a human happiness.

Too often we imagine that, to divinize a being is to dehumanize, to destroy its corporeal existence. But the Assumption of Mary reveals to us that our divinization, far from destroying our humanity, will be the harmonious restitution of our basic unity of body and soul.

There are those who represent heaven as a sort of suspension of our human faculties, an eternal and immobile contemplation of the infinite majesty of God. But the one and only being who has returned from the other side of the grave to show us what the total divinization of man is like, is Christ Himself, the Risen Christ. There has never been a person more natural, simpler,

275

more amicable, more obliging, and more warmhearted than the Christ of the apparitions after the Resurrection.

It may be that, in the future, instead of losing ourselves in contemplation, bearing up under ascetic practices, and detaching ourselves from the world and our brethren, religious life will become more human. Man is not human, but God is. God is love, and there is nothing more human—and rarer—than to love. Then our spiritual progress will not be measured by our mortifications, our hours of adoration, our visions or our stigmata, but by our serviceableness, by our politeness to our brothers and sisters, by our love and our respect for those who surround us.

The Risen Christ cooked for His Apostles. Mary Magdalene took Him for the gardener. The disciples of Emmaus walked miles with Him without recognizing Him because He was so much like anybody else, but they identified Him at last because He spoke to them so well regarding the Scriptures, and celebrated the Eucharist with them.

Mary is our mother in just this way. She does not bear a title of honor and glory that puts her on a pedestal or an inaccessible throne, but she is, rather, an example and a helper. Mother is not an honorific title but a function. To be a mother is to be capable of bringing to life, to beget sons and daughters to her own resemblance. The Blessed Virgin invites us today to keep in mind that she will one day unite us all in one same family, all the more human because it will be divine, and all the more divine because it will be so human.

FEAST OF CHRIST THE KING

"My Kingdom is not of this world." (John 18:33–37)

When this feast of Christ the King was first instituted by Pius XI, it aroused great astonishment at first and even some objections. Was this the proper time, when monarchial institutions were disappearing everywhere, or falling into disrepute, to reclaim this title for Christ? Above all, would not this seem to support the pretension with which our contemporaries reproach us and which is to them so odious, that of clericalism? Did Christ seek to govern people? And the Church, which represents Christ, did she want to clothe herself with political power?

It has become quite evident that this feast has no such signification. Christ ever refused to be made a king, and He hid Himself from His over-enthusiastic partisans who wished to make use of Him in order to obtain power. He did not declare Himself a king until that affirmation would no longer be a cause of danger. He was alone, a prisoner before Pilate, and He explained then, and also earlier, what that title meant, and in a way that no one could misunderstand.

"My Kingdom is not of this world. I am come to give testimony to the truth, and all those who are for the truth hear my voice, and they are my true Kingdom."

And He said elsewhere: "The kings of the earth lord it over their peoples and even have themselves called benefactors, but I am in the midst of you as one who serves. If anyone wishes to be first among you, let him make himself the last of all and the servant of all."

Thus all is made clear in a Christian sense.

Christ is the King of the world because He has so loved the world that He has given His life for it and nourishes it with His Body. He died in order to enable each generation to renew His sacrifice and to appease the hunger of the world.

Christ is our King because He is the only one whom we can love with totality. Probably He is the only one today who would give His life for you. He is the only one who fully justifies your existence, and for whom it is worth the trouble to remain in existence because He expects of you something that cannot be done by anyone else.

Contemplate any large city at night. See all those lights which signify so many isolated human beings, in sorrow, in pain, hun-

gry for love and so few capable of loving, and ask yourself what
it is that gives meaning to these lives, what it is that justifies all
these existences, so avid and so brief, and you will find the answer
only in the immense love of Christ which calls, solicits, invades
each of these beings and speaks to him in the depths of his heart.

All Christian authority imitates the authority of Christ.

The primacy of the pope is a primacy of function and of
service. The Greek Orthodox, as you know, are willing to grant
him a primacy of honor, but in Christianity there can be no
dignities which do not carry with them a responsibility. The
authority of the pope in the Church comes from the need that we
have of a head to unite us and for a rule of faith which guards
our fidelity to Christ. The most beautiful title which the popes
have ever used in signing documents, and which John XXIII
revived, is "Servant of the Servants of God."

And if Pope Paul has been able to make more progress in
bringing about the union of all the Churches in three years than
has been done in three centuries, it is because he has shown
himself to be the good shepherd and not a potentate who gives
orders and condemns, but a servant who loves, who calls by
name, and who respects those for whom he is responsible, and
the sheep, even those who are not of his flock, have begun to
listen to this voice and make some attempt to gather around him.

The Church herself began the Council by proclaiming in a
message, which I hope that you have all read and meditated
upon, "that the Church was for the service of all mankind, that,
like her Master, she has come, not to domineer, but to serve; that
she counted neither upon economic means nor upon earthly
power but upon the strength of Holy Spirit," whom you have
invoked for her, just a moment ago, at the beginning of Mass.

To satisfy the hunger of the world, a hunger which is both
material and spiritual, she renews every day the action of Christ
in giving Himself as food. And, because she recognizes that she
has a duty to perform towards all mankind, she everywhere
claims the right to accomplish this duty, which is to teach the

truth (so that all those who are of the truth may hear her voice); to administer the sacraments; to recall to every man his dignity and his supernatural vocation. Like her Master, she may be persecuted, humiliated, crucified, and even then, more especially then, when she shall be lifted up from the earth, she will draw all to her.

Yes, the Church is Christ, actually living among us, and He has abdicated the omnipotence of strength so that He may now exercise only the omnipotence of love.

All Christian authority conforms to this example.

For example, the authority of the husband over the wife is not a power of domination, it is an invitation to greater devotedness, to a better love. "Husbands, love your wives as Christ has loved the Church and delivered Himself for her, so that He might present her, this Church, resplendent, without spot or wrinkle, but holy and immaculate." It is said that a woman remains young as long as her husband loves her. She does not notice that she is growing old until a moment comes when she is no longer loved.

Between husband and wife there is not a rivalry of domination, but an emulation of devotedness and generosity. The one who loves most is the head. And that is why, in so many households, the mother is the one who reigns, because she has made herself the servant of all, because she most resembles Christ the King who is in the midst of us as one who serves.

This feast also gives us instruction on our state as militant Christians. We are not to seek after distinctions or titles; not to wait for recognition and respect; not to count upon success and felicitations. Not to domineer but to serve.

What changes there would be in our parishes, our works of charity, our families, our governments, if those who wish to be first would make themselves the servants of all and the last of all!

A Christian is, above all, a responsible person, and one who believes in his responsibility. He is one who, when meeting with some weakness, some sin, some betrayal, says to himself: "If I were better, others would be less wicked. If I desire that they change, let us begin by loving them better and serving them more. Let us begin by changing ourselves."

Christ won His triumph through failure, suffering, ingratitude, and death. It is extremely painful to realize that one must be lifted above the earth in order to attract all to oneself. We are always tempted to think that the most efficacious thing in this world is violence, money, lying, force. Even we, the friends of Christ, are tempted to address to Him the same demand that His enemies hurled at Him: "Come down from the cross! Stop hanging there, motionless, powerless, achieving nothing. Come down gloriously, come down triumphantly, come down and cause terror and we will all believe in you!"

But Jesus tells us: "You know not of what spirit you are. It is in remaining lifted up above the earth that I will draw all to myself."

Yes, it was in remaining upon the cross that Jesus best revealed the infinite patience and the infinite power of the love of God. It is by fixing upon us that look of love, eyes filled with tears and with blood, that He is certain to move the best among us and to put us freely and lovingly down upon our knees.

The whole nobility of Christ consists in His not wishing to have any other Kingdom nor any other followers but the poor and needy. We belong to Him and we can inaugurate our royalty in our own families, in our neighborhood, in our work and in our church, by becoming in the midst of them as one who serves.

MISSION SUNDAY

"Go, teach all nations!"   (Matthew 28:16–19)

You will not enter heaven alone. Either you will bring with you all those whom you have loved, influenced, aided, converted, —or you will be lost with all those who were with you, those for whom you were supernaturally responsible and whom you betrayed.

Out of the Church, no salvation: you will not save yourself apart from a community. You will not be received into the love of God if you have never loved anyone, —and it is a very poor kind of love that you have for those near to you if you do not save them.

The purpose of the Christian religion is not save yourself if you can, it is more than a religion of the "saved"; rather, it is a religion of "saviours."

The world will end with the same frightening question that was asked in its beginning: "What have you done to your brother?"

Recall the servant in the parable who did not use his talents productively. He wrapped them in a napkin and buried them in the earth. When he presented them with no additional gain, they were taken from him and he was condemned. So it will be with us. If we think that we can present our precious soul, all by itself, solitary, carefully protected and apparently immaculate, we are going to be asked: "Where are the others? Go and find the others!"

The reason for this universal solidarity, the catholic responsibility, is our baptism. In heaven, as in the Gospel of today, our Lord will ask: "With whose image have you been marked? Whose name do you bear?"

At our baptism we have been indelibly marked in the name of the Father. The Father is the One who has so loved the world that He has sent His Son into the world to save it. He still sends, each day, His son—yourself—into the world to save it. He wills that none of His little ones should perish.

In the name of the Son, who, as we shall say in an instant, at the Offertory, has offered Himself for the salvation of the entire world, who—at the Consecration—shed His Blood for many in remission of sins, and whom we proclaim with pride at the Last Gospel, "enlightens every man coming into this world."

In the name of the Holy Spirit of love and of exchange who enables us to give testimony with assurance of our faith and of our charity.

Hence, how can a Christian be anything else but a missionary?

Alas, the greater part of Christians have not lived up to the obligations of their baptism. They could so easily recall it every day by the Sign of the Cross or by the "Our Father"—"Hallowed be thy name. Thy kingdom come!" Instead, they remain in their passivity and their unconsciousness. They sleep on and their Sunday Masses do not interrupt their spiritual slumber.

And all the while, God does not assemble His faithful here to amuse them in a peaceful nursery. Doubtless, He does assemble them to encourage them. "Fear not, little flock, for it has pleased your Father to give you a Kingdom." But, once they are assembled and fed, He disperses the little flock. He sends them as sheep, since they are a little flock, into the midst of wolves. That is where they belong.

If Christians are going to gather together in their ghetto, if they are going to try to hide their spiritual treasures within the walls of their churches, it will be with them as with the manna in the desert; those who wanted to preserve it for the next day found that it had spoiled.

Whatever the Church does for the missions, the missions return with interest. The Church would not be the Church of Christ, the living Church, capable of giving you nourishment and your children life, generosity, and profound conviction that they seek and which they require if she were not the Church of the missions.

St. Paul says: "Woe to me if I preach not the Gospel." Woe to the Church, woe to us, if we are not missionaries. And he adds: "All that I do, I do it because of the Gospel, so that I may have a share in it," showing us plainly by this that, if we want to have a share in the Gospel, we must share it with others.

There is only one sign that we have passed from death to life, and that is if we love the brethren. There is only one proof that we know God, and that is if we resemble Him. There is only one sign that we are on the way to eternal salvation, and that is our capacity for opening that way to others.

All those who have had some encounter with God have had their hearts modelled after His Heart, and He has sent them out to others, He has made them missionaries.

Mary, first of all, the Queen of Apostles, what was the first thing that she did after receiving the Annunciation? Her first act was the "Visitation," she went out to others, she became a missionary in her own way, —humble, discreet, serviceable, —in the way that we can all follow, for she went to be of service to her relative. So efficacious was her act that Elizabeth was enlightened and even John the Baptist leaped for joy in her womb.

Mary Magdalene was favored with an apparition of the Risen Christ. She wanted to put her arms around Him but He would not allow it. He told her: "Go to my brethren." St. Peter, in a fervent moment, repeated: "I love you! I love you! You know that I love you!" And the Lord replied: "Yes, Peter, feed my lambs; feed my sheep!" *Occupy yourself with others.*

And at Pentecost, when the disciples were filled with the Holy Spirit, they were immediately sent forth into the street to communicate to others what they had just received!

Each of us, also, is sent by Christ. "Go, preach the Gospel to every creature. What has been murmured in your ear, go and preach it from the house-tops!"

And you all know that, in our days, in order to become a missionary, it is not an indispensable requirement that one set off for far distant countries.

Certainly, the Church has an urgent need for missionaries for all those places that are asking for them, or for places where they are desired, but for this kind of missionary effort we would adjure in vain a people who are hard, cold, and lacking in enthusiasm.

Certainly, the Church has more need than ever for lay missionaries. What is most lacking at the present day in missionary countries are Catholic doctors, engineers, economists, agronomists, and Catholic homes, —Catholic lay people who will give their services in a disinterested way and show what a militant Christian really is. In these days no Catholic student should complete his studies without asking himself if he ought not to devote two or three years to work in some undeveloped country in order to fulfill his missionary obligation and his baptismal engagement.

But, this is not the only missionary work. The entire Church should be in a missionary state. The first Christians converted their world because their Christianity was contagious. If we were like them, if our faith illumined, intrigued, disquieted our non-Christian neighbors, we would meet with like success.

Think: there are 600 million Christians out of two and a half billion men. These figures may seem discouraging when one recalls that, out of four infants that are born, only a single one is ever brought to the Church for baptism. But it can be considered in another way. It also means that if every Christian, during the course of his life, converted but two or three persons, in a very few years the entire world would be won for Christ.

With twelve poor Jews, Jesus converted the Roman world. And we, with 600 million Christians, are we going to despair of converting the globe?

The moment is decisive. The immense continents of Africa and Asia are awakening from their long sleep and are facing a choice, —whether to become Christian or atheistic. The whole world is seeking unity—it is indispensable to survival—, and it will come whether we want it or not.

We have reason to fear lest, if we be too slow in doing our part, the world will fall into the hands of another kind of missionary, terrible missionaries who will drive us out everywhere. In twenty or thirty years from now it will be decided whether the Church has ceased to be catholic and is but Western, or whether the Church has won over all these people who are now undecided.

You have immense power in your hands.

First, there is your example. Your words, your actions should all be missionary. Are we Christians in our professional relations, in our workshops, in our families? Have we ever tried to speak of religion to our friends who are not of our faith?

A member of the Legion of Mary was expressly charged to bring up the subject of religion with a man whom he knew either through his work or in some business way. He was so embarrassed, so disturbed, by this commission that, before going to ring the doorbell, he stopped in at the church, and guess what his prayer was? "Lord, grant that he may not be at home!" Such is our missionary courage.

But it happened that his friend was at home, and when he had gotten through the painful task of explaining the purpose of his visit, his friend remarked: "I have been wondering, and with astonishment, why you have never spoken to me of religion."

After your example, you have your prayer. Christ has promised that He will hear all those who pray in His name, and that if two or three among you agree, they shall obtain whatever they ask. What have we done up to now with this extraordinary power in regard to the conversion of our brethren? Have we asked the Master, with faith, to send workers to harvest in His fields, even if that worker should be—ourselves?

FEAST OF ALL SAINTS

It takes a little more effort than we feel capable of producing for us to turn our eyes sharply away from the innumerable cares of today and tomorrow, so that we may think for a few hours on the happiness of the saints and find our way into that lovely society where optimism triumphs and justice prevails.

We are so much more inclined to sorrow than to joy that we have made this beautiful, radiant feast of all the saints a feast of sorrow. We have annexed to it the dead and of that which is most sad about death, the feast of the cemeteries, of funeral flowers, and black vestments.

Instead of living this day with our souls filled with the thought of those whose loss caused us so much suffering, and whom it is such a joy to recall and to think of one day being united with them again, instead of thinking of what has truly happened to them, of the repose that they enjoy, of the recompense that they have found, of Him who loves them more than we ever knew how to love them, who loves them as they deserve to be loved, —instead of all this, we pass them over with but an instant of recollection and turn inward upon ourselves and our sorrow at our having lost them.

It is in this state of gloom that our Lord finds us and out of which He tries to lift us by telling us in the Gospel of today: "I know that you are poor, that you suffer and weep; you are weak and others torment you and you long for relief. Nevertheless, I tell you that you are truly happy, for the Kingdom of God belongs to you. You can be called the children of God and you shall possess the earth. I want to open to you a supernatural world where you will be reassured and consoled, where you will obtain mercy, where you will rejoice and regard as the most precious of gifts a little suffering here on earth."

It is only in heaven that all that has taken place upon earth can be judged, explained, and understood. Human existence is absurd if you try to understand it without taking into account this eternity which continues it and gives it equilibrium. All our calculations are false if they look only to below, if they seek to justify, by themselves, a life which is only the preparation for another life. Why have I failed in my life, in my career, in spite of my honesty, my labor, and my uprightness? Because a far more beautiful recompense awaits you in heaven. Why have I prayed and not been heard? Because your prayers have obtained for you far more than you would ever have asked for. Why have I lost those whom I loved? Because you will soon be reunited in Eternity. Why have I loved and received nothing but ingratitude in return, or not been loved in return? Because it is only in heaven that you will be loved as you deserve to be.

Be careful! Do not let yourself be deceived. You must not regard as lost what is your most precious possession here below: your tears, your prayers, your sorrows, and your sufferings. You think that you are weeping in vain over the loss of a loved one and all the while this trial is purifying that affection with which you will surround anew her whom you will never lose again but rejoin. You suffer from your own weaknesses and from those of others, but by this means you are learning to detach yourself from the world and turn to Him who is all strength and all joy. You despair of justice and of peace when you see that men can be so violent and so egoistic, but it is because of this that you open your soul to another peace and another justice infinitely more consoling. That is what has happened to the elect and to the saints whose feast we are celebrating today. Let us not represent them to ourselves as spoiled children during life and enriched with a happiness that has cost them nothing.

The dwellers in the house of the Father, the invited guests at His banquet, are the poor, the crippled, the blind, and the lame of this world. They have known our miseries, they have shared all our troubles, but they have regarded them as good. They have firmly believed that God has not lied. They have believed, in spite of everything, that God was right, that He knew better than we what was good, and they have received their recompense. They have entered into their repose. If our parents, our friends, our brothers and sisters could speak to us today, do you know what they would say? What they would teach us? What secret they would share with us? "Ah," they would tell us, "when we arrived in heaven, after this long pilgrimage on earth, do you

287

know what we discovered? It is a marvellous and unbelievable thing, but you should meditate on it patiently until you discover its meaning. We found nothing new. When we awakened from this long sleep with its nightmares, by which we mean our life down below, we found ourselves embraced, tightly clasped in arms that have always held us. That wonderful face which was disclosed to us in tenderness and tears of joy was the same that we had always felt bent over us in times of sadness and mourning. It was explained then why it always seemed to us that we were living a life which we did not understand very well. We recognized that elusive yet faithful friend who had disquieted us by his mysterious presence. We began to comprehend why we had always felt, in some obscure way, that, at bottom, life was really kind and favorable, and why, even when we were skeptic and blasé, when we said that life was horrible and not worth the trouble of living, we knew in our hearts that it was pure perversity on our part, and that we did it only to provoke by our complaints a goodness of which we were but too sure. We could guess something of what our friends, who were without faith, felt at the moment of their deaths and what made it so painful for them. They were leaving, for the first time, and for always, a Presence, a Source of goodness, a fireside of warmth and love which had warmed their lives but to which they had never yielded themselves, nor upon which they had ever acknowledged their dependence. We recall the years of our youth and we see clearly now why they seemed to us to be so radiant and pure. In those days the divine Presence illuminated our souls, souls which were more confiding and open. Now we strike our breasts, saying: 'If we had known! If we had thought!' And we all begged to be allowed to go to purgatory to expiate. Now we find no greater joy in heaven than to live over again in this light the marvellous moments of our earthly existence. At each step we pause, overwhelmed by the generosity of our God and ashamed of our past stupidity. Even a single moment affords us cause for

288

infinite joy and gladness. From what dangers we have escaped! What a gentle, yet strong, hand has turned us back from precipices towards which we were running with all the perversity of an obstinate child. What patience God had with us! All those things which we called failures, deceptions, mourning, catastrophes, mishaps, and contradictions were the moments when the mercy of God was taking the most care of us. Fortunately, God was there; fortunately, He did not listen to us; fortunately, He opposed us and obtained, in spite of ourselves, what was necessary for us.

"We are moved to tears when we consider the direction our lives took. Certainly, we were not left to ourselves, and, had we been, how quickly it all would have ended in a catastrophe. If you would only open your eyes and see all the care, all the attention, all the love, all the vigilance that surrounds you! It is God who is leading you, He walks by your side. But He keeps one hand over your eyes to hide His presence from you and the other hand upon your shoulder to guide you. All grows clear for him who believes in his adorable Guide. And everything is repugnant to him who distrusts Him and turns from Him. The world without God is a world of tears and misery, but the world, with God, is Paradise begun. The one conquers by violence but without the power to give contentment. The other lifts its eyes to the face of the Giver and reads therein a tenderness and a beauty which satisfies him forever."

That is what our relatives and friends would say to us from above if we would listen to them today. They would tell us that, if God loves them so much in heaven, it is because He already loved them like that when they were on earth. If God is to love us like that one day in heaven, God already loves us like that now when we are on earth. And if we do not discover during our lifetime the proofs of the love that He bears us, it is because our too-rarely-made prayers leave us unaware of His influence. It is because our eagerness to enjoy His gifts makes us forget the One who gave them. It is because our attachment to material goods makes us forget the princely gift of the friendship of God.

Let us pray to all the saints in heaven that we may be convinced of these truths, and that they may unite our souls to their joy and their gratitude so that we may one day rejoice with them in heaven after having suffered a little and believed much.

FOR A SUNDAY IN NOVEMBER

Hell

People pretend that the modern Christian scarcely ever thinks about hell, so seldom, in fact, that it seems that he no longer believes in its existence. They even say that priests no longer preach on that subject because they know that no one will listen to them. However, the existence of hell is a dogma of faith, and no one can be a Christian while refusing to believe in it. We have no right to eliminate this truth of revelation because we find it disagreeable. It suffices to open the Gospel to see with what insistence Jesus speaks to us regarding hell, and the eternal consequences of our choice.

But preachers have often so maltreated this subject that they have discouraged us from believing in it. In an attempt to make it more frightful, they have succeeded only in making it either rejected altogether or having its existence placed in doubt. It seems impossible to make their pictures, both infantine and cruel, agree with what we know from other sources of the goodness and the love of God.

In order that we may believe in hell, it is perhaps sufficient for us to know just what is the exact object of our faith.

To begin with, God did not create hell. God did not create a place of torture, a world of suffering, a universe of demons where He could visit His vengeance upon His enemies. Evil, according to Christian philosophy, is a privation. God did not create evil. Whatever God created is good, and very good (Genesis 1:31), and hell, which is the supreme evil, is uncreated.

First of all, hell is not a place but a state of soul. It is a kingdom that is just as spiritual as heaven. It is the state of a soul, made for God and having need of God as much as we have need of air; it is a place where the soul, having refused the air, is asphyxiated.

The second error which is in common use and which must be corrected is that God damns men. This is not true. It is men who damn themselves. God loves all that He has created. God loves even the damned because they are His creatures. The damned are those who refuse the love of God and thus punish themselves. They are like a house on a hilltop, receiving all the light of the sun, but closing its doors and its windows in order to remain in darkness. So, too, in hell, the light shines in the darkness and the darkness will not accept it.

Consequently, we must not imagine God chasing souls and pushing them into hell. Such an imaginary scene is false. It is also dangerous because of the idea that we form of God. He is not a torturer. Quite the contrary. Hell is the expression of the respect that God has for our liberty. If God saved, by force, all men and imposed His presence upon them, heaven would be nothing more than a huge concentration camp. God constrains no one to love Him. Throughout all eternity each one will go where he desires to go. Where your treasure is, there also will be your heart, your body, and your soul.

There are two sorts of beings: those who say to God: "Father, may your will be done!" and those to whom, sorrowfully and sick at heart, God ends by saying: "Very well. May your will be done now and forever!"

In fact, my brothers, heaven and hell are already begun for us.

291

Heaven and hell are already present in your souls, —and they will never be present anywhere else. Those to whom the goodness, the love, and the presence of God have not been a source of joy here below, would not find them above any more suited to their taste. God, other persons, friendship, faithful and generous love, will remain just as insipid in heaven as on earth. They would be as out of place in heaven as a cow in a church, as a deaf person at a concert, asking themselves what enjoyment these people find in this place!

In fact, we shall not choose our eternal destination intelligently if we do not have a foretaste of it. Our daily lives, our Sunday Masses, our Christian communities are given to us so that we may experiment and see whether we find it good to be with God and our brethren, to find out whether we desire this kind of heaven. In our bursts of piety, of hope, of confidence, or of tenderness, in the fervor of true prayer, in the joy of generous forgiveness, in the peace of a good confession, in all these we already taste something of the joys of heaven. And when we are insupportable to ourselves and to others, discontented, vindictive, stubborn in wrong-doing, sterile in love and sympathy, we have a foretaste of hell.

Thus it is with full liberty that a man damns himself. Even in eternity, God never constrains the liberty of man. He forces no one to love Him, but neither does He repulse anyone who loves Him or even desires to love Him. An act of love, an act of repentance, an appeal to His pity or His pardon, and hell immediately ceases to be.

"In that case," you are saying to yourself, "I can be tranquil! Under those conditions, hell should be empty, for there is no one who would be so hardened in sin. Nobody would want to be like that, unhappy forever. No one can be so bad that he closes himself off eternally from God."

You say this because you do not know how much perversity there can be in the heart of man, how we can be wicked and at the same time quite sane, unhappy and headstrong, suffering and loving our misfortune.

Undoubtedly, the greater number of our sins are sins of frailty, and if these are recognized and repaired, far from being an obstacle to the love of God, they can serve as a spring-board, or a spur, to our confidence in Him and to our humility.

But, unfortunately, our sins of weakness become sins of malice. What at first escaped us through weakness, we make worse by pride. We refuse to confess a sin which we detest, either because of shame, or ill-humor, or laziness. We hate it and yet we will not admit it, and all the while we are refusing the peace and the pardon of God! We put off the reparation which we know is due, and we barricade ourselves with great obstinacy in the trap into which we fell by accident.

Even a little child is capable of this. Recall the time when we were children. What cries of anger, what absurd stubbornness! The whole family pleaded with us, affectionately tried to reason with us, and we remained in our corner. "Rather die than ask pardon! Better to stay forever like this! Let the whole world come to an end before we will ask pardon!"

Did it ever happen, when you were in your teens, that you took the wrong bus? Because you were both too timid and too sure of yourself to ask for direction, to consult someone who knew, you climbed into the bus which you should not have taken.

Soon it became evident that you had made a mistake, that you were going in the wrong direction. Then, had you been simple and modest, you would have questioned the driver. But the idea of admitting your mistake in this way, of such a public confession, then the necessity of going, red-faced, the length of the car amid the amused glances of the other passengers, made you give up, and you slipped further back into your seat and tried to hide your uneasiness. Delays suggested themselves, —a little further on, or when there are fewer passengers, or in a few minutes.

Hell is like that. To remain in the evil that one sees, from which one suffers, and of which one refuses to repent. One has a grudge against the whole world, declaring everybody else responsible, but never humiliating oneself and avowing one's own guilt and asking pardon for it. It is to prefer to be unhappy all alone, in one's pride, in one's independence, in one's own sufficiency, rather than to be happy with Another, thanks to the grace of Another, and with others. We make hell for ourselves, we need no one to help us, it is a product of our own personal workmanship. Heaven is to live with all the others. Hell is to send everybody else to the devil and to be there oneself!

There is a pleasure in hell. If there were not, no one would go there. It is the somber pleasure of destroying oneself, of installing oneself in a place where one will definitely be left to oneself. It is a place where we shall love no one, where no one will come to us, where we will be definitely retired, excommunicated, damned to a kind of horrible peace.

Man has not only the capacity to damn himself, but he even has a taste for it! There is such a thing as a passion for evil just because it is evil. A man chooses and savors hell with full knowledge. There is not much difference between hell and what we already know here below. To die is to open oneself to that for which one has lived on earth. For what do you live? Money? You will have money. The flesh? You shall live of the flesh. For yourself? You shall have yourself.

Hell can be the continuation of certain pleasures which we seek without loving them, of numberless contacts in which there is no love. A fever and agitation over nothing, an atrocious fear of solitude and an incapacity for communion with others. Perhaps we shall never have that which we seek so eagerly now, —success, distractions, money, liberty, agitation, noise, —things which we have often noticed were leading us astray but to which we returned again and again with perverse obstinacy.

Will there be many damned?

About that we know nothing because that depends upon yourself. The Church canonizes, she does not damn. She declares with authority that certain ones are in heaven but she does not command you to believe that a single man is in hell.

If we pray, if we love enough, it is still possible that the whole world may be saved, for God has foreseen from all eternity those prayers. The prayers that you say today, those that you will say tomorrow, God has known them from all eternity, and also the souls that will be lost unless those prayers are offered. Until the last saint has offered his last prayer, we are not sure but that all mankind may be saved.

The horror of hell and our immense responsibility, our universal solidarity in regard to the eternal salvation of souls ought to place us on our knees in prayer. If Jesus willed to become incarnate, if He came on earth to speak, to teach, to suffer, to pray, and to die, it is because He knew what hell really is. Not the burlesque or mythological hell of Dante or Virgil, but the hell that is already gnawing at the souls of many among ourselves and which makes them seek to escape by forgetfulness, miserable distractions, strenuous pleasures, unconsciousness, and even death. He saw, even while He was speaking, those among His auditors who learned as they listened to Him that they were in hell, that they were tasting the pains of hell, and that they would remain there because they lacked all courage, all desire, all wish to change. It was this horror that placed Him upon the Cross.

Forgetfulness and lack of belief in hell is what makes sinners. Faith in hell makes redeemers. Our immense pity, our immense love for all men, living or dead, who are menaced by hell, leads us to come to their assistance by prayer and also by action. Our redemptive capacity is equal to the measure of our love. The Church prays every day at Mass "for the salvation of the entire world." Whatever is the object of prayer is likewise the object of hope. As long as we have life, we cannot resign ourselves to the loss of any man. It is still possible that, thanks to you, the whole world may be saved!